Voices of Early Christianity

Recent Titles in Voices of an Era

Voices of Early Christianity

Documents from the Origins of Christianity

Kevin W. Kaatz, Editor

Voices of an Era

GREENWOOD

AN IMPRINT OF ABC-CLIO, LLC
Santa Barbara, California • Denver, Colorado • Oxford, England

7804812600

All Biblical quotations are reprinted from the *New Revised Standard Version Bible*. Division of Christian Education of the National Council of Churches of Christ in the United States of America, 1989.

Library of Congress Cataloging-in-Publication Data

Voices of early Christianity : documents from the origins of Christianity / Kevin W. Kaatz, editor.
     pages cm. — (Voices of an era)
   Includes bibliographical references (pages   ) and index.
   ISBN 978-1-59884-952-3 (hardcopy : alk. paper) — ISBN 978-1-59884-953-0 (ebook)
1. Church history— Primitive and early church, ca. 30-600—Sources.   I. Kaatz, Kevin.
   BR167.V65   2013
     270.1—dc23   2012041162

ISBN: 978-1-59884-952-3
EISBN: 978-1-59884-953-0

17 16 15 14 13   1 2 3 4 5

This book is also available on the World Wide Web as an eBook.
Visit www.abc-clio.com for details.

Greenwood
An Imprint of ABC-CLIO, LLC

ABC-CLIO, LLC
130 Cremona Drive, P.O. Box 1911
Santa Barbara, California 93116-1911

This book is printed on acid-free paper ∞

Manufactured in the United States of America

As always, to Doug.

CONTENTS

PREFACE

Christianity is the largest religion in the world, and its early history determined what modern Christianity looks like today. Most of what is known about the early Christians comes primarily from documentary evidence. This volume includes some texts from the Old Testament, some from the New Testament, and many from Christians who wrote after the Bible was composed. The Arch of Constantine, which stands next to the Roman Coliseum, a section on the catacombs, and two images related to the resurrection are also included. The volume is broken up into six major sections: Early Christian Life, The Church, Early Christian Women, Conflicts of the Early Church, Persecution, and Church and Politics. There are 42 subsections. Each subsection contains an Introduction, which gives a basic background as to who was writing and why it was being written, as well as a Keep in Mind While You Read section, which helps the reader understand the context of the text. After the ancient text is presented, several additional sections are provided: an Aftermath section, which describes some of the effects the particular writings had on the early Christian community; an Ask Yourself section, which gives a number of questions that are designed to help the reader think about what the text is saying, not only to ancient Christians but also how it might be interpreted by modern readers; a Topics to Consider section, which lists possible exercises that the readers can do or think about that are related to a particular topic; and, finally, a Further Information section, which gives an extensive bibliography of books, journals, and, occasionally, websites, to which the reader can refer. This volume also includes sidebars that contain more information on the social context for some of these texts. For example, the sidebar for "Sources for Christ Outside of the New Testament" contains information on the political situation of Judea during the early part of the first century CE. There are also fact boxes for some of the texts, which contain definitions of words or phrases used in the ancient texts. The Glossary contains words that are not found in the fact boxes.

Many of the texts given here are excerpts, and the very act of cutting them into smaller (and therefore incomplete) parts means that understanding the context for a particular text may not be clear. It is hoped that the reader will read the entire work to get the full meaning. Nearly all of the primary texts used for this volume are in the public domain, and websites are given in the Further Information sections, referring to where the whole text can be found. As with most public domain texts, the language is often archaic, and this is particularly the case for early Christian texts that use words such as *thee, thy,* and *thou*. I have changed these texts to modern English, and in some cases I have retranslated the entire text.

Finally, it should be remembered that these writings were composed all over the Roman Empire, and even though it is tempting to think that the rules set down in one text applied to all Christians everywhere, that probably was not the case. These texts cannot speak for all Christians—even those texts found in the New Testament. Everyone had their own view, and although there was agreement on most of the principles laid down by the New Testament writers, people disagreed on what constituted true Christianity, sometimes violently. Some manuscripts documenting these arguments survived from antiquity, but many others did not. Each text presented here is, for the most part, just one voice out of many.

ACKNOWLEDGMENTS

The importance of reading primary texts was impressed on me when I started my PhD program in the Ancient History Department at Macquarie University, Sydney, Australia. Of course I had read primary texts in ancient history before, but when I first arrived at Macquarie in 1998, my PhD supervisor, Professor Sam Lieu, asked me to read all of Augustine's anti-Manichaean works so that I could form my own view before tackling the secondary literature. This has played a big part in my career as a researcher in early Christianity. For that, and other things, I am very grateful to Sam. It was also at Macquarie when I first started my teaching career. It was under the tutelage of Professor Andrew Gillett that I understood the importance of having students read and study the primary texts, and this has played a large role in the way I now teach my own courses. I am very grateful to Andrew for all the support he has given me throughout the years. I would like to thank George Butler, Michael Wilt and Anthony Chiffolo at ABC-CLIO for all of their help putting this volume together. I would also like to thank the students in my Fall 2012 History of Early Christianity course for allowing me to try this volume in a classroom setting. Finally, I would like to thank Doug McCulloch for spending many hours looking over the manuscript. Of course, any mistakes are my own.

INTRODUCTION

This book will explore the life of the early Christians by way of writings, the earliest of which are the Old Testament and the latest the Nicene Creed and its canons (or laws), issued in 325 CE. Christianity began as an offshoot of Judaism, and because of this the first Christians were Jewish converts and their religious texts were still the Old Testament (usually referred to as "Scripture" in the New Testament). Their earliest religious beliefs were created by way of this collection, along with the teachings of Jesus. Once Christians began to see themselves as different from the Jews, they began to use the Old Testament in new ways, and this included seeing in it a foretelling of Christ. For example, many Christians began to see the figure of Jonah as a Christ-like figure. This was also the case for the story of Abraham and the sacrifice of his son. In other words, Christians believed that the Old Testament was predicting the coming of the Messiah. Once early Christians became a larger group, they had a growing realization that they needed their own traditions and writings that were outside of the Old Testament. The earliest Christian writing is Paul's 1 Thessalonians, which dates to around 50 CE. Paul the Apostle made it his mission to include into his newly found religion people who were not Jews. He did this by traveling through Asia Minor (now Turkey) and either creating new Christian churches from the Gentile population or converting the Jewish population to Christianity. In order to control these new converts, Paul wrote letters which now make up the majority of the New Testament. Paul became the primary voice for the first century Christians, but he certainly was not the only voice. The books that make up the New Testament have at least nine different authors and range from the four Gospels, which tell the story of Jesus, to Revelation, an account of what will happen at the end of time. These are the texts and voices that survive from early Christian history, but they were not the only ones. Paul, as he was traveling through Asia Minor, came across many Christian teachers who had arrived before he did. In many cases he tried to convince them that he had the correct interpretation of Christianity. His writings are full of these confrontations. Unfortunately, Paul failed to provide names, but the arguments of these unnamed Christians can be at least partially recreated from his writings.

The New Testament contains a wealth of information about what these early Christians were thinking and doing. While these texts are an extremely important witness (and sometimes the only witness) to the lives of first-century Christians, this volume does not contain the whole books from this important source; if it did, it could have easily escalated into just reprinting the New Testament. Each section contains multiple texts, and they are put in chronological order so that the reader will see the progression of thought over time.

Outside of the biblical texts, Christians started writing sometime in the late first century and certainly by the beginning of the second. Many of these early sources are letters, much like those of Paul. Ignatius of Antioch is a perfect example. During his time as bishop there was a persecution directed at Christians by the Romans. As a church leader, he drew the attention of Roman authorities and was taken to Rome to stand trial. As he was taken through Asia Minor he wrote letters to Christian communities on various subjects that reveal quite a bit about the state of Christianity in this early period. Other Christians wrote to defend Christianity and, in the process, to define it. The most famous of these early writers was Justin Martyr. His *First Apology* was directed at the emperor, and in it he discussed how unfair it was to target Christians. His *Apology* also gave descriptions of early Christian thought and behavior, which have proven very useful to historians trying to discover what was happening in these communities.

Another part of this volume will include writings about early Christian women. Women played an essential role in the spreading of Christianity, especially in the first century. Many times Paul's missionary activity was supported by them. Although the subject of the roles of women in the early church is controversial, it is clear that some women held the office of deaconess. Later, as Christianity spread and differing types of Christianities were created, some women, especially those involved in Montanism, such as Priscilla and Maximilla, were prophets. Over time it appears that women's roles were reduced and many rules were set on them (such as the rules for widows). Women were actively involved in early Christianity, and their voices deserve to be heard, even though in nearly all cases their voices are heard through male writers.

One major factor in the lives of many early Christians was persecution. After the death of Jesus (the first martyr) there were persecutions in various Christian communities. One of the more serious in the first century occurred during the reign of Emperor Nero (54–68 CE). After Nero there were sporadic persecutions, and many Christians wrote about either their own experiences or the experiences of those who became martyrs. Examples included in this volume are Polycarp, Cyprian, Priscilla and Felicitas, and Origen (although Origen was tortured, he died from his treatment after the persecution had ended).

The political position (or lack thereof) of the early Christians usually led to their persecution. This changed with Emperor Constantine, the first Christian emperor. With his elevation the persecution of Christianity stopped, and it became the preferred religion of the Roman Empire. At the same time, many Christians began fighting with each other over who had the correct type of Christianity. One major conflict was between the Arians and the Nicenes (or those who followed the Nicene Creed). The Arians believed that God came first, followed by the Son and the Holy Spirit, while the Nicenes believed that the God, the Son, and the Holy Spirit existed forever. Emperor Constantine found himself in the middle of this fight, and in 325 CE he called the Council of Nicea together to end it. The Council produced the Nicene Creed, one of the most important documents from early Christianity.

How to Evaluate a Primary Source

For ancient history, the primary sources for information come from documents that were written and archaeology that was constructed during a particular time period being studied. Since this volume concentrates primarily on texts, it is important to understand what needs to be considered when reading a book or a letter written by someone nearly 2,000 years ago. Modern people, when examining primary texts, need to think about a number of questions beyond the actual message found in the text. Questions that are usually asked are: What is the history of the text itself? Do the originals exist and, if not, how was the text reconstructed? It is then important to think about: Who wrote it? To whom was it written? What are the circumstances that led to the creation of the letter or book?

Before looking at authorship, audience, and context, some observations should be made about the texts, or manuscripts (from the Latin *manus,* hand and *scripto,* to write). First, many texts from the first centuries of Christianity are not the originals. For example, the oldest part of the New Testament that exists today is a very small fragment of the Gospel of John, dated to the early part of the second century. It isn't until the 300s CE when we find manuscripts that contain large parts of the New Testament. Second, to make matters more difficult, there are over 5,000 manuscripts of the Greek New Testament (Greek was the original language), and there are differences found throughout these thousands of texts, sometimes small, sometimes large. To manage these differences, the manuscripts are organized into families that often originate from a particular geographical area. In the case of the Alexandrian family of manuscripts, they originate near Alexandria, Egypt. The modern printing of the Greek and Latin New Testament will contain a critical apparatus, found at the bottom of the page, which contains some of the major variations found between different manuscript families or differences between individual texts. For example, the title of the Gospel of John is "According to John" in most manuscripts, but the critical apparatus notes that in other manuscripts, the title is "The Gospel According to John." Thus, the texts of the Old and New Testaments we have today are essentially put together by modern scholars who are trying to determine what the original wording was.

The originals of many Christian writings that came after the composition of the biblical texts also do not exist anymore. Over time they have disappeared or were destroyed, either on purpose or by accident, so modern readers are reliant on copies or even copies of copies. An example of this is found in Eusebius of Caesarea's *Church History* (written in the late 200s or early 300s). Eusebius was the first historian to actively cite his sources. Sometimes the citations he gives are the only evidence we have of these writings. When we are lucky enough to have a number of copies of the same book they are usually not exactly the same, which is similar to the problems with the biblical texts. These difficulties with the biblical and later texts usually stem from the process of producing books or letters in the ancient world. Books were time-consuming and expensive to produce. The process began when one person would sit down to copy a book by hand, or someone would stand up in front of a group of scribes and read the original while the scribes would copy down what they heard. Many mistakes can enter a text in this way. The person copying the text could start to day-dream and miss whole sections. A word could be misspelled or even misplaced in the copied version. The person reading could accidently skip a part of the text causing the scribes to replicate the same mistake. Sometimes the problem lies with the copy itself—pages could have been missing, and then this missing section could have been transferred wholesale to the copy being made. The original being used could have also been corrupted in some way and the mistakes carried over into the copy.

Another item to consider when reading primary texts is that they were obviously not written in English. The texts provided in this volume were originally in Greek, Latin, and Coptic (an Egyptian language). This is something to take into account when reading ancient texts. Translation is a difficult process, and mistakes can also be made. A problem with translating is that it isn't as easy as giving a word-for-word account. Sometimes the translator is forced to add something that the original does not have in order to make it understandable to a modern reader. For example, Latin lacks definite and indefinite articles, which are *the* for definite and *a* and *an* for indefinite ("the book," as opposed to "a book"). This means that when it is translated into English, the translator must make a decision as to whether the original author meant something very specific ("the book") or more general ("a book"). Usually, the context will guide the translator.

Once these issues are dealt with, the contents of the text can then examined. As mentioned previously, there are three things that need to be looked at: authorship, the intended audience, and the context of the message. If the author is known, this can give the reader some background (if we are lucky enough to know something about the author) as to why the text was written. If the name of the author is attached, the reader then should also consider whether that person is actually the real author. Many texts from early Christianity were supposedly written by a famous person, but scholars have discovered that for some the authorship was by someone else. For example, some of the Gnostic texts from Nag Hammadi, Egypt, have the names of some of the Twelve Disciples attached to them, but many times the texts were written centuries after their deaths. This is also the case for some texts from the New Testament. There are many writings attributed to Paul that are now believed to have been written by Paul's followers, probably after his death. If the text is anonymous, then the reader needs to ask why that is the case. Modern readers do not need to necessarily mistrust an anonymous text, but it could lead to other questions, such as "Was it dangerous to put the name of the author on the text?"

Modern readers also need to consider the intended audience (to whom was the original author specifically writing) and the context (the reason for the text being written and/or information on the social environment of the author and the intended audience). Knowing who the intended audience was will help readers discover why it was written in the first place. Ancient letters usually include the addressee. For example, Paul the Apostle states the intended audience in his Letter to the Romans (the title of which was given later) in Romans 1:7: "To all God's beloved in Rome, who are called to be saints." Many books during this period were also addressed to particular people. For example, Justin Martyr addressed his *First Apology* "To the Emperor Titus Aelius Adrianus Antoninus Pius Augustus Cæsar, and to his son Verissimus the Philosopher, and to Lucius the Philosopher, the natural son of Caesar, and the adopted son of Pius, a lover of learning, and to the sacred Senate, with the whole People of the Romans." Sometimes, as in the case of Justin's *First Apology*, the context can be better determined by looking to whom the author was directing his book. Many times the context can also be discovered just by reading the text. Other times, modern readers will have to do a bit of historical investigation on the manuscript itself to gain a better understanding of the text. It is hoped that the Introduction, Keep in Mind While You Read, and the Aftermath sections will help with this process.

CHRONOLOGY

All dates are CE, unless noted.

31 BCE–14 CE	Rule of Emperor Augustus
ca. 33–36	Death of Christ
44	Persecution under Herod Agrippa
ca. 65	Death of Paul the Apostle
ca. 50	1 Thessalonians (earliest writing of the New Testament)
54–68	Rule of Emperor Nero
64	The Great Fire in Rome
ca. 64–67	Death of Peter and Paul
66	Jewish Revolt
70	Destruction of the Second Temple
ca. 70 to ca. 135	*Epistle of Barnabas*
112	Letters from Pliny the Younger to Emperor Trajan on the Christians
Late first century/early second century	*The Didache*
ca. 90–150	*Shepherd of Hermas*
Beginning of second century	Ignatius
ca. 115–202	Irenaeus
ca. 154	Death of Marcion
ca. 156	Death of Polycarp
ca. 165	Death of Justin Martyr

Middle/late second century	Montanus
ca. 160 to early third century	Tertullian
ca. 185 to ca. 251	Origen
ca. 200	*Muratorian Canon*
202	*Passion of Perpetua and Felicitas*
216–276	Mani
ca. 240–320	Lactantius
ca. 250	Decian Persecution
253–260	Rule of Emperor Valerian
ca. 260–336	Arius
ca. 260 to ca. 339	Eusebius of Caesarea
284–305	Rule of Diocletian
ca. 297	Great Persecution under Diocletian
ca. 300–373	Athanasius
306–324	Rule of Emperor Constantine in the west
306–324	Rule of Emperor Licinius in the east
312–328	Alexander of Alexandria, Bishop of Alexandria
313	Edict of Milan
315	Arch of Constantine
324–337	Rule of Emperor Constantine as sole emperor
325	Council of Nicea
325	Exile of Arius
342	Death of Eusebius of Nicomedia

EARLY CHRISTIAN LIFE

1. Sources for Christ Outside of the New Testament

INTRODUCTION

While the New Testament documents much of the life of Christ, there are some who question whether Jesus was an actual person. Was he figment of the imagination created by the New Testament authors? Or if he was real, was he really the Son of God, or was he just a good person? When evidence outside of the New Testament exists for people mentioned in the text, it is always cause for excitement. In the first and second century, there are three sources outside of the New Testament that lend credence to the existence of Christ: Josephus, Tacitus, and Suetonius.

KEEP IN MIND WHILE YOU READ

1. Josephus was a Jewish historian who lived from 37 to 100 CE and fought against the Romans when the Jews revolted against them in 66–70 CE. He ultimately surrendered, and became an advisor to the Romans when they attacked Jerusalem. He later moved to Rome, where he wrote his *Antiquities of the Jews*.
2. Tacitus was a Roman historian and senator.
3. Suetonius was a Roman historian who lived sometime between 69 and 130 CE. He became famous after writing *The Twelve Caesars*.

Josephus, Antiquities *18:2–3*

2. But Pilate undertook to bring a current of water to Jerusalem, and did it with the sacred money, and derived the origin of the stream from the distance of two hundred furlongs. However, the Jews were not pleased with what had been done about this water; and many ten thousands of the people got together, and made a clamor against him, and insisted that he should leave off that design. Some of them also used reproaches, and abused the man, as crowds of such people usually do. So he habited a great number of his soldiers in their

habit, who carried daggers under their garments, and sent them to a place where they might surround them. So he bid the Jews himself go away; but they boldly casted reproaches upon him. He gave the soldiers that signal which had been beforehand agreed on, who laid upon them much greater blows than Pilate had commanded them, and equally punished those that were tumultuous, and those that were not, nor did they spare them in the least: and since the people were unarmed, and were caught by men prepared for what they were about, there were a great number of them slain by this means, and others of them ran away wounded. And thus an end was put to this sedition.

3. Now there was about this time Jesus, a wise man, if it be lawful to call him a man; for he was a doer of wonderful works, a teacher of such men who receive the truth with pleasure. He drew over to him both many of the Jews and many of the Gentiles. He was (the) Christ. And when Pilate, at the suggestion of the principal men amongst us, had condemned him to the cross, those that loved him at the first did not forsake him; for he appeared to them alive again the third day; as the divine prophets had foretold these and ten thousand other wonderful things concerning him. And the tribe of Christians, so named from him, are not extinct at this day.

Source: *The Works of Flavius Josephus,* translated by William Whiston. London: Chatto and Windus, 1897, 48–49.

Tacitus, Annals 15.44

Such indeed were the precautions of human wisdom. The next thing was to seek means of propitiating the gods, and recourse was had to the **Sibylline books**, by the direction of which prayers were offered to Vulcanus, Ceres, and Proserpina. Juno, too, was entreated by the matrons, first, in the Capitol, then on the nearest part of the coast, whence water was procured to sprinkle the **fane** and image of the goddess. And there were sacred banquets and nightly vigils celebrated by married women. But all human efforts, all the lavish gifts of the emperor, and the propitiations of the gods, did not banish the sinister belief that the **conflagration** was the result of an order. Consequently, to get rid of the report, Nero fastened the guilt and inflicted the most exquisite tortures on a class hated for their abominations, called Christians by the populace. Christus, from whom the name had its origin, suffered the extreme penalty during the reign of Tiberius at the hands of one of our procurators, Pontius Pilatus, and a most mischievous superstition, thus checked for the moment, again broke out not only in Judaea, the first source of the evil, but even in Rome, where all things hideous and shameful from every part of the world find their center and become popular. Accordingly, an arrest was first made of all who pleaded guilty; then, upon their information, an immense multitude was convicted, not so much of the crime of firing the city, as of hatred against mankind. Mockery of every sort was added to their deaths. Covered with the skins of beasts, they were torn by dogs and perished, or were nailed to crosses, or were doomed to the flames and burnt, to serve as a nightly illumination, when daylight had expired. Nero offered his gardens for the spectacle, and was exhibiting a show in the circus, while he mingled with the people in the dress of a charioteer or stood aloft on a car. Hence, even for criminals who deserved extreme and exemplary

conflagration The Great Fire of Rome in 64 CE.

fane A temple.

Sibylline books Books used by the Romans to help tell the future or to help guide the government.

punishment, there arose a feeling of compassion; for it was not, as it seemed, for the public good, but to glut one man's cruelty, that they were being destroyed.

Source: *Annals of Tacitus,* translated by Alfred John Church and William Jackson Brodribb. London: Macmillan, 1906, 304–5.

Suetonius, Lives of the Caesars, Claudius 5.25.3–5

He forbade men of foreign birth to use the Roman names so far as those of the clans were concerned. Those who usurped the privileges of Roman citizenship he executed in the Esquiline field. He restored to the Senate the provinces of Achaia and Macedonia, which Tiberius had taken into his own charge. He deprived the Lykians of their independence because of deadly **intestine** feuds, and restored theirs to the Rhodians, since they had given up their former faults. He allowed the people of Ilium perpetual exemption from tribute, on the ground that they were the founders of the Roman race, reading an ancient letter of the Senate and People of Rome written in Hellenic to King Seleukos, in which they promised him their friendship and alliance only on condition that he should keep their kinsfolk of Ilium free from every burden. Since the Jews constantly made disturbances at the instigation of **Chrestus**, he expelled them from Rome. He allowed the envoys of the Germani to sit in the orchestra, led by their naive self-confidence; for when they had been taken to the seats occupied by the common people and saw the Parthian and Armenian envoys sitting with the Senate, they moved of their own accord to the same part of the theater, protesting that their merits and rank were no whit inferior. He utterly abolished the cruel and inhuman religion of the Druids among the Gauls, which under Augustus had merely been prohibited to Roman citizens; on the other hand he even attempted to transfer the Eleusinian rites from Attica to Rome, and had the temple of Venus Erykina in Sicily, which had fallen to ruin through age, restored at the expense of the treasury of the Roman people. He struck his treaties with foreign princes in the Forum, sacrificing a pig and reciting the ancient formula of the **fetial** priests. But these and other acts, and in fact almost the whole conduct of his reign, were dictated not so much by his own judgment as that of his wives and freedmen, since he nearly always acted in accordance with their interests and desires.

> **Chrestus/Christus** Christ.
> **fetial** Priests who would advise the Roman senate, especially on foreign matters.
> **intestine** Internal or civil. Here it means civil strife.

Source: Suetonius. *De Vita Caesarum,* translated by J. C. Rolfe. Cambridge, MA: Harvard University Press, 1920, 51–53.

AFTERMATH

The common link of these texts is persecution, which is especially evident in the Suetonius passage. The persecution of the Christians continued, on and off, until the early 300s, when Constantine became the Roman emperor in the west. In terms of the texts, these have been used for evidence of Christ outside of the New Testament, although they certainly have not been accepted by everyone (especially the Josephus passage).

ASK YOURSELF

1. There is quite a bit of discussion on the exact nature of these texts. It isn't clear whether they can be used as evidence for the existence of Jesus, or whether they are just hearsay. The text of Josephus has raised the most discussion. Do you think that Josephus, who was Jewish, would have described Christ the way he did? If your answer is no, then who could have written this?
2. Are any of the writers sympathetic to the Christians?
3. Do you think Suetonius knew what Christianity was like? Or do you think that what he wrote was just hearsay?

TOPICS TO CONSIDER

- Consider the background to these particular texts. What were the conditions in the Roman Empire when these three people were writing?
- Consider the modern idea of the separation of church and state. Consider how this idea would have been received during the first and second centuries in the Roman Empire.
- Religious persecution was fairly common during the Roman period. Do modern governments persecute their citizens because of their religious beliefs?

THE DATING OF CHRIST

It is generally thought that Christianity began with the birth of Christ. While the exact date for this event is unknown, what is known is that he was born sometime in the time of Emperor Augustus (who ruled from 31 BCE to 14 CE) and died sometime in the reign of Emperor Tiberius (ruled 14 CE to 37 CE). He was born in Judea, which had come under Roman control as early as 63 BCE. Shortly after the takeover, the Roman Senate declared Herod to be the King of the Jews in 40 BCE, and he ruled the area, under Roman protection, until 4 BCE. It wasn't until 6 CE when the area became the Roman province of Judea. The Romans put prefects (or governors) in charge, and in 23 CE they chose Pontius Pilate to be the prefect of Judea from 23 to 36 CE. According to the four Gospels and Acts, Pilate was the governor at the time of Jesus's death and was responsible for enacting the death sentence. In 1961, archaeologists, digging in a theater in Caesarea Maritima, found an inscription that stated that Pilate was a prefect.

Further Information

Hülsen, Ch. "The Burning of Rome under Nero." *American Journal of Archaeology* 13, no. 1 (Jan.–Mar., 1909): 45–48.

Laupot, Eric. "Tacitus' Fragment 2: The Anti-Roman Movement of the 'hristiani' and the Nazoreans." *Vigiliae Christianae* 54, no. 3 (2000): 233–47.

Slingerland, Dixon. "Suetonius 'Claudius' 25.4 and the Account in Cassius Dio." *Jewish Quarterly Review,* n.s., 79, no. 4 (Apr., 1989): 305–22.

Zeitlin, Solomon. "The Christ Passage in Josephus." *Jewish Quarterly Review,* n.s., 18, no. 3 (Jan., 1928): 231–55.

2. SYNOPTIC GOSPELS

INTRODUCTION

Readers of the Gospels (Matthew, Mark, Luke, and John) may notice that the texts sometimes contain very similar accounts, especially Matthew, Mark, and Luke. These three texts are called the Synoptic Gospels (from the Greek *syn*, meaning together, and *optic*, seen, or seen together) because of these similarities. Scholars have worked for centuries to determine why three of the four Gospels contain much of the same material, which is called the Synoptic Problem. One way they have examined the texts is to put them into a chart, with verses from Matthew, Mark, and Luke in parallel. When this was done, the differences became clear. One explanation for these differences is that the Gospel of Mark is the oldest Gospel, and the authors of the Gospels of Matthew and Luke borrowed material both from Mark and elsewhere. Another explanation is that Luke was written later, using both Matthew and Mark.

If Matthew and Luke are compared with the text of Mark, it will be seen that there is material found in Matthew and Luke that is not found in Mark. Where did this new material come from? And, more important, why did the authors of these two Gospels feel it necessary to add more (assuming they added more)? Further, the question remains: Where did Matthew and Luke find all the extra information that Mark did not have? Some scholars believe that there was another source that both Matthew and Luke used called Q (which stands for the German word *Quelle*, or source). Q is believed to have been a collection of the sayings of Jesus, possibly both oral and written. The existence of Q has been questioned by some, but if it actually existed, it would have been important to the early Christians.

KEEP IN MIND WHILE YOU READ

1. There is no consensus on who actually wrote these Gospels. The names Matthew, Mark, Luke, and John were applied later to the texts.
2. The order of the Gospels as we have it printed today is Matthew, Mark, Luke, and John. This order was set down in some early manuscripts and is accepted in nearly

all translations. However, there are other ancient manuscripts in which the order found is Matthew, John, Luke, and Mark.

3. The Gospels were originally written in Greek. Sometimes English translations do not reflect the differences found in the Greek manuscripts.

4. As mentioned in the "How to Evaluate a Primary Source" section, the original manuscripts of the Christian Bible do not exist. The earliest scrap of manuscript comes from the middle of the second century. Scholars examine these manuscripts, piece them together, and then try to determine what the original wording was.

Below are the texts that illustrate some of the problems with the Synoptic Gospels. The three texts tell the story of the betrayal and the arrest of Jesus. The spaces represent areas that do not occur in one or more of the three texts.

Selections from Matthew, Mark, and Luke

Synoptic Gospel Table 1

Matt 26:47–56	Mark 14:43–52	Luke 22:47–53
26:47 While he was still speaking, Judas, one of the twelve, arrived;	14:43 Immediately, while he was still speaking, Judas, one of the twelve, arrived;	22:47 While he was still speaking, suddenly a crowd came, and the one called Judas, one of the twelve, was leading them.
with him was a large crowd with swords and clubs, from the **chief priests and the elders** of the people. 26:48 Now the betrayer had given them a sign, saying, "The one I will kiss is the man; arrest him."	and with him there was a crowd with swords and clubs, from the chief priests, the scribes, and the elders. 14:44 Now the betrayer had given them a sign, saying, "The one I will kiss is the man; arrest him and lead him away under guard." 14:45 So when he came, he went up to him at once and said, **"Rabbi!"** and kissed him.	He approached Jesus to kiss him; 22:48 but Jesus said to him, "Judas, is it with a kiss that you are betraying the Son of Man?" 22:49 When those who were around him saw what was coming, they asked, "Lord, should we strike with the sword?"
26:49 At once he came up to Jesus and said, "Greetings, Rabbi!" and kissed him. 26:50 Jesus said to him, "Friend, do what you are here to do."		22:50 Then one of them struck the slave of the high priest and cut off his right ear.
Then they came and laid hands on Jesus and arrested him. 26:51 Suddenly, one of those with Jesus put	14:46 Then they laid hands on him and arrested him.	22:51 But Jesus said, "No more of this!"
		And he touched his ear and healed him.
		22:52 Then Jesus said to the chief priests, the officers of the temple police, and the elders who had come for him, "Have you come out with swords and clubs as if I were a bandit? 22:53 When I was with you day after day in the temple, you did not lay hands on me. But this is your hour, and the power of darkness!"

> **chief priests and the elders** These chief priests and elders were the leaders of the synagogue.
> **Rabbi** A religious teacher. Here the text is referring to Jesus as a rabbi.

his hand on his sword, drew it, and struck the slave of the high priest, cutting off his ear. 26:52 Then Jesus said to him, "Put your sword back into its place; for all who take the sword will perish by the sword. 26:53 Do you think that I cannot appeal to my Father, and he will at once send me more than twelve legions of angels? 26:54 But how then would the scriptures be fulfilled, which say it must happen in this way?" 26:55 At that hour Jesus said to the crowds, "Have you come out with swords and clubs to arrest me as though I were a bandit? Day after day I sat in the temple teaching, and you did not arrest me. 26:56 But all this has taken place, so that the scriptures of the prophets may be fulfilled." Then all the disciples deserted him and fled.

14:47 But one of those who stood near drew his sword and struck the slave of the high priest, cutting off his ear.

14:48 Then Jesus said to them, "Have you come out with swords and clubs to arrest me as though I were a bandit? 14:49 Day after day I was with you in the temple teaching, and you did not arrest me. But let the **scriptures** be fulfilled." 14:50 All of them deserted him and fled.

14:51 A certain young man was following him, wearing nothing but a linen cloth. They caught hold of him, 14:52 but he left the linen cloth and ran off naked.

> **scriptures** The Hebrew Bible (called the Old Testament by the Christians). Many of the texts that make up the Christian Bible were not yet written.
>
> **the temple** Technically the Second Temple, built after the Persian king Cyrus the Great let many Israelites go back to Israel after they had been taken to Babylon by King Nebuchanezzer II. It was completed around 515 BCE. This temple was destroyed by the Romans in 70 CE.

clubs as if I were a bandit? 22:53 When I was with you day after day in **the temple**, you did not lay hands on me. But this is your hour, and the power of darkness!"

Source: Society of Biblical Literature, eds. *Harper Collins Study Bible: New Revised Standard Version.* Rev. ed. New York: HarperCollins, 2006. All Scripture quotations appear from the *New Revised Standard Version Bible.* Division of Christian Education of the National Council of Churches of Christ in the United States of America, 1989.

AFTERMATH

Ancient readers knew that there were differences in the texts that were passed down, but in many cases the differences were ignored or explained away. Many Christians (both ancient and modern) would pick certain phrases that agreed with their point of view and ignore the near-parallel phrases. The Synoptic texts on divorce are a good example. In Matthew 5:32, Jesus states that the only reason to get a divorce would be unfaithfulness. He also states that anyone who marries a divorced woman commits adultery. Jesus, in Mark 10:2, states that divorce is not allowed, and if people who are divorced remarry, they are committing adultery. Those who support divorce will use Matthew to support their view, and those who do not support divorce will use Mark. Other early Christians, especially Tatian, believed that the Gospels were originally one story and later were written down by four people. Tatian then produced a work called the *Diatesseron,* which was his attempt to harmonize the four Gospels (see sidebar).

ASK YOURSELF

1. Who do you think the naked young man was, and why do Matthew and Luke not include this part?

2. Why would Luke include the details of the group that came to get Jesus (the chief priests, the officers of the temple police, and the elders) while Matthew and Mark do not give these details?

3. Should the texts of the Christian Bible be ordered according to the date they were created?

TOPICS TO CONSIDER

- ✍ Does it matter that there are three texts that tell slightly different versions of the same story? How does the fact that these are sacred texts to Christians affect your answer?

- ✍ The Gospel of John is not considered part of the Synoptic Problem. Looking at the *Synopsis of the Four Gospels* by Kurt Aland (see Further Information below), compare the text of John with the Synoptic Gospels and explain why the text of John was different. Be sure to use examples from the text to illustrate your answer.

- ✍ Many people have thought that the text by Matthew was the first because it appears first in the New Testament. Consider the history of this particular text in terms of its importance to both early and modern Christians and why it is now placed first.

THE HARMONIZATION OF THE GOSPELS

Many early Christians knew that there were similar accounts found in the various Gospels. The cost of producing a book was expensive, primarily because each book had to be copied out by hand. For this and other reasons, some decided to shorten the four Gospels down to one account. One such person was Tatian, who lived sometime in the second century. His compilation is the *Diatessaron*. This book was very popular in the churches of Syria and was mainly used until the 400s CE when they started to use the four separate Gospels. Theodoret of Cyrus, a Christian living in the 400s, stated that he had collected over 200 copies of the *Diatessaron*, put them away, and replaced them with the four Gospels. Creating a harmony of the Gospels was not just an ancient endeavor. Thomas Jefferson, the primary author of the Declaration of Independence and the third president of the United States, also created his own compilation of the Gospels. He titled it *The Life and Morals of Jesus of Nazareth*, or as it is known today, the *Jefferson Bible*. In it he took out all references to angels, miracles, and the divinity of Jesus, and he literally took a razor to the Greek, Latin, French, and English editions and arranged the pieces in what he thought was the correct order. Jefferson did not want it published during his lifetime.

Further Information

Abakuks, Adris. "A Statistical Study of the Triple-Link Model in the Synoptic Problem." *Journal of the Royal Statistical Society*, Series A (Statistics in Society), 169, no. 1 (2006): 49–60.

Aland, Kurt, ed. *Synopsis of the Four Gospels: Greek-English Edition of the Synopsis Quattuor Evangeliorum*. 10th ed. Stuttgart: Biblia-Druck, 1993.

Bultmann, Rudolf. "The New Approach to the Synoptic Problem." *Journal of Religion* 6, no. 4 (Jul., 1926): 337–62.

Farmer, William R. *The Synoptic Problem: A Critical Analysis.* New York: Macmillan, 1964.

Honoré, A. M. "A Statistical Study of the Synoptic Problem." *Novum Testamentum* 10, Fasc. 2/3 (Apr.–Jul., 1968): 95–147.

Porúbčan, Štefan. "Form Criticism and the Synoptic Problem." *Novum Testamentum* 7, Fasc. 2 (Mar., 1964): 81–118.

Sanders, E. P., and Margaret Davies. *Studying the Synoptic Gospels.* London: SCM Press, 1989.

The Synoptic Gospels: Our Primary Sources for the Study of Jesus, by James F. McGrath. http://blue.butler.edu/˜jfmcgrat/jesus/synoptics.htm.

The Synoptic Gospels: Structural Outlines and Unique Materials, by Felix Just. http://catholic-resources.org/Bible/Synoptic_Outlines.htm.

3. BAPTISM

INTRODUCTION

Baptism was one of the most important ceremonies in early Christianity. In this period, to become a Christian, one had to accept Jesus as the savior and at some point be baptized. The ceremony usually took place among other believers. Jesus was baptized by John the Baptist, which many believe was the start of his ministry. The Gospels record that the voice of God was heard at Jesus's baptism: "You are my Son, the Beloved; with you I am well pleased" (Luke 3:22). The Book of Acts records that many of the disciples were baptized, and Jesus also told the disciples to go out and baptize others, so at the very beginning of Christianity it was a ritual in which most Christians had to participate.

However, some question whether the writings of the New Testament on this issue reflect what was happening in the earliest Christian communities. It was common later in the fourth century for adults who were Christian to wait until they were on their deathbed to ask for baptism, since it was believed they would then enter heaven sinless (Emperor Constantine is a good example). There are three texts listed below that relate to baptism: a section from the Gospel of Mark, a section from 1 Corinthians, and a large section from Tertullian's *On Baptism*.

KEEP IN MIND WHILE YOU READ

1. The many examples from the New Testament that mention baptism were used over and over by the later Christian authors. Tertullian is a prime example of this, especially in chapter 9 where he lists all of the places where Jesus used water. The scriptural quotations Tertullian uses are listed within the text.
2. Paul, in the passage from 1 Corinthians, is dealing with a problem in Corinth over baptism. Some people believed that they were more important because of who baptized them. Paul, as an apostle, could and did baptize, but he doesn't seem to be too interested in performing this ritual often.
3. Tertullian, in his *On Baptism,* is arguing against those who think that Christians do not need baptism. This is especially clear if one reads the entire text. Tertullian also

        lists who should be in charge of this ceremony, when it should be done, and what should happen immediately after being baptized.

4. Tertullian looks back at many examples from the Old Testament in order to explain the importance of baptism to Christians, especially to those who believed that baptism was not important.

5. Tertullian's *On Baptism* was meant to be a guidebook for those who wanted to be baptized, as well as an instructional tool for those who would be performing it. He gives a list of who would be responsible for dealing with problems in other Christian communities.

Mark 16:14–16

Later he appeared to the eleven themselves as they were sitting at the table; and he up-braided them for their lack of faith and stubbornness, because they had not believed those who saw him after he had risen. And he said to them, "Go into all the world and proclaim the good news to the whole creation. The one who believes and is baptized will be saved; but the one who does not believe will be condemned."

1 Corinthians 1:13–17

Has Christ been divided? Was Paul crucified for you? Or were you baptized in the name of Paul? I thank God that I baptized none of you except Crispus and Gaius, so that no one can say that you were baptized in my name. (I did baptize also the household of Stephanas; beyond that, I do not know whether I baptized anyone else.) For Christ did not send me to baptize but to proclaim the gospel, and not with eloquent wisdom, so that the cross of Christ might not be emptied of its power.

Source: Society of Biblical Literature, eds. *Harper Collins Study Bible: New Revised Standard Version*. Rev. ed. New York: HarperCollins, 2006. All Scripture quotations appear from the *New Revised Standard Version Bible*. Division of Christian Education of the National Council of Churches of Christ in the United States of America, 1989.

Tertullian, On Baptism, *Selections*

Chapter 1

Happy is our sacrament of water, in that, by washing away the sins of our early blindness, we are set free and admitted into eternal life! A treatise on this matter will not be superfluous; instructing not only such as are just becoming formed (in the faith), but those who, content with having simply believed, without full examination of the reasons of the traditions, carry (in mind), through ignorance, an untried though probable faith. The consequence is, that a viper of the **Cainite heresy,** lately conversant in this quarter, has carried away a great number with her most venomous doctrine, making it her first aim to destroy baptism, which is quite in accordance with nature; for vipers and asps and basilisks themselves generally do affect arid and waterless places. But we, little fishes, after the example of our **IChThUS** Jesus Christ, are born in water, nor have we safety in any other way than by permanently abiding in water; so that most monstrous creature, who had no right to teach even sound doctrine (See 1 Tim. 2:11–12), knew full well how to kill the little fishes, by taking them away from the water!

Chapter 6

Not that in the waters we obtain the Holy Spirit; but in the water, under (the witness of) the angel, we are cleansed, and prepared for the Holy Spirit. In this case also **a type** has preceded; for thus was John beforehand the Lord's forerunner, "preparing His ways" (Luke 1:76). Thus, too, does the angel, the witness of baptism, "make the paths straight" (Isa. 40:3; Matt. 3:3) for the Holy Spirit, who is about to come upon us, by the washing away of sins, which faith, sealed in (the name of) the Father, and the Son, and the Holy Spirit, obtains. For if "in the mouth of three witnesses every word shall stand:" (Deut. 19:15; Matt. 18:16; 2 Cor. 13:1)—while, through the benediction, we have the same (three) as witnesses of our faith whom we have as sureties of our salvation too—how much more does the number of the divine names suffice for the assurance of our hope likewise! Moreover, after the pledging both of the attestation of faith and the promise of salvation under "three witnesses," there is added, of necessity, mention of the Church; inasmuch as, wherever there are three, that is, the Father, the Son, and the Holy Spirit, there is the Church, which is a body of three (see Matt. 18:20).

Chapter 8

In the next place the hand is laid on us, invoking and inviting the Holy Spirit through benediction. Shall it be granted possible for human ingenuity to summon a spirit into water, and, by the application of hands from above, to animate their union into one body with another spirit of so clear sound; and shall it not be possible for God, in the case of His own organ, to produce, by means of "holy hands," a sublime spiritual modulation? But this, as well as the former, is derived from the old sacramental rite in which Jacob blessed his grandsons, born of Joseph, Ephrem and Manasses; with his hands laid on them and

a type Many Christian writers looked to other sections of the Bible that did not outwardly appear to be related to the subject. In this case, Tertullian believed that John the Baptist was a forerunner of Christ. In chapter 9 Tertullian believed that the Hebrews escaping from the Egyptians by crossing water was a symbol of baptism.

Cainite heresy The Cainites were a Gnostic group that venerated Cain, the brother of Abel. According to the Cainites, the God described in the Old Testament was evil and had killed Cain. For them, Cain was the first victim of this evil God.

IChThUS An acronym. The Greek word for fish is *ichthus,* and it became a very important symbol in Christianity, and remains so today (for example, the fish symbol on cars). The Greek words are: **I**esus **Ch**ristus, **Th**eu **u**ius, **s**oter, or Jesus Christ, son of God, Savior.

interchanged, and indeed so transversely slanted one over the other, that, by delineating Christ, they even portended the future benediction into Christ. Then, over our cleansed and blessed bodies willingly descends that Holiest Spirit from the Father. Over the waters of baptism, recognizing as it were His primeval seat, He came down on the Lord" in the shape of a dove," (Matt. 3:16; Luke 3:22) in order that the nature of the Holy Spirit might be declared by means of the creature (the emblem) of simplicity and innocence, because even in her bodily structure the dove is without literal gall. And accordingly He says, "Be simple as doves" (Matt. 10:16). Even this is not without the supporting evidence of a preceding figure. For just as, after the waters of the deluge, by which the old iniquity was purged—after the baptism, so to say, of the world—a dove was the herald which announced to the earth the assuagement of celestial wrath, when she had been sent her way out of the ark, and had returned with the olive-branch, a sign which even among the nations is the fore-token of peace; so by the self-same law of heavenly effect, to earth—that is, to our flesh—as it emerges from the font, after its old sins flies the dove of the Holy Spirit, bringing us the peace of God, sent out from the heavens where is the Church, the typified ark. But the world returned unto sin; in which point baptism would ill be compared to the deluge. And so it is destined to fire; just as the man too is, who after baptism renews his sins: (2 Pet. 2:9; Heb. 10: 26–27, 29) so that this also ought to be accepted as a sign for our admonition.

Chapter 9

How many, therefore, are the pleas of nature, how many the privileges of grace, how many the solemnities of discipline, the figures, the preparations, the prayers, which have ordained the sanctity of water? First, indeed, when the people, set unconditionally free, escaped the violence of the Egyptian king by crossing over through water, it was water that extinguished the king himself, with his entire forces (Exodus 14:27–30). What figure more manifestly fulfilled in the sacrament of baptism? The nations are set free from the world by means of water, to wit: and the devil, their old tyrant, they leave quite behind, overwhelmed in the water. Again, water is restored from its defect of "bitterness" to its native grace of "sweetness" by the tree of Moses (See Exodus 15:24–25). That tree was Christ, restoring, from within Himself, the veins of sometime envenomed and bitter nature into the all-healthful waters of baptism. This is the water which flowed continuously down for the people from the "accompanying rock;" for if Christ is "the Rock," without doubt we see baptism blest by the water in Christ. How mighty is the grace of water, in the sight of God and His Christ, for the confirmation of baptism! Never is Christ without water: if, that is, He is Himself baptized in water (Matt. 3:13–17); inaugurates in water the first rudimentary displays of His power, when invited to a marriage (John 2:1–11); invites the thirsty, when He makes a discourse, to His own sempiternal water (John 7:37, 38); approves, when teaching concerning love, among works of charity, the cup of water offered to a poor (child) (Matt. 10:42); recruits His strength at a well (John 4:6); walks over the water (Matt. 14:25); willingly crosses the sea (Mark 4:36); ministers water to His disciples (John 13:1–12). Onward even to the passion does the witness of baptism last: while He is being surrendered to the cross, water intervenes; witness Pilate's hands (Matt. 27:24); when He is wounded, forth from His side bursts water; witness the soldier's lance (John 19:34)!

Chapter 14

But they roll back an objection from that apostle himself, in that he said, "For Christ sent me not to baptize" (1 Cor. 1:17), as if by this argument baptism were done away! For if so, why did he baptize Gaius, and Crispus, and the house of Stephanas (1 Corinthians 1:14–16)? However, even if Christ had not sent him to baptize, yet He had given other apostles the precept to baptize. But these words were written to the Corinthians in regard of the circumstances of that particular time; seeing that schisms and dissensions were agitated among them, while one attributes everything to Paul, another to Apollos (1 Cor. 1: 11–12; 3: 3–4). For which reason the "peace-making" apostle, for fear he should seem to claim all gifts for himself, says that he had been sent "not to baptize, but to preach." For preaching is the first thing, baptizing after. Therefore the preaching came first: but I think baptizing was lawful to one who preaches.

Chapter 16

We have indeed, likewise, a second font, (itself one with the former,) that of blood, concerning which the Lord said, "I have to be baptized with a baptism," (Luke 12:50) when He had been baptized already. For He had come "by means of water and blood," (1 John 5:6) just as John has written; that He might be baptized by the water and glorified by the blood, to make us, in like manner, called by water and chosen by blood. These two baptisms He sent out from the wound in His pierced side, in order that they who believed in His blood might be bathed with the water; they who had been bathed in the water might likewise drink the blood (John 6:53). This is the baptism which both stands in lieu of the fontal bathing when that has not been received, and restores it when lost.

Chapter 17

For concluding our brief subject, it remains to put you in mind also of the due observance of giving and receiving baptism. Of giving it, the chief priest (who is the bishop) has the right: in the next place, the presbyters and deacons, yet not without the bishop's authority, on account of the honor of the Church, which when it is preserved, peace is preserved. Beside these, even laymen have the right; for what is equally received can be equally given. Unless bishops, or priests, or deacons, be on the spot, other disciples are called i.e. to the work. The word of the Lord ought not to be hidden by any: in like manner, too, baptism, which is equally God's property, can be administered by all. But how much more is the rule of reverence and modesty incumbent on laymen—seeing that these powers belong to their superiors—lest they assume to themselves the specific function of the bishop! Emulation of the episcopal office is the mother of schisms. The most holy apostle has said, that "all things are lawful, but not all expedient" (1 Cor. 10:23). Let it suffice assuredly, in cases of necessity, to avail yourself (of that rule, if at any time circumstance either of place, or

> **Thecla** The main character (along with the Apostle Paul) in *The Acts of Paul and Thecla*, which was an apocryphal work. This means that the authorship was believed to be Paul, but in fact it was written sometime in the middle of the second century.

of time, or of person compels you (so to do); for then the steadfast courage of the rescuer, when the situation of the endangered one is urgent, is exceptionally admissible; inasmuch as he will be guilty of a human creature's loss if he shall refrain from bestowing what he had free liberty to bestow. But the woman of pertness, who has usurped the power to teach, will of course not give birth for herself likewise to a right of baptizing, unless some new beast shall arise like the former; so that, just as the one abolished baptism, so some other should in her own right confer it! But if the writings which wrongly go under Paul's name, claim **Thecla**'s example as a license for women's teaching and baptizing, let them know that, in Asia, the presbyter who composed that writing, as if he were augmenting Paul's fame from his own store, after being convicted, and confessing that he had done it from love of Paul, was removed from his office. For how credible would it seem, that he who has not permitted a woman even to learn with over-boldness, should give a female the power of teaching and of baptizing! "Let them be silent," he says, "and at home consult their own husbands" (1 Cor. 14:34–35).

Source: Roberts, Rev. Alexander, and James Donaldson, eds. *The Ante-Nicene Fathers: Translations of the Writings of the Fathers Down to A.D. 325*, vol. 3. New York: Charles Scribner's Sons, 1905, 669, 672–673, 676, 677.

AFTERMATH

By the time of Tertullian, baptism was a common feature of early Christianity, but as he points out, there were some who did not believe that it held any religious power. Over time, these groups disappeared (either through persecution or the lack of new followers). Another topic that starts to appear around the time of Tertullian is that of infant baptism: Is an infant saved if the child is unbaptized at the time of death? Should infant baptism occur when the infant is not making the active choice to become a Christian? These questions became extremely important in early Christianity.

There were at least three early Christians who had read Tertullian's *On Baptism* and had used it in their own arguments. These were Didymus the Blind, Jerome, and, later, Isidore of Seville (Evans xxxiv–xxxvi). Didymus in particular made use of the same biblical comparisons as Tertullian. Tertullian made it abundantly clear that women should not perform baptisms. In the modern period, women still have had problems becoming priests and especially doing baptisms; this is primarily because of the Apostle Paul but also because of Tertullian.

ASK YOURSELF

1. Tertullian, a Christian, makes use of examples from the Old Testament. Why do you think the Old Testament was so important to Tertullian?
2. Clearly, Tertullian is writing in response to some complaints about the efficacy of baptism. Using the text of Tertullian, why does this person or group think that baptism is useless? Do you think Tertullian has given a good response?
3. Tertullian makes it clear that women cannot perform baptisms under any circumstances. How does he back up this command with the use of the New Testament? Do you think this is reason enough to prevent women from baptizing someone, both in the ancient world and in the modern?

TOPICS TO CONSIDER

- ❧ There were not too many controversies in early Christianity about baptism. However, problems arose when people switched churches and became rebaptized. Rebaptism still occurs in churches today. Do research on the trends of baptism in the modern Christianity (both Protestant and Catholic) and discuss what these various Christianities say in terms of baptizing someone again.
- ❧ One of the biggest topics in Christianity today is whether or not to allow women to become priests. Consider how the views of Tertullian and other early Christian writers affect the controversy today.
- ❧ Paul seems to put little effort into baptism or think that it is totally unimportant. Of course, he is responding to particular problems. Consider how Paul's view of baptism is similar to or different from that of the other New Testament writers. Also consider how his view affected early Christian writers up through the fourth century.

Further Information

The Acts of Paul and Thecla. http://www.fordham.edu/halsall/basis/thecla.asp.

Beasley-Murray, G. R. *Baptism in the New Testament*. London: MacMillan, 1962.

Evans, E., ed. *Tertullian's Homily on Baptism*. London: SPCK, 1964.

Ferguson, Everett. *Baptism in the Early Church: History, Theology, and Liturgy in the First Five Centuries*. Grand Rapids, MI: Eerdman, 2009.

Hamman, André, ed., and Thomas, Halton, trans. *Baptism: Ancient Liturgies and Patristic Texts*. New York: Alba House, 1967.

McDonnell, Kilian. *Christian Initiation and Baptism in the Holy Spirit: Evidence from the First Eight Centuries*. 2nd rev. ed. Collegeville, MN: Liturgical Press, 1994.

The Tertullian Project. http://www.tertullian.org/index.htm.

4. CASTRATION

INTRODUCTION

Castration was the act of cutting off the testicles, either voluntarily or not. At no time was castration a ritual in early Christianity. It is mentioned in the New Testament, and in the following centuries it had an interesting history in early Christianity. While it does not seem to have been a problem in the first century, castration was a problem for some early Christian groups by the 300s CE when it is mentioned in the very first canon of the ecumenical Council of Nicea, which declares that men who castrate themselves cannot become priests. Eunuchs (castrated males) were also known outside of Christian circles, and it appears that the rise of eunuchs in Christianity corresponds to a rise of eunuchs in the Roman Empire during the second to the fourth centuries (see Stevenson 496–511). The following texts are from Galatians 5:1–14; Matthew 19:8–12; Clement of Alexandria, *Miscellanies* 3.1; Canon 1 from the Council of Nicea; and Eusebius of Caesarea, *Ecclesiastical History* 6.8.1–5.

KEEP IN MIND WHILE YOU READ

1. Part of the desire to castrate oneself was taken from the statement of Jesus about eunuchs (see Matthew, below). Some took this literally and castrated themselves.
2. By far the most famous eunuch in early Christianity was Origen, who lived from 185 to 251 CE. Origen was one who had taken the statement of Jesus literally. It may be that he regretted his decision later, or at least regretted that his self-castration had become open news.
3. As asceticism became more popular, especially among women, the desire for some men to castrate themselves also increased. Part of the reason for this was that men, to reduce the impact of their exposure to women, decided to control their sexual desires by castration.

Galatians 5:1–14

For freedom Christ has set us free. Stand firm, therefore, and do not submit again to a yoke of slavery. Listen! I, Paul, am telling you that if you let yourselves be circumcised, Christ will be of no benefit to you. Once again I testify to every man who lets himself be circumcised that he is obliged to obey the entire law. You who want to be justified by the law have cut yourselves off from Christ; you have fallen away from grace. For through the Spirit, by faith, we eagerly wait for the hope of righteousness. For in Christ Jesus neither circumcision nor uncircumcision counts for anything; the only thing that counts is faith working through love. You were running well; who prevented you from obeying the truth? Such persuasion does not come from the one who calls you. A little yeast leavens the whole batch of dough. I am confident about you in the Lord that you will not think otherwise. But whoever it is that is confusing you will pay the penalty. But my friends, why am I still being persecuted if I am still preaching circumcision? In that case the offense of the cross has been removed. I wish those who unsettle you would castrate themselves! For you were called to freedom, brothers and sisters; only do not use your freedom as an opportunity for self-indulgence, but through love become slaves to one another. For the whole law is summed up in a single commandment, "You shall love your neighbor as yourself."

Matthew 19:8–12

He (Jesus) said to them, "It was because you were so hard-hearted that Moses allowed you to divorce your wives, but from the beginning it was not so. And I say to you, whoever divorces his wife, except for unchastity, and marries another commits adultery." His disciples said to him, "If such is the case of a man with his wife, it is better not to marry." But he said to them, "Not everyone can accept this teaching, but only those to whom it is given. For there are eunuchs who have been so from birth, and there are eunuchs who have been made eunuchs by others, and there are eunuchs who have made themselves eunuchs for the sake of the kingdom of heaven. Let anyone accept this who can."

Source: Society of Biblical Literature, eds. *Harper Collins Study Bible: New Revised Standard Version*. Rev. ed. New York: HarperCollins, 2006. All Scripture quotations appear from the *New Revised Standard Version Bible*. Division of Christian Education of the National Council of Churches of Christ in the United States of America, 1989.

> **Valentinians** A Gnostic Christian group that started in the second century. It was started by Valentinus. Irenaeus, who lived from about 115 to 202, wrote quite a bit about the Valentinians in his *Against Heresies*.

Clement of Alexandria, Miscellanies *3.1*

The **Valentinians**, who described the union of man and woman as derived from the divine emanation above, approve of marriage.

The followers of **Basilides**, on the other hand, say when the apostles asked whether it was better not to take a wife, the Lord replied: "Not all can receive this saying: there are some eunuchs from birth, others from necessity." And their explanation of this saying is that some men, from their birth, by nature avoid women, and those who are naturally of this temperament, do well if they do not consider a wife. These, they say, are eunuchs from birth. Those, however, who are eunuchs from necessity, are those theatrically trained who only control themselves because they have a repeated eagerness for glory. Furthermore, those who have suffered accidental castration have become eunuchs of necessity. Those, then, who are eunuchs of necessity are not eunuchs by word or reason. But those who castrated themselves for the sake of the eternal kingdom, will avoid for that reason, the troubles marriage makes, because they are afraid of the burden and also the worry of attending to family life.

Basilides Another Gnostic Christian who started his own religious movement in Egypt during the second century. Clement of Alexandria mentions them often in his writings.

Source: Clement of Alexandria. *Miscellanies,* 182–202 CE. Translated by Kevin Kaatz, 2012.

Eusebius of Caesarea, Ecclesiastical History *6.8.1–5*

At this time while Origen was conducting catechetical instruction at Alexandria, a deed was done by him which proved an immature and youthful mind, but at the same time gave the highest proof of faith and continence. For he took the words, "There are eunuchs who have made themselves eunuchs for the kingdom of heaven's sake," in too literal and extreme a sense. And in order to fulfill the Savior's word, and at the same time to take away from the unbelievers all opportunity for scandal,—for, although young, he met for the study of divine things with women as well as men,—he carried out in action the word of the Savior. He thought that this would not be known by many of his acquaintances. But it was impossible for him, though desiring to do so, to keep such an action secret. When Demetrius, who presided over that parish, at last learned of this, he admired greatly the daring nature of the act, and as he perceived his zeal and the genuineness of his faith, he immediately exhorted him to courage, and urged him the more to continue his work of catechetical instruction. Such was he at that time. But soon afterward, seeing that he was prospering, and becoming great and distinguished among all men, the same Demetrius, overcome by human weakness, wrote of his deed as most foolish to the bishops throughout the world. But the bishops of Caesarea and Jerusalem, who were especially notable and distinguished among the bishops of Palestine, considering Origen worthy in the highest degree of the honor, ordained him a presbyter. Thereupon his fame increased greatly, and his name became renowned everywhere, and he obtained no small reputation for virtue and wisdom. But Demetrius, having nothing else that he could say against him, except this deed of his boyhood, accused him bitterly, and dared to include with him in these accusations those who had raised him to the presbyterate.

Source: Wace, Henry, and Philip Schaff, eds. *A Select Library of Nicene and Post-Nicene Fathers of the Christian Church,* vol. 1. Oxford: Parker, 1890, 254–55.

Canon 1 from the Council of Nicea

barbarians A term used by both the Romans and the Greeks to describe people who lived outside of their borders. Usually (although not always) they were considered to be savage and without civilization.

If anyone in sickness has been subjected by physicians to a surgical operation, or if he has been castrated by **barbarians,** let him remain among the clergy; but, if any one in sound health has castrated himself, it behooves that such an one, if [already] enrolled among the clergy, should cease [from his ministry], and that from henceforth no such person should be promoted. But, as it is evident that this is said of those who willfully do the thing and presume to castrate themselves, so if any have been made eunuchs by barbarians, or by their masters, and should otherwise be found worthy, such men the Canon admits to the clergy.

Source: Schaff, Philip, and Henry Wace, eds. *A Select Library of Nicene and Post-Nicene Fathers of the Christian Church*, vol. 14. New York: Charles Scribner's Sons, 1900, 8.

AFTERMATH

Males who castrated themselves were a minor problem in the 300s CE, since the topic continued to be brought up. During this period (and slightly earlier), many Christian writers used the passage from Matthew, not to promote physical castration, but to promote asceticism and celibacy. The making of a eunuch meant that a person would abstain from all sexual activity, as if a physical castration had taken place. Despite Canon 1 from Nicea, the practice continued. As noted by Caner (406), Epiphanius of Salamis, writing in 377 CE, noted that there were a number of monks who castrated themselves, and in 390 CE, John Chrysostom wrote that there were people doing this in Antioch (Caner 407).

ASK YOURSELF

1. If you are male, does the statement made by Jesus in Matthew make you want to castrate yourself? If not, what does the passage mean to you? If you are a woman, what does this passage mean to you? Can a female be a eunuch?
2. Eusebius states that Bishop Demetrius was at first happy with the choice that Origen made. Do you think this statement is true, or does Eusebius have a reason to stretch the truth? Why do you think that Demetrius changed his mind and went against Origen?
3. What do you think made Paul so upset that he wished that those causing problems would castrate themselves?

TOPICS TO CONSIDER

- ✒ Self-castration may have had a following in early Christianity, but it is certainly not very popular among modern Christians. Consider the history of castration and how it affects Christianity today, especially the text from Matthew.
- ✒ Origen's writings had an important impact on many writers. Later, however, he was seen as a heretic. Consider why there was a change in how Christians saw Origen. Consider whether his castration had anything to do with this change.

    Eusebius mentions that men who have been castrated either by barbarians or by their masters are still eligible to be clergy. Consider how popular it was for the barbarians and/or owners of slaves to castrate someone. Consider why this would have been done and what purpose it would have served.

Further Information

Caner, Daniel F. "The Practice and Prohibition of Self-Castration in Early Christianity." *Vigiliae Christianae* 51, no. 4 (Nov., 1997): 396–415.

Hanson, R.P.C. "A Note on Origen's Self-Mutilation." *Vigiliae Christianae* 20, no. 2 (Jun., 1966): 81–82.

Kuefler, Mathew. *The Manly Eunuch: Masculinity, Gender Ambiguity, and Christian Ideology in Late Antiquity*. Chicago: University of Chicago Press, 2001.

Stevenson, Walter. "The Rise of Eunuchs in Greco-Roman Antiquity." *Journal of the History of Sexuality* 5, no. 4 (Apr., 1995): 495–511.

Talbott, Rick. "Imagining the Matthean Eunuch Community: Kyriarchy on the Chopping Block." *Journal of Feminist Studies in Religion* 22, no. 1 (Spring, 2006): 21–43.

Taylor, Gary. *Castration: An Abbreviated History of Western Manhood*. New York: Routledge, 2002.

5. CIRCUMCISION

INTRODUCTION

Circumcision was an important rite in Judaism, with it being a covenant between God and his people. As seen below, eight days after birth, Jewish males would have their foreskin removed. Jesus was circumcised (Luke 2:21). Paul, who was a Jew, was circumcised (Philippians 3:5), and we know that Paul himself circumcised Timothy when Timothy was an adult (Acts 16:3). However, as Christians began to spread the message of Christ to the Gentile population (the non-Jewish population), circumcision was holding back these men from joining. They clearly did not want to have their foreskin cut off in order to join this new religious movement. After this early Christian leaders began to wonder if circumcision was a requirement for all Gentile men who wanted to become Christians. The first church council was held in Jerusalem, probably around 50 CE, to discuss this. By now Paul and Barnabas had been allowing Gentile men to join Christianity without being circumcised. According to Acts 14:26–15:29 and Galatians 2:11–17 (given below), Peter stood up at the meeting and declared that new Christian males did not need it, and Paul and Barnabas were allowed to preach to noncircumcised men. It was a break from Judaism, but Christians adopted the language of circumcision in that it now became spiritual rather than physical. The texts below include Genesis 17:9–19 and 17:22–27; Romans 2:12–3:5; 3:28–4:17, 1 Corinthians 7:18–20; and Galatians 2:1–10.

KEEP IN MIND WHILE YOU READ

1. The council that met in Jerusalem to decide the fate of circumcision decided that there were four rules that the new Gentile converts had to follow: they had to "abstain only from things polluted by idols and from fornication and from whatever has been strangled and from blood" (Acts 15:20).
2. Before Paul, early Christians only targeted the Jewish population for proselytizing. Because of this, early Christianity spread through the Mediterranean by way of Jewish communities. After Paul, membership was open to anyone who could follow a few rules and who believed in Christ.

3. For Christians, faith in Christ was the first "commandment," and it was through this belief that they broke away from Judaism, their mother religion. This new faith allowed Christians to move away from many of the Jewish laws, including restrictions on eating certain foods and working on the Sabbath.

Genesis 17:9–14, 17:22–27

God said to Abraham, "As for you, you shall keep my covenant, you and your offspring after you throughout their generations. This is my covenant, which you shall keep, between me and you and your offspring after you: Every male among you shall be circumcised. You shall circumcise the flesh of your foreskins, and it shall be a sign of the covenant between me and you. Throughout your generations every male among you shall be circumcised when he is eight days old, including the slave born in your house and the one bought with your money from any foreigner who is not of your offspring. Both the slave born in your house and the one bought with your money must be circumcised. So shall my covenant be in your flesh an everlasting covenant. Any uncircumcised male who is not circumcised in the flesh of his foreskin shall be cut off from his people; he has broken my covenant."

. . . And when he had finished talking with him, God went up from Abraham. Then Abraham took his son Ishmael and all the slaves born in his house or bought with his money, every male among the men of Abraham's house, and he circumcised the flesh of their foreskins that very day, as God had said to him. Abraham was ninety-nine years old when he was circumcised in the flesh of his foreskin. And his son Ishmael was thirteen years old when he was circumcised in the flesh of his foreskin. That very day Abraham and his son Ishmael were circumcised; and all the men of his house, slaves born in the house and those bought with money from a foreigner, were circumcised with him.

Romans 2:12–3:5; 3:28–4:17

All who have sinned apart from **the law** will also perish apart from the law, and all who have sinned under the law will be judged by the law. For it is not the hearers of the law who are righteous in God's sight, but the doers of the law who will be justified. When Gentiles, who do not possess the law, do instinctively what the law requires, these, though not having the law, are a law to themselves. They show that what the law requires is written on their hearts, to which their own conscience also bears witness; and their conflicting thoughts will accuse or perhaps excuse them on the day when, according to my gospel, God, through Jesus Christ, will judge the secret thoughts of all. But if you call yourself

> **the law** The law was taken from the Old Testament. For early Christians, this was the only religious text they had.

a Jew and rely on the law and boast of your relation to God and know his will and determine what is best because you are instructed in the law, and if you are sure that you are a guide to the blind, a light to those who are in darkness, a corrector of the foolish, a teacher of children, having in the law the embodiment of knowledge and truth, you, then, that teach others, will you not teach yourself? While you preach against stealing, do you steal? You that forbid **adultery**, do you commit adultery? You that abhor idols, do you rob temples? You that boast in the law, do you dishonor God by breaking the law? For, as it is written, "The name of God is blasphemed among the Gentiles because of you."

> **adultery** Having sexual intercourse with someone outside of marriage.

Circumcision indeed is of value if you obey the law; but if you break the law, your circumcision has become uncircumcision. So, if those who are uncircumcised keep the requirements of the law, will not their uncircumcision be regarded as circumcision? Then those who are physically uncircumcised but keep the law will condemn you that have the written code and circumcision but break the law. For a person is not a Jew who is one outwardly, nor is true circumcision something external and physical. Rather, a person is a Jew who is one inwardly, and real circumcision is a matter of the heart—it is spiritual and not literal. Such a person receives praise not from others but from God. Then what advantage has the Jew? Or what is the value of circumcision? Much, in every way. For in the first place the Jews were entrusted with the oracles of God. What if some were unfaithful? Will their faithlessness nullify the faithfulness of God? By no means! Although everyone is a liar, let God be proved true, as it is written, "So that you may be justified in your words, and prevail in your judging." But if our injustice serves to confirm the justice of God, what should we say? That God is unjust to inflict wrath on us? (I speak in a human way.) . . .

For we hold that a person is justified by faith apart from works prescribed by the law. Or is God the God of Jews only? Is he not the God of Gentiles also? Yes, of Gentiles also, since God is one; and he will justify the circumcised on the ground of faith and the uncircumcised through that same faith. Do we then overthrow the law by this faith? By no means! On the contrary, we uphold the law. What then are we to say was gained by Abraham, our ancestor according to the flesh? For if Abraham was justified by works, he has something to boast about, but not before God. For what does the scripture say? "Abraham believed God, and it was reckoned to him as righteousness." Now to one who works, wages are not reckoned as a gift but as something due. But to one who without works trusts him who justifies the ungodly, such faith is reckoned as righteousness. So also David speaks of the blessedness of those to whom God reckons righteousness apart from works: "Blessed are those whose iniquities are forgiven, and whose sins are covered; blessed is the one against whom the Lord will not reckon sin." Is this blessedness, then, pronounced only on the circumcised, or also on the uncircumcised? We say, "Faith was reckoned to Abraham as righteousness." How then was it reckoned to him? Was it before or after he had been circumcised? It was not after, but before he was circumcised. He received the sign of circumcision as a seal of the righteousness that he had by faith while he was still uncircumcised. The purpose was to make him the ancestor of all who believe without being circumcised and who thus have righteousness reckoned to them, and likewise the ancestor of the circumcised who are not only circumcised but who also follow the example of the faith that our ancestor Abraham had before he was circumcised. For the promise that he would inherit the world did not come to Abraham or to his descendants through the law but through the righteousness of faith. If it is the adherents of the law who are to be the heirs, faith is null and the promise is void. For the law brings wrath; but where there is no law, neither is there violation. For this reason it depends on faith, in order that the promise may rest on grace and be guaranteed to all his descendants, not only to the adherents of the law but also to those who share the faith of Abraham (for he is the father of all of us, as it is written, "I have made you the father of many nations")—in the presence of the God in whom he believed, who gives life to the dead and calls into existence the things that do not exist.

1 Corinthians 7:18–20

Was anyone at the time of his call already circumcised? Let him not seek to remove the marks of circumcision. Was anyone at the time of his call uncircumcised? Let him not seek circumcision. Circumcision is nothing, and uncircumcision is nothing; but obeying the commandments of God is everything. Let each of you remain in the condition in which you were called.

Galatians 2:1–10

Then after fourteen years I went up again to Jerusalem with Barnabas, taking Titus along with me. I went up in response to a revelation. Then I laid before them (though only in a private meeting with the acknowledged leaders) the gospel that I proclaim among the Gentiles, in order to make sure that I was not running, or had not run, in vain. But even Titus, who was with me, was not compelled to be circumcised, though he was a Greek. But because of false believers secretly brought in, who slipped in to spy on the freedom we have in Christ Jesus, so that they might enslave us—we did not submit to them even for a moment, so that the truth of the gospel might always remain with you. And from those who were supposed to be acknowledged leaders (what they actually were makes no difference to me; God shows no partiality)—those leaders contributed nothing to me. On the contrary, when they saw that I had been entrusted with the gospel for the uncircumcised, just as Peter had been entrusted with the gospel for the circumcised (for he who worked through Peter making him an apostle to the circumcised also worked through me in sending me to the Gentiles), and when James and Cephas and John, who were acknowledged pillars, recognized the grace that had been given to me, they gave to Barnabas and me the right hand of fellowship, agreeing that we should go to the Gentiles and they to the circumcised. They asked only one thing, that we remember the poor, which was actually what I was eager to do.

Source: Society of Biblical Literature, eds. *Harper Collins Study Bible: New Revised Standard Version*. Rev. ed. New York: HarperCollins, 2006. All Scripture quotations appear from the *New Revised Standard Version Bible*. Division of Christian Education of the National Council of Churches of Christ in the United States of America, 1989.

AFTERMATH

In the end, it was probably Paul and Barnabas's decision to go to the Gentile community that helped Christianity spread as fast as it did. Paul's persuasiveness (along with some of the other apostles—Acts 14:26–15:29) at explaining why circumcision was not important won the day, and thereafter males did not have to go through this particular procedure. Some early Christian communities, especially the Jewish Christians, continued to practice circumcision. Irenaeus, in his *Against Heresies* 1.26.2, describes a group called the Ebionites who require circumcision. Not surprisingly, this group rejected the writings of Paul. Most

Christian groups, however, kept the language of circumcision while rejecting the physical aspects. As seen, Paul discussed spiritual circumcision. Examples of spiritual circumcision can been found in numerous early Christian documents that come after the time of Paul. One example is in Justin Martyr's *Dialogue with Trypho the Jew*. He states, "The blood of that circumcision is obsolete, and we trust in the blood of salvation; there is now another covenant and another law has gone forth from Zion" (chapter 24). Christians like Justin also began to write about how baptism had become the new circumcision. He states, "And we, who have approached God through Him, have received not carnal, but spiritual circumcision, which Enoch and those like him observed. And we have received it through baptism, since we were sinners, by God's mercy; and all men may equally obtain it" (*Dialogue with Trypho* 43). This became the standard vocabulary of Christians when discussing circumcision.

ASK YOURSELF

1. All of these texts have to do with men joining Christianity. Why do the texts not discuss rituals that a Gentile woman would have to go through to join? Do you think there were rituals that women had to go through to become Christians?
2. Circumcision was a requirement for Jewish males. Why do you think cutting off the foreskin was so important to God in the Old Testament? What do you think it represented?
3. Do you think Christianity changed when it did not require circumcision for Christian males? Or do you think the change was done primarily to attract new members? Why do you think there was a change between the Old and the New Testaments in terms of circumcision?
4. In Romans, Paul states, "Real circumcision is a matter of the heart—it is spiritual and not literal." What do you think he means by that? What is a spiritual circumcision? Do you think that term would apply to males only, or are women included in this?

TOPICS TO CONSIDER

- ❧ It is hard to estimate how many male children are circumcised today in the United States. Most of the reporting is done by hospitals, where it is a medical procedure, and usually does not include procedures done outside of a hospital. The percentages vary anywhere from over 50 percent in 2006 to around 33 percent in 2009. The religion of the parent is not given in these statistics. Consider the message of Paul and consider why so many male children are circumcised today anyway.
- ❧ Recreate the church council that took place in Jerusalem, with people playing the part of the various apostles, including those who were against spreading Christianity to the Gentiles. Consider the role of persuasive speech in the argument for and against this. Consider the methods of argument that these early Christians would use to convince the council to either accept or deny circumcision.
- ❧ Paul won his argument to not have Gentiles circumcised. Consider how Christianity would have spread if he had lost his argument and uncircumcised men were not allowed to become Christians. Consider too how this would have affected Christianity today, especially in terms of theology.

MALE CIRCUMCISION

Male circumcision had a long history in the ancient world. It was practiced in ancient Egypt as early as the Old Kingdom (2649–2150 BCE), although it isn't clear if it was done for a religious or some other cultural purpose (for example, to reduce the desire for sex or for hygiene). It also appears that it was not performed on infants, but closer to the time of puberty. Based on archaeological evidence, circumcision was practiced in northern Syria sometime in the early 3000s BCE. If the Old Testament book of Jeremiah can be taken as a historical document, Jeremiah 9:25–26 lists not only Egypt but the kingdoms of "Judah, Edom, the Ammonites and Moab" as groups whose males were also circumcised. Unfortunately the text does not state the reason why this was performed. This was also practiced in the Aztec civilization; a painting depicts a young male being circumcised with a sharp seashell. For many early peoples, circumcision was probably a rite of passage into adulthood. With the Hebrews and some early Christians, it was the only way to be a proper member of the religion.

Further Information

Cohen, Shaye J. D. "Judaism without Circumcision and 'Judaism' without 'Circumcision' in Ignatius." *Harvard Theological Review* 95, no. 4 (Oct., 2002): 395–415.

Jacobs, Andrew S. "A Jew's Jew: Paul and the Early Christian Problem of Jewish Origins." *Journal of Religion* 86, no. 2 (April 2006): 258–86.

Johnson, Luke Timothy. *Religious Experience in Earliest Christianity: A Missing Dimension in New Testament Study*. Minneapolis, MN: Fortress Press, 1998.

Martin, Troy W. "The Covenant of Circumcision (Genesis 17:9–14) and the Situational Antitheses in Galatians 3:28." *Journal of Biblical Literature* 122, no. 1 (Spring, 2003): 111–25.

Paget, J.N.B. Carleton. "Barnabas 9:4: A Peculiar Verse on Circumcision." *Vigiliae Christianae* 45, no. 3 (Sep., 1991): 242–54.

Thiessen, Matthew. *Contesting Conversion: Genealogy, Circumcision, and Identity in Ancient Judaism and Christianity*. New York: Oxford University Press, 2011.

6. ON EATING

INTRODUCTION

Food purity laws had been commonplace in the Jewish community for centuries before Christianity appeared. These laws were fairly strict but were important in keeping the Jewish community as a community. When Christianity began, the early groups of people to convert were Jewish. Naturally, they kept to some of their previous rules. It was probably not much of a problem until Paul began to travel throughout modern-day Turkey on his mission to convert the Gentile population. The Gentiles were not willing to follow some of the Jewish rules that many early converts to Christianity were still following. The Apostle Peter had a dream (see the passage from Acts, below) whereby the food purity laws were thrown out and Christians could essentially eat what they wanted (except for blood and what was strangled). Paul, who had convinced the apostles to allow uncircumcised men to become Christians, also wrote about food issues. Some Christians were refusing to eat food sacrificed to idols. Paul's compromise probably made many happy. The following texts are from Leviticus 11:1–47, Acts 10:9–17, and 1 Corinthians 8:1–13.

KEEP IN MIND WHILE YOU READ

1. The title Leviticus is taken from the Greek, and the book is named after the Levites, the Jewish priesthood. It is so named because Leviticus is made up of lists of laws for the Jewish people, and the Levites had to make sure that the people kept these laws. The Hebrew title is translated as "And He Called." Although the exact date of writing is unknown, it is thought that the material found in it dates to at least the 500s BCE.
2. Archaeological digs in Corinth (modern-day Turkey) have shown that there were numerous temples dedicated to the many Greek and Roman gods during the first century CE, which is when the Apostle Paul was there. His comments regarding Christians being worried about eating meat sacrificed to the gods were almost certainly true.

3. Paul was meeting with Gentiles who were interested in becoming Christians. He had already solved the problem of circumcision by generating official support to allow uncircumcised men to join. His next problem was that these same Gentiles were used to eating meat sacrificed to the gods. Paul constantly sought to balance the needs of the new Christians who were originally Gentiles with those of the new Christians who used to be Jews.

Leviticus 11:1–47

The LORD spoke to Moses and Aaron, saying to them: Speak to the people of Israel, saying: From among all the land animals, these are the creatures that you may eat. Any animal that has divided hoofs and is cleft-footed and chews the cud—such you may eat. But among those that chew the cud or have divided hoofs, you shall not eat the following: the camel, for even though it chews the cud, it does not have divided hoofs; it is unclean for you. The rock badger, for even though it chews the cud, it does not have divided hoofs; it is unclean for you. The hare, for even though it chews the cud, it does not have divided hoofs; it is unclean for you. The pig, for even though it has divided hoofs and is cleft-footed, it does not chew the cud; it is unclean for you. Of their flesh you shall not eat, and their carcasses you shall not touch; they are unclean for you. These you may eat, of all that are in the waters. Everything in the waters that has fins and scales, whether in the seas or in the streams—such you may eat. But anything in the seas or the streams that does not have fins and scales, of the swarming creatures in the waters and among all the other living creatures that are in the waters—they are detestable to you and detestable they shall remain. Of their flesh you shall not eat, and their carcasses you shall regard as detestable. Everything in the waters that does not have fins and scales is detestable to you. These you shall regard as detestable among the birds. They shall not be eaten; they are an abomination: the eagle, the vulture, the osprey, the buzzard, the kite of any kind; every raven of any kind; the ostrich, the nighthawk, the sea gull, the hawk of any kind; the little owl, the cormorant, the great owl, the water hen, the desert owl, the carrion vulture, the stork, the heron of any kind, the hoopoe, and the bat. All winged insects that walk upon all fours are detestable to you. But among the winged insects that walk on all fours you may eat those that have jointed legs above their feet, with which to leap on the ground. Of them you may eat: the locust according to its kind, the bald locust according to its kind, the cricket according to its kind, and the grasshopper according to its kind. But all other winged insects that have four feet are detestable to you. By these you shall become unclean; whoever touches the carcass of any of them shall be unclean until the evening, and whoever carries any part of the carcass of any of them shall wash his clothes and be unclean until the evening. Every animal that has divided hoofs but is not cleft-footed or does not chew the cud is unclean for you; everyone who touches one of them shall be unclean. All that walk on their paws, among the animals that walk on all fours, are unclean for you; whoever touches the carcass of any of them shall be unclean until the evening, and the one who carries the carcass shall wash his clothes and be unclean until the evening; they are unclean for you.

These are unclean for you among the creatures that swarm upon the earth: the weasel, the mouse, the great lizard according to its kind, the gecko, the land crocodile, the lizard, the sand lizard, and the chameleon. These are unclean for you among all that swarm; whoever touches one of them when they are dead shall be unclean until the evening. And anything upon which any of them falls when they are dead shall be unclean, whether an article of wood or cloth or skin or sacking, any article that is used for any purpose; it shall be dipped into water, and it shall be unclean until the evening, and then it shall be clean. And if any of them falls into any earthen vessel, all that is in it shall be unclean, and you shall break the vessel. Any food that could be eaten shall be unclean if water from any such vessel comes upon it; and any liquid that could be drunk shall be unclean if it was in any such vessel. Everything on which any part of the carcass falls shall be unclean; whether an oven or stove, it shall be broken in pieces; they are unclean, and shall remain unclean for you. But a spring or a cistern holding water shall be clean, while whatever touches the carcass in it shall be unclean. If any part of their carcass falls upon any seed set aside for sowing, it is clean; but if water is put on the seed and any part of their carcass falls on it, it is unclean for you. If an animal of which you may eat dies, anyone who touches its carcass shall be unclean until the evening. Those who eat of its carcass shall wash their clothes and be unclean until the evening; and those who carry the carcass shall wash their clothes and be unclean until the evening. All creatures that swarm upon the earth are detestable; they shall not be eaten. Whatever moves on its belly, and whatever moves on all fours, or whatever has many feet, all the creatures that swarm upon the earth, you shall not eat; for they are detestable. You shall not make yourselves detestable with any creature that swarms; you shall not defile yourselves with them, and so become unclean. For I am the LORD your God; sanctify yourselves therefore, and be holy, for I am holy. You shall not defile yourselves with any swarming creature that moves on the earth. For I am the LORD who brought you up from the land of Egypt, to be your God; you shall be holy, for I am holy. This is the law pertaining to land animal and bird and every living creature that moves through the waters and every creature that swarms upon the earth, to make a distinction between the unclean and the clean, and between the living creature that may be eaten and the living creature that may not be eaten.

Acts 10:9–17

About noon the next day, as they were on their journey and approaching the city, Peter went up on the roof to pray. He became hungry and wanted something to eat; and while it was being prepared, he fell into a trance. He saw the heaven opened and something like a large sheet coming down, being lowered to the ground by its four corners. In it were all kinds of four-footed creatures and reptiles and birds of the air. Then he heard a voice saying, "Get up, Peter; kill and eat." But Peter said, "By no means, Lord; for I have never eaten anything that is profane or unclean." The voice said to him again, a second time, "What God has made clean, you must not call profane." This happened three times, and the thing was suddenly taken up to heaven. Now while Peter was greatly puzzled about what to make of the vision that he had seen, suddenly the men sent by Cornelius appeared. They were asking for Simon's house and were standing by the gate.

1 Corinthians 8:1–13

Now concerning food sacrificed to idols: we know that "all of us possess knowledge." Knowledge puffs up, but love builds up. Anyone who claims to know something does not yet have the necessary knowledge; but anyone who loves God is known by him. Hence, as to the eating of food offered to idols, we know that "no idol in the world really exists," and that "there is no God but one." Indeed, even though there may be so-called gods in heaven or on earth—as in fact there are many gods and many lords—yet for us there is one God, the Father, from whom are all things and for whom we exist, and one Lord, Jesus Christ, through whom are all things and through whom we exist. It is not everyone, however, who has this knowledge. Since some have become so accustomed to idols until now, they still think of the food they eat as food offered to an idol; and their conscience, being weak, is defiled. "Food will not bring us close to God." We are no worse off if we do not eat, and no better off if we do. But take care that this liberty of yours does not somehow become a stumbling block to the weak. For if others see you, who possess knowledge, eating in the temple of an idol, might they not, since their conscience is weak, be encouraged to the point of eating food sacrificed to idols? So by your knowledge those weak believers for whom Christ died are destroyed. But when you thus sin against members of your family, and wound their conscience when it is weak, you sin against Christ. Therefore, if food is a cause of their falling, I will never eat meat, so that I may not cause one of them to fall.

Source: Society of Biblical Literature, eds. *Harper Collins Study Bible: New Revised Standard Version*. Rev. ed. New York: HarperCollins, 2006. All Scripture quotations appear from the *New Revised Standard Version Bible*. Division of Christian Education of the National Council of Churches of Christ in the United States of America, 1989.

AFTERMATH

Although Christians were no longer under the dietary restrictions found in Judaism, they still had some restrictions of their own. According to Acts 15:20, Christians should "abstain only from things polluted by idols and from fornication and from whatever has been strangled and from blood." Clement of Alexandria included a chapter in his book titled *The Instructor*, which was dedicated to eating (*The Instructor* 2.1). Clement states that Christians should abstain from meat sacrificed to idols, not because the gods have power, but because the meat is offered to "demons." However, like Paul, he states that Christians should be able to eat what they want: "We are not, then, to abstain wholly from various kinds of food, but only are not to be taken up about them." Clement also makes use of the passage from Acts and states that Christians are indifferent to eating pork because of Peter's dream. By the 300s, it seems that Christians can eat all animals, but still not blood (Grant 304, 305). A possible reason for this is that by the 300s Christianity was a legalized religion, and by the end of the 300s it was the only legal religion, thereby making meat sacrificed to the gods relatively rare and no longer a concern.

ASK YOURSELF

1. These dietary restrictions were taken very seriously. Why do you think all of the animals found in the Leviticus passage are off limits to Jewish people (even today)?
2. There are many animals listed in the Leviticus passage. Many of the animals listed are not eaten today in western society—for example, the buzzard, raven, owl, and the bat. Why do you think that is? Do you think it is a cultural issue, or are these animals just not edible?

3. Why do you think that the laws in Leviticus also make it clear that even touching the dead bodies of these forbidden animals is "detestable"? Why do you think there is no difference between touching and eating?
4. In the passage from Acts, Peter has a dream that is sent by God. In the dream God makes all animals acceptable to eat that were previously unacceptable. Why do you think that God would not make them clean in the Old Testament, but clean in the New Testament? What do you think had changed with the belief in Christ?

TOPICS TO CONSIDER

- Jewish Christian groups still exist today (for example, Jews for Jesus). Consider how these groups are treated in today's society.
- Paul allows Christians to eat meat if it does not upset or confuse people who have not thought about the issue. As seen, he himself would not eat it if it would trouble anyone. Consider how his view would have helped Christians who were reading his letter.
- There are many archaeological remains from Corinth and other cities that Paul had visited. Consider how the temples found in these cities would have affected the early Christians, not only with the sacrifice of animals but with all the other activities associated with these temples.

Further Information

Bazell, Dianne M. "Strife among the Table-Fellows: Conflicting Attitudes of Early and Medieval Christians toward the Eating of Meat." *Journal of the American Academy of Religion* 65, no. 1 (Spring, 1997): 73–99.

Bulmer, Ralph. "The Uncleanness of the Birds of Leviticus and Deuteronomy." *Man,* n.s., 24, no. 2 (Jun., 1989): 304–32.

Cheung, Alex T. *Idol Food in Corinth: Jewish Background and Pauline Legacy.* Sheffield, England: Sheffield Academic Press, 1999.

Clement of Alexandria, *Instructor.* http://www.ccel.org/ccel/schaff/anf02.vi.iii.i.i.html.

Grant, Robert M. "Dietary Laws among Pythagoreans, Jews, and Christians." *Harvard Theological Review* 73, no. 1/2 (Jan.–Apr., 1980): 299–310.

Murphy-O'Connor, Jerome. "The Corinth That Saint Paul Saw." *Biblical Archaeologist* 47, no. 3 (Sep., 1984): 147–59.

Murphy-O'Connor, Jerome. *St. Paul's Corinth: Texts and Archaeology.* Collegeville, MN: Liturgical Press, 1983.

Neusner, Jacob. "The Idea of Purity in Ancient Judaism." *Journal of the American Academy of Religion* 43, no. 1 (Mar., 1975): 15–26.

7. EUCHARIST

INTRODUCTION

The celebration of the Eucharist (the changing of bread and wine into the body and blood of Christ) was one of the most important ceremonies in early Christianity, second only to baptism. The Eucharistic ceremony was held in remembrance of the Last Supper, which was literally the last meal that Jesus ate with his disciples before he was crucified. A member of the clergy would bless the bread and the wine, and the congregants would then be offered some of each. The symbols of the bread (his body) and especially the wine (his blood) became the best-known symbols of Christian community, and the term "blood of Christ" became one of the most used phrases in early Christian writing. The Eucharist ceremony was also known to non-Christians and was used against them many times, especially since the phrase "eat my body and drink my blood" lent itself to charges of cannibalism. In dealing with this charge, Christian writers then had to defend this important ceremony, and, in the process, they had to define what exactly the symbols meant. The texts of the Last Supper below are Mark and Luke, the *Didache,* and Justin Martyr's *First Apology.*

KEEP IN MIND WHILE YOU READ

1. Justin Martyr (died around 165 CE) addressed his *First Apology* to "Emperor Titus Aelius Adrianus Antoninus Pius Augustus Cæsar, and to his son Verissimus the Philosopher, and to Lucius the Philosopher, the natural son of Cæsar, and the adopted son of Pius, a lover of learning, and to the sacred Senate, with the whole People of the Romans." It is clear in the first sentence that he wrote to all of the Romans in order to defend Christianity. The section of the apology on the Eucharist was written to make it clear the Christians did not practice cannibalism.
2. Christians began meeting to have community meals because of the accounts found in the Synoptic Gospels. The meal was eaten after the blessing of the bread and wine.
3. The word "Eucharist" comes from the Greek *eucharistia,* which means "thanksgiving." This word appears in Mark 14:23 and Luke 22:17 ("and after giving *thanks . . .*"). This thanksgiving, or Eucharist, became an important part of Christianity.
4. The title *Didache* means "teaching." The full title of the *Didache* is the *Teaching of the Twelve Apostles.* It was probably written sometime in the second century.

Mark 14:16–26

So the disciples set out and went to the city, and found everything as he had told them; and they prepared the Passover meal. When it was evening, he came with the twelve. And when they had taken their places and were eating, Jesus said, "Truly I tell you, one of you will betray me, one who is eating with me." They began to be distressed and to say to him one after another, "Surely, not I?" He said to them, "It is one of the twelve, one who is dipping bread into the bowl with me. For the Son of Man goes as it is written of him, but woe to that one by whom the Son of Man is betrayed! It would have been better for that one not to have been born." While they were eating, he took a loaf of bread, and after blessing it he broke it, gave it to them, and said, "Take; this is my body." Then he took a cup, and after giving thanks he gave it to them, and all of them drank from it. He said to them, "This is my blood of the covenant, which is poured out for many. Truly I tell you, I will never again drink of the fruit of the vine until that day when I drink it new in the kingdom of God." When they had sung the hymn, they went out to the Mount of Olives.

Luke 22:13–22

So they went and found everything as he had told them; and they prepared the Passover meal. When the hour came, he took his place at the table, and the apostles with him. He said to them, "I have eagerly desired to eat this Passover with you before I suffer; for I tell you, I will not eat it until it is fulfilled in the kingdom of God." Then he took a cup, and after giving thanks he said, "Take this and divide it among yourselves; for I tell you that from now on I will not drink of the fruit of the vine until the kingdom of God comes." Then he took a loaf of bread, and when he had given thanks, he broke it and gave it to them, saying, "This is my body, which is given for you. Do this in remembrance of me." And he did the same with the cup after supper, saying, "This cup that is poured out for you is the new covenant in my blood. But see, the one who betrays me is with me, and his hand is on the table. For the Son of Man is going as it has been determined, but woe to that one by whom he is betrayed!" Then they began to ask one another, which one of them it could be who would do this.

Source: Society of Biblical Literature, eds. *Harper Collins Study Bible: New Revised Standard Version*. Rev. ed. New York: HarperCollins, 2006. All Scripture quotations appear from the *New Revised Standard Version Bible*. Division of Christian Education of the National Council of Churches of Christ in the United States of America, 1989.

Didache 9–10

(9) Now about the Eucharist: this is how to give thanks: First in connection with the cup: "We thank you, our Father, for the holy vine of David, your child, which you have revealed

through Jesus, your child. To you be glory forever." Then in connection with the piece (broken off the loaf): "We thank you, our Father, for the life and knowledge which you have revealed through Jesus, your child. To you be glory forever. "As this piece (of bread) was scattered over the hills and then was brought together and made one, so let your Church be brought together from the ends of the earth into your Kingdom. For yours is the glory and the power through Jesus Christ forever." You must not let anyone eat or drink of your Eucharist except those baptized in the Lord's name. For in reference to this the Lord said, "Do not give what is sacred to dogs."

(10) After you have finished your meal, say grace in this way: "We thank you, holy Father, for your sacred name which you have lodged in our hearts, and for the knowledge and faith and immortality which you have revealed through Jesus, your child. To you be glory forever. "Almighty Master, 'you have created everything' for the sake of your name, and have given men food and drink to enjoy that they may thank you. But to us you have given spiritual food and drink and eternal life through Jesus, your child. "Above all, we thank you that you are mighty. To you be glory forever. "Remember, Lord, your Church, to save it from all evil and to make it perfect by your love. Make it holy, 'and gather' it 'together from the four winds' into your Kingdom which you have made ready for it. For yours is the power and the glory forever." "Let Grace come and let this world pass away." "Hosanna to the God of David!" "If anyone is holy, let him come. If not, let him repent." "Our Lord, come!" "Amen." In the case of prophets, however, you should let them give thanks in their own way.

Source: Didache, translated by Kirsopp Lake, in *The Apostolic Fathers,* vol. 1. New York: MacMillan, 1912, 323–25.

Justin Martyr, First Apology, *65–66*

(65) But we, after we have thus washed him who has been convinced and has assented to our teaching, bring him to the place where those who are called brethren are assembled, in order that we may offer hearty prayers in common for ourselves and for the baptized person, and for all others in every place, that we may be counted worthy, now that we have learned the truth, by our works also to be found good citizens and keepers of the commandments, so that we may be saved with an everlasting salvation. Having ended the prayers, we salute one another with a kiss. There is then brought to the president of the brethren bread and a cup of wine mixed with water; and he taking them, gives praise and glory to the Father of the universe, through the name of the Son and of the Holy Spirit, and offers thanks at considerable length for our being counted worthy to receive these things at His hands. And when he has concluded the prayers and thanksgivings, all the people present express their assent by saying "Amen." This word "Amen" answers in the Hebrew language to *genoito* (so be it). And when the president has given thanks, and all the people have expressed their assent, those who are called by us deacons give to each of those present to partake of the bread and wine mixed with water over which the thanksgiving was pronounced, and to those who are absent they carry away a portion.

(66) And this food is called among us *Eucharistia* (the Eucharist), of which no one is allowed to partake but the man who believes that the things which we teach are true, and

who has been washed with the washing that is for the remission of sins, and unto regeneration, and who is so living as Christ has enjoined. For not as common bread and common drink do we receive these; but in like manner as Jesus Christ our Savior, having been made flesh by the Word of God, had both flesh and blood for our salvation, so likewise have we been taught that the food which is blessed by the prayer of His word, and from which our blood and flesh by transmutation are nourished, is the flesh and blood of that Jesus who was made flesh. For the apostles, in the memoirs composed by them, which are called Gospels, have thus delivered unto us what was enjoined upon them: that Jesus took bread, and when He had given thanks, said, "Do this in remembrance of Me, this is My body;" and that, after the same manner, having taken the cup and given thanks, He said, "This is My blood;" and gave it to them alone. Which the wicked devils have imitated in the mysteries of Mithras, commanding the same thing to be done. For, that bread and a cup of water are placed with certain incantations in the mystic rites of one who is being initiated, you either know or can learn.

Source: Roberts, Rev. Alexander, and James Donaldson, eds. *The Ante-Nicene Fathers: Translations of the Writings of the Fathers Down to A.D. 325,* vol. 1. New York: Charles Scribner's Sons, 1903, 185.

AFTERMATH

The ceremony of the Eucharist still plays an important role in some forms of the Christian religion, especially Catholicism. After the time of Justin there was a movement in the clergy for saying specific prayers to convert the bread and wine into the body and blood of Christ. Justin, in his *First Apology,* chapter 67, states that the clergy can offer prayers in whatever way they like to do this conversion. Ambrose, the bishop of Milan at the end of the fourth century, states that certain words had to be spoken. The ceremony also became much more elaborate in the later part of the 300s, and this is clear from the *Apostolic Constitutions,* chapters 8–13. Here, very elaborate prayers are given before the bread and wine are given out.

ASK YOURSELF

1. Justin, in chapter 65, states that the Christians say "Amen" in Hebrew when they have finished the Eucharist, prayers, and thanksgivings. Why would Christians not say amen in Greek or Latin? Why in Hebrew? Do you think that Christians in the middle of the second century would have understood this particular language?
2. Justin, who wrote the *First Apology* sometime in the 150s CE, states in chapter 66: "For the apostles, in the memoirs composed by them, which are called Gospels ..." Why do you think he had to explain this to his readers? Who is his audience?
3. The passages from the Synoptic Gospels all record Jesus discussing his betrayal along with the taking of the wine and bread. What link do you think there is between the two? Also, the order of the betrayal is different between Luke and Mark. Why do you think Luke put the betrayal account after the Eucharist, as opposed to Mark, who put it first?

TOPICS TO CONSIDER

- ❧ The *Didache* and Justin Martyr give two accounts of the Eucharistic ceremony. Consider why there are two accounts of an extremely important ceremony and what this might mean for Christians, both ancient and modern.

- ❧ Some Christians today (especially the Catholics) believe that they are actually eating the body of Christ and drinking his blood when they take Communion. Consider the roots of this particular ceremony. Were there precedents in Judaism or in the Greco-Roman society in which the Christians were living?

- ❧ Recreate the account of the Eucharist (and the other ceremonies) that the *Didache* describes. Now consider how modern Christians celebrate the Eucharist (including the prayer that the clergy give). How are they the same? How are they different? If the ceremonies are different, account for these differences.

- ❧ The title "Son of Man" is given many times in the Gospels as a title for Jesus. Consider what that title might have meant to a first-century Christian, as well as to modern Christians.

Further Information

Apostolic Constitutions, chapter 8. http://www.newadvent.org/fathers/07158.htm.

Billy, Dennis. *Beauty of the Eucharist: Voices from the Church Fathers.* New York: New City Press, 2010.

Bouman, C. A. "Variants in the Introduction to the Eucharistic Prayer." *Vigiliae Christianae* 4, no. 2 (Apr., 1950): 94–115.

Brooks, Oscar S. "The Johannine Eucharist: Another Interpretation." *Journal of Biblical Literature* 82, no. 3 (Sep., 1963): 293–300.

Feeley-Harnik, Gillian. *The Lord's Table: Eucharist and Passover in Early Christianity.* Philadelphia: University of Pennsylvania Press, 1981.

LaVerdiere, Eugene A. *The Eucharist in the New Testament and the Early Church.* Collegeville, MN: Liturgical Press, 1996.

Petzer, J. H. "Luke 22:19b-20 and the Structure of the Passage." *Novum Testamentum* 26, Fasc. 3 (Jul., 1984): 249–52.

Van de Sandt, Huub. " 'Do Not Give What Is Holy to the Dogs' (Did 9:5D and Matt 7:6A): The Eucharistic Food of the Didache in Its Jewish Purity Setting." *Vigiliae Christianae* 56, no. 3 (Aug., 2002): 223–46.

8. Marriage

INTRODUCTION

Marriage was considered to be an extremely important ritual in early Christianity and was later a sacrament. The main purpose of a Christian marriage was to have a partner, and not necessarily to produce children (although this changes later). This was quite different from the Roman view of marriage, which was to produce children (Nathan 41–42). That being said, there were some Christians during the time of Paul who believed that people should not marry nor have sexual relations. The passage from 1 Corinthians given below is Paul's response to a letter he received, and his response gives a good overview of Christian marriage. The first two passages are the creation story from Genesis. Christian and Jews understood this as being the first marriage.

KEEP IN MIND WHILE YOU READ

1. Below are two versions of the creation of Adam and Eve. The first account is very basic, while the second account discusses the creation of the first woman from the rib of Adam. The two versions are called the Priestly and the Yahwist accounts. It is believed that the Yahwist account was written first, and it gets its name because of the use of the personal name of God, Yahweh. Afterward, a priest or priests added a number of legal texts to the Yahwist account. Genesis 1:24–30 is from the Priestly account, while Genesis 2:15–24 is from the Yahwist account.
2. Not all Christians had the same view of marriage. Some did not believe in marriage at all. Paul, who stressed that people should remain unmarried, thought that people should get married if they could not control their sexual desires. He was not, however, against marriage, but he preferred that people remain single and celibate like himself.
3. Paul's view of marriage rested on his belief that the end of time was near and Christ was coming back. He believed that people should be focusing on Christ and not on worldly issues.
4. The minimum age for marriage in the Roman Empire was 14 for men and 12 for women (Nathan 16), and there are cases where girls younger than this were arranged to be married (St. Augustine, in the later 300s, is a good example).

Genesis 1:24–30

And God said, "Let the earth bring forth living creatures of every kind: cattle and creeping things and wild animals of the earth of every kind." And it was so. God made the wild animals of the earth of every kind, and the cattle of every kind, and everything that creeps upon the ground of every kind. And God saw that it was good. Then God said, "Let us make humankind in our image, according to our likeness; and let them have dominion over the fish of the sea, and over the birds of the air, and over the cattle, and over all the wild animals of the earth, and over every creeping thing that creeps upon the earth." So God created humankind in his image, in the image of God he created them; male and female he created them. God blessed them, and God said to them, "Be fruitful and multiply, and fill the earth and subdue it; and have dominion over the fish of the sea and over the birds of the air and over every living thing that moves upon the earth." God said, "See, I have given you every plant yielding seed that is upon the face of all the earth, and every tree with seed in its fruit; you shall have them for food. And to every beast of the earth, and to every bird of the air, and to everything that creeps on the earth, everything that has the breath of life, I have given every green plant for food." And it was so.

Genesis 2:15–24

The Lord God took the man and put him in the garden of Eden to till it and keep it. And the Lord God commanded the man, "You may freely eat of every tree of the garden; but of the tree of the knowledge of good and evil you shall not eat, for in the day that you eat of it you shall die." Then the Lord God said, "It is not good that the man should be alone; I will make him a helper as his partner." So out of the ground the Lord God formed every animal of the field and every bird of the air, and brought them to the man to see what he would call them; and whatever the man called every living creature, that was its name. The man gave names to all cattle, and to the birds of the air, and to every animal of the field; but for the man there was not found a helper as his partner. So the Lord God caused a deep sleep to fall upon the man, and he slept; then he took one of his ribs and closed up its place with flesh. And the rib that the Lord God had taken from the man he made into a woman and brought her to the man. Then the man said, "This at last is bone of my bones and flesh of my flesh; this one shall be called Woman, for out of Man this one was taken." Therefore a man leaves his father and his mother and clings to his wife, and they become one flesh.

1 Corinthians 7:1–17, 7:24–40

Now concerning the matters about which you wrote: "It is well for a man not to touch a woman." But because of cases of sexual immorality, each man should have his own wife and each woman her own husband. The husband should give to his wife her conjugal rights, and likewise the wife to her husband. For the wife does not have authority over her own body, but the husband does; likewise the husband does not have authority over his own body, but the wife does. Do not deprive one another except perhaps by agreement for a set time, to devote yourselves to prayer, and then come together again, so that Satan may not tempt you because of your lack of self-control. This I say by way of concession, not of command. I wish that all were as I myself am. But each has a particular gift from God, one having one kind and another a different kind. To the unmarried and the widows I say that it is well for them to remain unmarried as I am. But if they are not practicing self-control, they should marry. For it is better to marry than to be aflame with passion. To the married I give this command—not I but the Lord—that the wife should not separate from her husband (but if she does separate, let her remain unmarried or else be reconciled to her husband), and that the husband should not divorce his wife. To the rest I say—I and not the Lord—that if any believer has a wife who is an unbeliever, and she consents to live with him, he should not divorce her. And if any woman has a husband who is an unbeliever, and he consents to live with her, she should not divorce him. For the unbelieving husband is made holy through his wife, and the unbelieving wife is made holy through her husband. Otherwise, your children would be unclean, but as it is, they are holy. But if the unbelieving partner separates, let it be so; in such a case the brother or sister is not bound. It is to peace that God has called you. Wife, for all you know, you might save your husband. Husband, for all you know, you might save your wife. However that may be, let each of you lead the life that the Lord has assigned, to which God called you. This is my rule in all the churches. . .

In whatever condition you were called, brothers and sisters, there remain with God. Now concerning virgins, I have no command of the Lord, but I give my opinion as one who by the Lord's mercy is trustworthy. I think that, in view of the **impending crisis,** it is well for you to remain as you are. Are you bound to a wife? Do not seek to be free. Are you free from a wife? Do not seek a wife. But if you marry, you do not sin, and if a virgin mar-

> **impending crisis** Paul believed that Jesus would be returning during his lifetime.

ries, she does not sin. Yet those who marry will experience distress in this life, and I would spare you that. I mean, brothers and sisters, the appointed time has grown short; from now on, let even those who have wives be as though they had none, and those who mourn as though they were not mourning, and those who rejoice as though they were not rejoicing, and those who buy as though they had no possessions, and those who deal with the world as though they had no dealings with it. For the present form of this world is passing away. I want you to be free from anxieties. The unmarried man is anxious about the affairs of the Lord, how to please the Lord; but the married man is anxious about the affairs of the world, how to please his wife, and his interests are divided. And the unmarried woman and the virgin are anxious about the affairs of the Lord, so that they may be holy in body and spirit; but the married woman is anxious about the affairs of the world, how to please her husband. I say this for your own benefit, not to put any restraint upon you, but to promote good order and unhindered devotion to the Lord. If anyone thinks that he is not behaving properly toward his fiancée, if his passions are strong, and so it has to be, let him marry as he wishes; it is no sin. Let them marry. But if someone stands firm in his resolve, being under no necessity but having his own desire under control, and has determined in his own mind to keep her as his fiancée, he will do well. So then, he who marries his fiancée does well; and he who refrains from marriage will do better. A wife is bound as long as her husband lives. But if the husband dies, she is free to marry anyone she wishes, only in the Lord. But in my judgment she is more blessed if she remains as she is. And I think that I too have the Spirit of God.

Source: Society of Biblical Literature, eds. *Harper Collins Study Bible: New Revised Standard Version*. Rev. ed. New York: HarperCollins, 2006. All Scripture quotations appear from the *New Revised Standard Version Bible*. Division of Christian Education of the National Council of Churches of Christ in the United States of America, 1989.

AFTERMATH

It is unfortunate that not much is known about the family unit in early Christianity. While Paul makes it clear that his advice is extremely important, he gives no advice on the actual marriage ceremony. In the early 100s, Ignatius of Antioch writes to Polycarp, bishop of Smyrna. Ignatius tells Polycarp that people should get married "with the advice of the bishop" and that they should marry, not because of lust, but to be "in the lord." This appears to be opposite of what Paul stated—that people should get married if they can't control their lust. Of course, Paul also states that the married couple needed to make time for prayers. Tertullian, in the late 190s or early 200s CE, also appears to reject Paul's advice on widows getting remarried after the death of their spouses (see Remarriage, below). However, marriage remained the norm for early Christians.

ASK YOURSELF

1. As stated, Paul is responding to a letter about sex. Just by looking at Paul's letter, what are the main points of this now lost letter? What do you think led to this particular group to believe that a man should not touch a woman?
2. Why does Paul spend so much time discussing a mixed marriage of an unbeliever and a believer? What does that tell us about the makeup of early Christian communities?
3. Paul believed the End was near. How do you think this affected his views of marriage? How do you think this belief affected these new Christian communities?

TOPICS TO CONSIDER

- ✑ Paul gives some rules that are his own advice and some that are commandments of God. Make a table that separates the two and consider why Paul stressed the difference. Consider how early Christians would have accepted Paul's advice, as opposed to God's commandments.
- ✑ Paul sets the foundation for sexual equality between married couples. Consider how Roman non-Christian husbands treated their non-Christian wives, and compare that to how Roman Christian husbands were to treat their Christian wives. Also consider whether Paul's view would have encouraged people to join Christianity.
- ✑ Many groups responded differently to the idea that the End was coming. Consider how this view affected these communities. Did it make a difference in their behavior? Consider how modern Christian communities have adapted to Paul's incorrect assumption that the End was going to happen, in his lifetime, or least very soon after his death.

MARRIAGE IN THE ROMAN EMPIRE

Marriage was one of the most common legal features found in the Roman Empire. It was the cornerstone of the society, with the husband the head of the family, just as the emperor was the head of the empire. The age when men and women could get married was 14 for males, 12 for females. Augustine, a North African Catholic bishop of Hippo (354–430 CE), was engaged to a girl of 10 but had to wait until she turned 12; in the end, he never married her. It was known that some girls were married even younger than this (Hopkins 313). For some pagan Romans, marriage was a way to cement political ties with another family, irrespective of the possible attraction between the man and woman. Before the first century BCE, at marriage the woman would become part of the husband's household (or if the husband was young, the couple would become part of the father-in-law's household). The new wife would have any property of hers transferred from her father to her new husband. Another type of marriage, which was the most common after the first century BCE, was a free marriage, where the wife was legally independent from her husband and the property that she had before she was married would remain hers. Regardless of the type of marriage, having children was highly encouraged.

Further Information

Balch, David L., and Carolyn Osiek. *Early Christian Families in Context: An Interdisciplinary Dialogue.* Grand Rapids, MI: Eerdmans, 2003.

Grubbs, Judith Evans. *Women and the Law in the Roman Empire: A Sourcebook on Marriage, Divorce and Widowhood.* New York: Routledge, 2002.

Hopkins, M. K. "The Age of Roman Girls at Marriage." *Population Studies* 18, no. 3 (Mar., 1965): 309–27.

Nathan, Geoffrey S. *The Family in Late Antiquity: The Rise of Christianity and the Endurance of Tradition.* New York: Routledge, 2000.

Rawson, Beryl, ed. *Marriage, Divorce, and Children in Ancient Rome.* Oxford: Clarendon Press, 1991.

Reynolds, Phillip L. *Marriage in the Western Church: The Christianization of Marriage during the Patristic and Early Medieval Periods.* Leiden, the Netherlands: Brill, 2001.

9. Divorce

INTRODUCTION

Divorce seemed to be a common occurrence in early Christian communities, if the biblical texts can be seen as being representative. There are a few places in the Old Testament where divorce is discussed, and early Christians somewhat adopted the position found in the Old Testament (for example, Deuteronomy 24:1, given below). In the Synoptic Gospels (Matthew, Mark, and Luke), divorce is discussed (also below). Jesus gives only one excuse for divorcing a spouse, and that is adultery. In the Roman world, after the time of Emperor Augustus, divorce could also be granted because of immorality, so it is possible that the early Christians had adopted both the Roman and the Jewish perspectives on divorce. Jesus also made it very clear that marriage after a divorce was severely frowned upon. It is no surprise that many early Christian writers also reject remarriage after a divorce, especially if adultery was involved. The passages below are from Deuteronomy, the Synoptic Gospels, and Tertullian, a second-century North African church father. Tertullian included in his writing a great many references to the Old and New Testaments. The biblical verse citations are listed within the text.

KEEP IN MIND WHILE YOU READ

1. The passage from Tertullian is taken from his *Against Marcion*. Marcion was a second-century Christian who believed that the Old Testament should not be used by Christians. Marcion attempted to find discrepancies in the text by finding what he thought were opposite statements (his book was called the *Antitheses*). Marcion thought the New Testament gave the opposite message from what the Old Testament said regarding divorce.

2. Marriage was considered to be a sacred act that began with Adam and Eve. The idea that it was a sanctified act led to the belief that the marriage bond should not be broken, and this is why divorce was not allowed in many cases.

3. The passages provided below from the New Testament are all related in that there must have been a similar root to these texts. As discussed earlier in this volume,

Matthew, Mark, and Luke are Synoptic Gospels. It is believed by most scholars that Mark was produced first, and Matthew and Luke used Mark, as well as their own independent sources.

4. It is believed by some scholars that Tertullian was a lawyer, mostly because of his legalistic language (see below). However, others believe that he was just highly educated, which would also explain his style of writing.

Deuteronomy 24:1–4

Suppose a man enters into marriage with a woman, but she does not please him because he finds something objectionable about her, and so he writes her a certificate of divorce, puts it in her hand, and sends her out of his house; she then leaves his house and goes off to become another man's wife. Then suppose the second man dislikes her, writes her a bill of divorce, puts it in her hand, and sends her out of his house (or the second man who married her dies); her first husband, who sent her away, is not permitted to take her again to be his wife after she has been defiled; for that would be abhorrent to the LORD, and you shall not bring guilt on the land that the LORD your God is giving you as a possession.

Mark 10:2–12

Some Pharisees came, and to test him (Jesus) they asked, "Is it lawful for a man to divorce his wife?" He answered them, "What did Moses command you?" They said, "Moses allowed a man to write a certificate of dismissal and to divorce her." But Jesus said to them, "Because of your hardness of heart he wrote this commandment for you. But from the beginning of creation, 'God made them male and female. For this reason a man shall leave his father and mother and be joined to his wife, and the two shall become one flesh.' So they are no longer two, but one flesh. Therefore what God has joined together, let no one separate." Then in the house the disciples asked him again about this matter. He said to them, "Whoever divorces his wife and marries another commits adultery against her; and if she divorces her husband and marries another, she commits adultery."

Matthew 5:27–32

"You have heard that it was said, 'You shall not commit adultery.' But I say to you that everyone who looks at a woman with lust has already committed adultery with her in his heart. If your right eye causes you to sin, tear it out and throw it away; it is better for you to lose one of your members than for your whole body to be thrown into hell. And if your right hand causes you to sin, cut it off and throw it away; it is better for you to lose one of your members than for your whole body to go into hell. "It was also said, 'Whoever divorces his wife, let him give her a certificate of divorce.' But I say to you that anyone who divorces his wife, except on the ground of unchastity, causes her to commit adultery; and whoever marries a divorced woman commits adultery."

Luke 16:18

Anyone who divorces his wife and marries another, commits adultery, and whoever marries a woman divorced from her husband commits adultery.

Source: Society of Biblical Literature, eds. *Harper Collins Study Bible: New Revised Standard Version*. Rev. ed. New York: HarperCollins, 2006. All Scripture quotations appear from the *New Revised Standard Version Bible*. Division of Christian Education of the National Council of Churches of Christ in the United States of America, 1989.

Tertullian, Against Marcion 4.34

But Christ prohibits divorce, saying, "Anyone who divorces his wife and marries another commits adultery, and whoever marries a woman divorced from her husband commits adultery" (Luke 16:18). In order to forbid divorce, He makes it unlawful to marry a woman that has been **put away**. Moses, however, permitted repudiation in Deuteronomy: "When a man has taken a wife, and lived with her, and it comes to pass that she does not please him, because he found her unfaithful, then let him write her a bill of divorcement and give it in her, and send her away, out of his house" (Deuteronomy 24:1). You see, therefore, that there is a difference between the law and the gospel—between Moses and Christ? To be sure there is! But then you have rejected that other gospel which witnesses to the same verity and the same Christ. There, while prohibiting divorce, He has given us a solution of this special question respecting it: "Moses," says He, "because of the hardness of your hearts, allowed you to give a bill of divorcement; but from the beginning it was not so" (Matthew 19:8)—for this reason, indeed, because He who had "made them male and female" had likewise said, "They shall become one flesh; what therefore God has joined together, let not man put asunder" (Matthew 19:4, 6). Now, by this answer of His (to the Pharisees), He both sanctioned the provision of Moses, who was His own (servant), and restored to its primitive purpose the institution of the Creator, whose Christ He was.

Since, however, you are to be refuted out of the Scriptures which you have received, I will meet you on your own ground, as if your Christ were mine. When, therefore, He prohibited divorce, and yet at the same time represented the Father, even Him who united male and female, must He not have rather exculpated than abolished the enactment of Moses? But, observe, if this Christ be yours when he teaches contrary to Moses and the Creator, on the same principle must He be mine if I can show that His teaching is not contrary to them. I maintain, then, that there was a condition in the prohibition which He now made of divorce; the case supposed being, that a man put away his wife for the express purpose of marrying another. His words are: "Anyone who divorces his wife and marries another, commits adultery, and whoever marries a woman divorced from her husband commits adultery,"—"divorce," that is, for the reason wherefore a woman ought not to be dismissed, that another wife may be obtained. For he who marries a woman who is unlawfully divorced is as much of an adulterer as the man who marries one who is undivorced. Permanent is the marriage which is not rightly dissolved; to marry, therefore, while matrimony is undissolved, is to commit adultery. Since, therefore, His prohibition

> **put away** To divorce.

of divorce was a conditional one, He did not prohibit absolutely; and what He did not absolutely forbid, that He permitted on some occasions, when there is an absence of the cause why He gave His prohibition. In very deed His teaching is not contrary to Moses, whose precept He partially defends, I will not say confirms.

If, however, you deny that divorce is in any way permitted by Christ, how is it that you on your side destroy marriage, not uniting man and woman, nor admitting to the sacrament of baptism and of the eucharist those who have been united in marriage anywhere else, unless they should agree together to repudiate the fruit of their marriage, and so the very Creator Himself? Well, then, what is a husband to do in your sect, if his wife commits adultery? Shall he keep her? But your own apostle, you know, does not permit "the members of Christ to be joined to a harlot" (1 Corinthians 6:15). Divorce, therefore, when justly deserved, has even in Christ a defender. So that Moses for the future must be considered as being confirmed by Him, since he prohibits divorce in the same sense as Christ does, if any unchastity should occur in the wife. For in the Gospel of Matthew he says, "anyone who divorces his wife, except on the ground of unchastity, causes her to commit adultery; and whoever marries a divorced woman commits adultery" (Matthew 5:32). He also is deemed equally guilty of adultery, who marries a woman divorced by her husband. The Creator, however, except on account of adultery, does not put asunder what He Himself joined together, the same Moses in another passage enacting that he who had married after violence to a woman, should thenceforth not have it in his power to divorce his wife. Now, if a compulsory marriage contracted after violence shall be permanent, how much rather shall a voluntary one, the result of agreement! This has the sanction of the prophet: "You shall not forsake the wife of your youth" (Malachi 2:15). Thus you have Christ following spontaneously the tracks of the Creator everywhere, both in permitting divorce and in forbidding it. You find Him also protecting marriage, in whatever direction you try to escape. He prohibits divorce when He will have the marriage inviolable; He permits divorce when the marriage is spotted with unfaithfulness. You should blush when you refuse to unite those whom even your Christ has united; and repeat the blush when you disunite them without the good reason why your Christ would have them separated.

I have now to show whence the Lord derived this decision of His, and to what end He directed it. It will thus become more fully evident that His object was not the abolition of the Mosaic ordinance by any suddenly devised proposal of divorce; because it was not suddenly proposed, but had its root in the previously mentioned John. For John reproved Herod, because he had illegally married the wife of his deceased brother, who had a daughter by her (a union which the law permitted only on the one occasion of the brother dying childless, when it even prescribed such a marriage, in order that by his own brother, and from his own wife, seed might be reckoned to the deceased husband), and was in consequence thrown into prison, and finally, by the same Herod, was even put to death. The Lord having therefore made mention of John, and of course of the occurrence of his death, hurled His censure against Herod in the form of unlawful marriages and of adultery, pronouncing as an adulterer even the man who married a woman that had been put away from her husband. This he said in order the more severely to load Herod with guilt, who had taken his brother's wife, after she had been loosed from her husband not less by death than by divorce; who had been impelled thereto by his lust, not by the prescription of the (Levirate) law—for, as his brother had left a daughter, the marriage with the widow could not be lawful on that very account; and who, when the prophet asserted against him the law, had therefore put him to death.

Source: Roberts, Rev. Alexander, and James Donaldson, eds. *The Ante-Nicene Fathers: Translations of the Writings of the Fathers Down to A.D. 325*, vol. 3. New York: Charles Scribner's Sons, 1905, 404–6.

AFTERMATH

The rules on divorce remained remarkably the same in the centuries that followed Tertullian, although there were certainly some changes. Many of these changes happened during the time of Emperor Constantine in the early 300s. The laws that were developed during this time discussed marriage and divorce, but this time the laws covered all Roman citizens. The biggest change was that Constantine tried to stop unilateral divorce, which is when only one spouse wanted a divorce (Nathan 62–63). On the ecclesiastical side, there was an early church council that met in Arles, France, in 314 CE. Canon (or law) 11 states that if a man catches his wife in the act of adultery, he should not take other wives while his first wife is still alive. This assumes that divorce is allowed in the case of adultery, which is what one would expect. It does, however, forbid remarriage when a spouse is living. Today, divorce is not granted in the Catholic Church, although it does grant annulments. However, a Catholic today can receive a divorce (in a civil proceeding) but may not remarry in the church until he or she receives an annulment.

ASK YOURSELF

1. As stated above, Tertullian is arguing against Marcion, a second-century Christian. How does this argument shape Tertullian's view of divorce? What are Marcion's views of marriage and divorce?

2. Knowing that the passages above from the New Testament are from parallel verses, why do you think there are differences between them? If the text of Luke was the only text that had survived, how would our view of divorce in early Christian communities change? How does having three views of the same subject help us understand divorce?

3. Tertullian states that God both prohibits and permits divorce. Do you think his explanation a useful one? Do you think it would have created confusion, or would it have helped Christians who were reading Tertullian?

TOPICS TO CONSIDER

- The divorce rate in the United States is close to 50 percent, which means that half of all marriages end in divorce. Consider how some Christian groups deal with divorce today and discuss their views of remarriage.

- In many (but not all) ancient texts, the man is the one to initiate the divorce on the grounds that the wife committed adultery. Examine the texts above and other early Christian writings and consider who is divorcing whom. Consider the position of women in these societies where they can initiate divorce. Also consider whether this "right" can tell us something about the status of women. Is there a correlation?

- Consider the various examples of divorce from the Old and New Testament, along with Tertullian, and compare and contrast these to the reasons why people divorce today. Consider how modern laws on divorce differ from the ancient laws.

DIVORCE IN THE ANCIENT WORLD

Divorce was common in the ancient world. Early laws vary on the justifications for divorce and on who could initiate the proceedings. The laws of Hammurabi date to the 18th century BCE and state that if a woman wishes to divorce her husband she has to present evidence that her husband has done something wrong (law code 142). If this proved to be the case, she could move back to her father's house and take her dowry back. However, if she was the one who was found guilty of causing the problems, then the woman could be drowned (law code 143). If the man wanted a divorce and children were involved, a type of alimony would have to be paid (law code 137). If there were no children, he would give her back her purchase price if she was bought, or her dowry if she was not bought (law code 138 and 139). Divorce also became very common in the Roman world. It was usually just an agreement to end the marriage. When a divorce occurred, the women would receive her dowry back and possibly move back into her father's house. If independent before the marriage (meaning that she was not under the legal control of her father), she would remain independent after. If she had committed adultery, she would not receive all of her dowry back. There was no legal punishment for men who committed adultery.

Further Information

Clark, Elizabeth A. "Antifamilial Tendencies in Ancient Christianity." *Journal of the History of Sexuality* 5, no. 3 (Jan., 1995): 356–80.

Geller, M. J. "Early Christianity and the Dead Sea Scrolls." *Bulletin of the School of Oriental and African Studies, University of London,* 57, no. 1 (1994): 82–86.

Nathan, Geoffrey S. *The Family in Late Antiquity: The Rise of Christianity and the Endurance of Tradition.* New York: Routledge, 2000.

Salter, Kenneth W. "Canon Law Divorce and Annulment of the Roman Catholic Church at the Parish." *Journal of Marriage and Family* 31, no. 1 (Feb., 1969): 51–60.

Schatkin, Margaret A. "Divorce." In *Encyclopedia of Early Christianity*, 2nd ed., edited by Everett Ferguson, 340–41. New York: Garland, 1998.

Tertullian. *Against Marcion.* http://www.ccel.org/ccel/schaff/anf03.v.iv.i.html.

10. REMARRIAGE

INTRODUCTION

The subject of remarriage of great interest to early Christians, especially when the main topic was either divorce or what was permissible after the death of a spouse. According to the New Testament, in the one case where divorce was allowed (adultery, see the section on Divorce), remarriage was not allowed, at least if the ex-spouse was still alive. Unfortunately there wasn't much written in the New Testament on remarriage if a spouse had died, but Paul does touch on the subject. He states that it is better for widows to remain unmarried, but if they cannot resist sexual desire, they should marry. The first text is from Matthew, while the next section is from Tertullian's first letter to his wife. In the early 200s CE, Tertullian wrote two letters to his wife on the possibility of her getting remarried if Tertullian died. In his first letter, Tertullian was adamant that his wife not remarry, and in the following letter he sets out his reasons why she should not. As usual, many of the reasons were based on biblical verses. The biblical verse citations are included within the texts.

KEEP IN MIND WHILE YOU READ

1. Tertullian, who lived in Carthage, North Africa, was the first Christian to write in Latin (at least that we know of). He was a lawyer by profession, and later in life he may have joined a Christian group called the Montanists.

2. Tertullian writes a second letter to his wife that is primarily concerned with mixed marriages consisting of Christians and non-Christians. Tertullian was totally against this type of marriage, especially when the marriage was of a non-Christian husband and a Christian wife. His main objection was that he believed that a woman should obey her husband and would therefore give up Christianity.

3. Tertullian was an apologist, meaning that he defended Christianity. In addition to his many books, these letters to his wife are some early examples of private correspondence between a husband and his wife. Unfortunately we don't have her response.

Matthew 22:23–33

The same day some Sadducees came to him, saying there is no resurrection; and they asked him a question, saying, "Teacher, Moses said, 'If a man dies childless, his brother shall marry the widow, and raise up children for his brother.' Now there were seven brothers among us; the first married, and died childless, leaving the widow to his brother. The second did the same, so also the third, down to the seventh. Last of all, the woman herself died. In the resurrection, then, whose wife of the seven will she be? For all of them had married her." Jesus answered them, "You are wrong, because you know neither the scriptures nor the power of God. For in the resurrection they neither marry nor are given in marriage, but are like angels in heaven. And as for the resurrection of the dead, have you not read what was said to you by God, 'I am the God of Abraham, the God of Isaac, and the God of Jacob'? He is God not of the dead, but of the living." And when the crowd heard it, they were astounded at his teaching.

Source: Society of Biblical Literature, eds. *Harper Collins Study Bible: New Revised Standard Version*. Rev. ed. New York: HarperCollins, 2006. All Scripture quotations appear from the *New Revised Standard Version Bible*. Division of Christian Education of the National Council of Churches of Christ in the United States of America, 1989.

Tertullian, **To His Wife,** *Letter 1*

1. I have thought it appropriate, my best beloved fellow-servant in the Lord, even from this early period, to provide for the course which you must pursue after my departure from the world, if I shall be called before you; (and) to entrust to your honor the observance of the provision. For in things worldly we are active enough, and we wish the good of each of us to be consulted. If we draw up wills for such matters, why shouldn't we much more to take forethought for our posterity in things divine and heavenly, and in a sense to bequeath a legacy to be received before the inheritance be divided,—(the legacy, I mean, of) admonition and demonstration touching those (bequests) which are allotted out of (our) immortal goods, and from the heritage of the heavens? Only, that you may be able to receive in its entirety this request in trust of my admonition, may God grant, to whom be honor, glory, renown, dignity, and power, now and to the ages of the ages! The precept, therefore, which I give you is, that, with all the restraint you may, that you, after our departure, renounce nuptials; not that you will on that score confer any benefit on me, except in that you will profit yourself. But to Christians, after their departure from the world, no restoration of marriage is promised in the day of the resurrection, translated as they will be into the condition and sanctity of angels (Luke 20:34–36). Therefore no solicitude arising from carnal jealousy will, in the day of the resurrection, even in the case of the woman whom they chose to represent as having been married to seven brothers successively, wound any one of her so many husbands; nor is any (husband) awaiting her to put her to confusion. The question raised by the Sadducees has yielded to the Lord's sentence (See Matt. 22:23–33; Mark 12:18–27; Luke 20:27–40). You shouldn't think that it is for the sake of preserving to the end for myself the entire devotion of your flesh, that I, suspicious of the pain of (anticipated) slight, am even at this early period instilling into you the counsel of (perpetual)

widowhood. There will at that day be no resumption of voluptuous disgrace between us. No such frivolities, no such impurities, does God promise to His (servants). But whether to you, or to any other woman whatever who pertains to God, the advice which we are giving shall be profitable, we take leave to treat of at large.

2. We do not indeed forbid the union of man and woman, blessed by God as the seminary of the human race, and devised for the replenishment of the earth and the furnishing of the world, and therefore permitted, yet singly. For Adam was the one husband of Eve, and Eve his one wife, one woman, one rib. We grant, that among our ancestors, and the patriarchs themselves, it was lawful not only to marry, but even to multiply wives. There were concubines, too, (in those days.) But although the Church did come in figuratively in the synagogue, yet (to interpret simply) it was necessary to institute (certain things) which should afterward deserve to be either lopped off or modified. For the Law was (in due time) to supervene. (Nor was that enough:) for it was right that causes for making up the deficiencies of the Law should have forerun (Him who was to supply those deficiencies). And so to the Law presently had to succeed the Word of God introducing the spiritual circumcision. Therefore, by means of the wide license of those days, materials for subsequent emendations were furnished beforehand, of which materials the Lord by His Gospel, and then the apostle in the last days of the (Jewish) age, either cut off the redundancies or regulated the disorders.

3. But let it not be thought that my reason for premising thus much concerning the liberty granted to the old, and the restraint imposed on the later time, is that I may lay a foundation for teaching that Christ's advent was intended to dissolve wedlock, (and) to abolish marriage talons; as if from this period onward I were prescribing an end to marrying. Let them see to that, who, among the rest of their perversities, teach the disjoining of the "one flesh in twain;" denying Him who, after borrowing the female from the male, recombined between themselves, in the matrimonial computation, the two bodies taken out of the consortship of the self-same material substance. In short, there is no place at all where we read that nuptials are prohibited; of course on the ground that they are "a good thing." What, however, is better than this "good," we learn from the apostle, who permits marrying indeed, but prefers abstinence; the former on account of the insidiousnesses of temptations, the latter on account of the straits of the times (1 Cor. 7). Now, by looking into the reason thus given for each proposition, it is easily discerned that the ground on which the power of marrying is conceded is necessity; but whatever necessity grants, she by her very nature depreciates. In fact, in that it is written, "To marry is better than to burn," what, pray, is the nature of this "good" which is (only) commended by comparison with "evil," so that the reason why "marrying" is more good is (merely) that "burning" is less? Nay, but how far better is it neither to marry nor to burn? Why, even in persecutions it is better to take advantage of the permission granted, and "flee from town to town," than, when apprehended and racked, to deny (the faith). And therefore more blessed are they who have strength to depart (this life) in blessed confession of their testimony. I may say, What is permitted is not good. For how stands the case? I must of necessity die (if I be apprehended and confess my faith). If I think (that fate) deplorable, (then flight) is good; but if I have a fear of the thing which is permitted, (the permitted thing) has some suspicion attaching to the cause of its permission. But that which is "better" no one (ever) "permitted," as being undoubted, and manifest by its own inherent purity. There are some things which are not to be desired merely because they are not forbidden, albeit they are in a certain sense forbidden when other things are preferred to them; for the preference given to the higher things is a dissuasion from the lowest. A thing is not "good" merely because it is not "evil," nor is it "evil" merely because it is not "harmful." Further: that which is fully

"good" excels on this ground, that it is not only not harmful, but profitable into the bargain. For you are bound to prefer what is profitable to what is (merely) not harmful. For the first place is what every struggle aims at; the second has consolation attaching to it, but not victory. But if we listen to the apostle, forgetting what is behind, let us both strain after what is before, and be followers after the better rewards. Thus, albeit he does not "cast a snare upon us," he points out what tends to utility when he says, "The unmarried woman thinks on the things of the Lord, that both in body and spirit she may be holy; but the married is solicitous how to please her husband" (Phil. 3:13–14). But he nowhere permits marriage in such a way as not rather to wish us to do our utmost in imitation of his own example. Happy the man who shall prove like Paul!

7. To us continence has been pointed out by the Lord of salvation as an instrument for attaining eternity, and as a testimony of (our) faith; as a commendation of this flesh of ours, which is to be sustained for the "garment of immortality," (1 Cor. 15:53; 2 Cor. 5:4) which is one day to supervene; for enduring, in fine, the will of God. Besides, reflect, I advise you, that there is no one who is taken out of the world but by the will of God, if, (as is the case,) not even a leaf falls from off a tree without it. The same who brings us into the world must of necessity take us out of it too. Therefore when, through the will of God, the husband is deceased, the marriage likewise, by the will of God, deceases. Why should you restore what God has put an end to? Why do you, by repeating the servitude of matrimony, spurn the liberty which is offered you? "You have been bound to a wife," says the apostle; "seek not loosing. You have been loosed from a wife; seek not binding" (1 Cor. 7:27). For even if you do not "sin" in re-marrying, still he says "pressure of the flesh ensues" (1 Cor. vii. 28). Wherefore, so far as we can, let us love the opportunity of continence; as soon as it offers itself, let us resolve to accept it, that what we have not had strength (to follow) in matrimony we may follow in widowhood. The occasion must be embraced which puts an end to that which necessity commanded. How detrimental to faith, how obstructive to holiness, second marriages are, the discipline of the Church and the prescription of the apostle declare, when he suffers not men twice married to preside (1 Tim. 2:2; Tit. 1:6), when he would not grant a widow admittance into the order unless she had been "the wife of one man" (1 Tim. 5:9–10); for it behooves God's altar to be set forth pure. That whole halo which encircles the Church is represented (as consisting) of holiness. Priesthood is (a function) of widowhood and of celibacies among the nations. Of course (this is) in conformity with the devil's principle of rivalry. For the king of heathendom, the chief pontiff, to marry a second time is unlawful. How pleasing must holiness be to God, when even His enemy affects it!—not, of course, as having any affinity with anything good, but as insultingly affecting what is pleasing to God the Lord . . .

Source: Roberts, Rev. Alexander, and James Donaldson, eds. *The Ante-Nicene Fathers: Translations of the Writings of the Fathers Down to A.D. 325*, vol. 4. New York: Charles Scribner's Sons, 1905, 39–42.

AFTERMATH

Unfortunately we don't know the response of Tertullian's wife to the proposal. It appears that she died before him, so we don't know how seriously she would have taken his recommendations. As far as we know, Tertullian did not remarry after the death of his wife. The topic of remarriage is tied to the topic of widowhood. In the New Testament writings widows were people that communities were supposed to take care of, and this was an idea that Christians borrowed from the Jews. A good example of this is 1 Timothy 5:3–5, which describes how widows (who do not remarry) should be treated. However, young widows were instructed to remarry and have children (1 Timothy 5:14). These conflicting views in the early Christian texts affected the belief in remarriage long after Tertullian. Two centuries later, another North African, Augustine of Hippo, wrote a book titled *On the Excellence of Widowhood*. In chapter 6 of that work he castigates Tertullian and his thoughts on remarriage. Augustine states specifically that remarriage is not a bad thing.

ASK YOURSELF

1. In the passage from Matthew, the last verse given mentioned that the crowd was astounded at the statements made by Jesus. Who were these people that were astounded, and why would this particular message be so shocking?

2. Tertullian lists a number of reasons why his decision to ask his wife not to remarry after his death was not based on possible jealousy. Do you think his reasons are really not based on jealousy that she might have another husband? Do you find the biblical verses reasonable?

3. Tertullian makes use of Luke 20:34–36, in which Jesus states: "Those who belong to this age marry and are given in marriage; but those who are considered worthy of a place in that age and in the resurrection from the dead neither marry nor are given in marriage. Indeed they cannot die anymore, because they are like angels and are children of God, being children of the resurrection." Tertullian states that there will be no marriage in heaven after the resurrection. Many Christians today look forward to being united with dead relatives, including spouses. If you are a Christian and married, how does this verse apply to your own marriage? Does it make you feel differently about marriage?

4. As stated in the introduction, Paul allowed widows to remarry in the case where they could not control their sexual desire. Paul was one of the most important writers for later Christians, including Tertullian. Why do you think the Tertullian advised just the opposite of Paul?

TOPICS TO CONSIDER

- Remarriage was common in early U.S. history, primarily because life expectancy was highly variable, so that one spouse often outlived the other by quite a few years. Childbirth was also dangerous for both the mother and the child. Examine this period and consider how the issue of remarriage was handled, especially in terms of the biblical passages that Tertullian used.

- Remarriage is extremely common in the United States today, primarily because divorce is extremely easy to receive. Examine how the issue of remarriage is handled in various religious organizations today, especially with respect to the biblical passages that Tertullian used.

- Like other ancient Christians, Tertullian makes extensive use of the New Testament. Consider how he might have formed his argument if he did not have the New Testament texts. Is the New Testament vitally important to his argument, or could he have written these letters to his wife without them?

Further Information

Beattie, Gillian. *Women and Marriage in Paul and His Early Interpreters.* London: Continuum, 2005.

Church, F. Forrester. "Sex and Salvation in Tertullian." *Harvard Theological Review* 68, no. 2 (Apr., 1975): 83–101.

Kraemer, Ross S. "The Conversion of Women to Ascetic Forms of Christianity." *Signs* 6, no. 2 (Winter, 1980): 298–307.

Methuen, Charlotte. "The 'Virgin Widow': A Problematic Social Role for the Early Church?" *Harvard Theological Review* 90, no. 3 (Jul., 1997): 285–98.

11. The End Times

INTRODUCTION

As Paula Fredriksen notes, "Christianity began with the announcement that time and history were about to end" (Fredriksen 151). Christians believed that Christ would come back to judge both the living and the dead. The idea of eternal judgment at the end of time was an important one for early Christians. The end times are mentioned on many occasions in the New Testament, with the earliest being in the writings of Paul. Paul believed and taught that the end of time would occur during his own lifetime. The book of Revelation describes what Christians believe will happen at the end of time, the study of which is called eschatology. According to the beginning chapter of Revelation, the revelation by Jesus was told to John, who according to tradition is the Apostle John. Revelation is one of the most graphic texts of the New Testament, while at the same time being one of the most enigmatic, primarily because of the heavy use of symbols. The following texts are taken from 1 Corinthians and Revelation.

KEEP IN MIND WHILE YOU READ

1. Paul's view should not be taken as representative of all early Christians. One needs to keep in mind that Paul was writing letters to various Christian groups that he founded or to Christians he discovered when he traveled through Asia Minor and when he was taken as a prisoner to Italy.
2. Not everyone in the early church accepted Revelation as canonical. It wasn't until the middle to end of the fourth century when it was considered to be part of the official canon to be read by Christians.
3. Christians were a persecuted group until the rise of Emperor Constantine at the beginning of the fourth century. During these first three centuries, the belief that Christ would return to judge believers and nonbelievers was fairly strong. After the persecution of Christians finished, the end times was still important, but its importance in early Christian groups seemed to decline.

1 Thessalonians 4:13–18

But we do not want you to be uninformed, brothers and sisters, about those who have died, so that you may not grieve as others do who have no hope. For since we believe that Jesus died and rose again, even so, through Jesus, God will bring with him those who have died. For this we declare to you by the word of the Lord, that we who are alive, who are left until the coming of the Lord, will by no means precede those who have died. For the Lord himself, with a cry of command, with the archangel's call and with the sound of God's trumpet, will descend from heaven, and the dead in Christ will rise first. Then we who are alive, who are left, will be caught up in the clouds together with them to meet the Lord in the air; and so we will be with the Lord forever. Therefore encourage one another with these words.

Revelation 1:1–20, 2:18–29, 8:1–9:16

The revelation of Jesus Christ, which God gave him to show his servants what must soon take place; he made it known by sending his angel to his servant John, who testified to the word of God and to the testimony of Jesus Christ, even to all that he saw. Blessed is the one who reads aloud the words of the prophecy, and blessed are those who hear and who keep what is written in it; for the time is near. John to the seven churches that are in Asia: Grace to you and peace from him who is and who was and who is to come, and from the seven spirits who are before his throne, and from Jesus Christ, the faithful witness, the firstborn of the dead, and the ruler of the kings of the earth. To him who loves us and freed us from our sins by his blood, and made us to be a kingdom, priests serving his God and Father, to him be glory and dominion forever and ever. Amen. Look! He is coming with the clouds; every eye will see him, even those who pierced him; and on his account all the tribes of the earth will wail. So it is to be. Amen. "I am the Alpha and the Omega," says the Lord God, who is and who was and who is to come, the Almighty. I, John, your brother who share with you in Jesus the persecution and the kingdom and the patient endurance, was on the island called Patmos because of the word of God and the testimony of Jesus. I was in the spirit on the Lord's day, and I heard behind me a loud voice like a trumpet saying, "Write in a book what you see and send it to the seven churches, to Ephesus, to Smyrna, to Pergamum, to Thyatira, to Sardis, to Philadelphia, and to Laodicea." Then I turned to see whose voice it was that spoke to me, and on turning I saw seven golden lampstands, and in the midst of the lampstands I saw one like the Son of Man, clothed with a long robe and with a golden sash across his chest. His head and his hair were white as white wool, white as snow; his eyes were like a flame of fire, his feet were like burnished bronze, refined as in a furnace, and his voice was like the sound of many waters. In his right hand he held seven stars, and from his mouth came a sharp, two-edged sword, and his face was like the sun shining with full force. When I saw him, I fell at his feet as though dead. But he placed his right hand on me, saying, "Do not be afraid; I am the first and the last, and the living one. I was dead, and see, I am alive forever and ever; and I have the keys of Death and of Hades. Now write what you have seen, what is, and what is to take place after this. As for the mystery of the seven stars that you saw in my right hand, and the seven golden lampstands: the seven stars are the angels of the seven churches, and the seven lampstands are the seven churches.

. . . 2:18 "And to the angel of the church in Thyatira write: These are the words of the Son of God, who has eyes like a flame of fire, and whose feet are like burnished bronze: "I know your works—your love, faith, service, and patient endurance. I know that your last works are greater than the first. But I have this against you: you tolerate that woman Jezebel, who calls herself a prophet and is teaching and beguiling my servants to practice fornication and to eat food sacrificed to idols. I gave her time to repent, but she refuses to repent of her fornication. Beware, I am throwing her on a bed, and those who commit adultery with her I am throwing into great distress, unless they repent of her doings; and I will strike her children dead. And all the churches will know that I am the one who searches minds and hearts, and I will give to each of you as your works deserve. But to the rest of you in Thyatira, who do not hold this teaching, who have not learned what some call 'the deep things of Satan,' to you I say, I do not lay on you any other burden; only hold fast to what you have until I come. To everyone who conquers and continues to do my works to the end, I will give authority over the nations; to rule them with an iron rod, as when clay pots are shattered—even as I also received authority from my Father. To the one who conquers I will also give the morning star. Let anyone who has an ear listen to what the Spirit is saying to the churches.

. . . 8:1 When the Lamb opened the seventh seal, there was silence in heaven for about half an hour. And I saw the seven angels who stand before God, and seven trumpets were given to them. Another angel with a golden censer came and stood at the altar; he was given a great quantity of incense to offer with the prayers of all the saints on the golden altar that is before the throne. And the smoke of the incense, with the prayers of the saints, rose before God from the hand of the angel. Then the angel took the censer and filled it with fire from the altar and threw it on the earth; and there were peals of thunder, rumblings, flashes of lightning, and an earthquake. Now the seven angels who had the seven trumpets made ready to blow them. The first angel blew his trumpet, and there came hail and fire, mixed with blood, and they were hurled to the earth; and a third of the earth was burned up, and a third of the trees were burned up, and all green grass was burned up. The second angel blew his trumpet, and something like a great mountain, burning with fire, was thrown into the sea. A third of the sea became blood, a third of the living creatures in the sea died, and a third of the ships were destroyed. The third angel blew his trumpet, and a great star fell from heaven, blazing like a torch, and it fell on a third of the rivers and on the springs of water. The name of the star is Wormwood. A third of the waters became wormwood, and many died from the water, because it was made bitter. The fourth angel blew his trumpet, and a third of the sun was struck, and a third of the moon, and a third of the stars, so that a third of their light was darkened; a third of the day was kept from shining, and likewise the night. Then I looked, and I heard an eagle crying with a loud voice as it flew in midheaven, "Woe, woe, woe to the inhabitants of the earth, at the blasts of the other trumpets that the three angels are about to blow!" And the fifth angel blew his trumpet, and I saw a star that had fallen from heaven to earth, and he was given the key to the shaft of the bottomless pit; he opened the shaft of the bottomless pit, and from the shaft rose smoke like the smoke of a great furnace, and the sun and the air were darkened with the smoke from the shaft. Then from the smoke came locusts on the earth, and they were given authority like the authority of scorpions of the earth. They were told not to damage the grass of the earth or any green growth or any tree, but only those people who do not have the seal of God on their foreheads. They were allowed to torture them for five months, but not to kill them, and their torture was like the torture of a scorpion when it stings someone. And in those days people will seek death but will not find it; they will long to die, but death will flee from them. In appearance the locusts were like horses equipped for battle. On their heads were what looked like crowns of gold; their faces were like human faces, their hair like women's hair, and their teeth like lions' teeth; they had scales like iron breastplates, and the noise of their wings was like the noise of many chariots with horses rushing into battle. They have tails like scorpions, with stingers, and in their tails is their power to harm people for five months. They have as king over them the angel of the bottomless pit; his name in Hebrew is Abaddon, and in Greek he is called Apollyon. The first woe has passed. There are still two woes to come. Then the sixth angel blew his trumpet, and I heard a voice from the four horns of the golden altar before God, saying to the sixth angel who had the trumpet, "Release the four angels who are bound at the great river Euphrates." So the four angels were released, who had been held ready for the hour, the day, the month, and the year, to kill a third of humankind. The number of the troops of cavalry was two hundred million; I heard their number . . .

Source: Society of Biblical Literature, eds. *Harper Collins Study Bible: New Revised Standard Version.* Rev. ed. New York: HarperCollins, 2006. All Scripture quotations appear from the *New Revised Standard Version Bible.* Division of Christian Education of the National Council of Churches of Christ in the United States of America, 1989.

AFTERMATH

The return of Jesus, the judgment of the living and the dead, and the end of life as usual were an important part of early Christianity. Belief in Jesus separated out the Christian community from other religions, but believing that Jesus would judge all people, Christians and non-Christians, tied these early Christian communities together. It also drove a wedge between those who believed and those who did not, since there was only one fate for nonbelievers. The idea that Jesus was coming back to judge also held a strong fascination for the writers in the second century. Like Paul, they believed that the end was imminent. The author of the *Epistle of Barnabas,* in chapter 4, states that the "tribulation" is at hand and Christians should be prepared for it. Ignatius, in his *Epistle to the Ephesians,* chapter 11, states that "the last times are come upon us. Let us therefore be of a reverent spirit, and fear the long-suffering of God, that it tend not to our condemnation. For let us either stand in awe of the wrath to come, or show regard for the grace which is at present displayed . . ." Despite its popularity for some, the book of Revelation was not accepted by all Christians until the middle of the 300s.

ASK YOURSELF

1. In his early writings, Paul believed that the end was very near. How do you think this would have affected the behavior of early Christians? Also, when the end did not appear as soon as Paul thought, he had to change his views of when it would actually arrive. How do you think early Christians felt about this when Paul believed it would come within his lifetime, but it didn't?
2. Why do you think it took so long for Revelation to be accepted as canonical? Just from reading the text, what problems can you imagine the early church had with it?
3. What do you think the relationship is between Revelation and the rest of the writings from the New Testament? Could Revelation be placed at the beginning or

the middle of the New Testament canon and still have the same impact? Why or why not?

4. Why do you think that having an end time was and is important to Christians? What benefit comes from believing that the world will end and believers will be taken to heaven?

5. Revelation is directed to seven churches. Why those churches? Why not to Rome or Jerusalem?

TOPICS TO CONSIDER

- ➣ Consider how modern churches discuss the contents of Revelation. Is eschatology an important part of modern churches? You may need to examine a few different kinds of churches. If it is not, how do they account for Revelation?

- ➣ There are many places in Revelation where symbols are used, and there is much discussion on what some of these symbols mean. Read through the passage provided and the rest of Revelation, picking out the symbols. What do you think they mean, for both ancient and modern Christians?

- ➣ Sometimes Revelation is very cryptic. Read the rest of Revelation and list the passages you find obscure. Consider what they might mean to early Christians, modern Christians, and non-Christians.

Further Information

Barnard, L. W. "Justin Martyr's Eschatology." *Vigiliae Christianae* 19, no. 2 (Jun., 1965): 86–98.

Bratten, Carl E., and Robert W. Jenson. *The Last Things: Biblical and Theological Perspectives on Eschatology*. Grand Rapids, MI: Eerdmanns, 2002.

Francis, Fred O. "Eschatology and History in Luke-Acts." *Journal of the American Academy of Religion* 37, no. 1 (Mar., 1969): 49–63.

Fredriksen, Paula. "Apocalypse and Redemption in Early Christianity from John of Patmos to Augustine of Hippo." *Vigiliae Christianae* 45, no. 2 (Jun., 1991): 151–83.

Holleman, Joost. *Resurrection and Parousia: A Traditio-Historical Study of Paul's Eschatology in 1 Corinthians 15*. Louvain, Belgium: Brill, 1996.

Kee, Howard C. "The Development of Eschatology in the New Testament." *Journal of Bible and Religion* 20, no. 3 (Jul., 1952): 187–93.

Kümmel, Werner Georg. "Futuristic and Realized Eschatology in the Earliest Stages of Christianity." *Journal of Religion* 43, no. 4 (Oct., 1963): 303–14.

12. Resurrection: Scenes from the Christian Catacombs

INTRODUCTION

The belief in resurrection at the end of time is a central belief in Christianity. Jesus was raised from the dead, and this became the hope for all Christians. This episode is mentioned many times in the New Testament, throughout the history of Christian writings, and it was natural that early Christians would have chosen the story of Lazarus as the symbol for the resurrection to come and of the power of Christ. The story of Lazarus is told only in the Gospel of John. It is here where we are told that Lazarus was the brother of Mary. Lazarus had died, and Jesus decided to bring him back from the dead. He had been dead for four days. The stone was rolled away from his tomb, and Jesus called out to him, "Lazarus, come out!" He did. The early Christians used the image of Lazarus, his tomb, and his resurrection. The image on the next page depicts a fresco at the Catacomb of Via Latina.

KEEP IN MIND WHILE YOU READ

1. The idea of resurrection can also be found in the Hebrew Bible. Daniel 12:1–2 states, "At that time Michael, the great prince, the protector of your people, shall arise. There shall be a time of anguish, such as has never occurred since nations first came into existence. But at that time your people shall be delivered, everyone who is found written in the book. Many of those who sleep in the dust of the earth shall awake, some to everlasting life, and some to shame and everlasting contempt." This idea is also found in 2 Maccabees 7.
2. The Via Latina catacomb dates to sometime in the 300s and is relatively small compared to other catacombs, consisting of about a dozen rooms.
3. Some people thought that the catacombs were used during times of persecution and that Christians would use them to hide, but most scholars do not accept this theory.
4. It is not known who the painters were. It is possible that some were done by the people who dug the catacombs (the *fossores*), or that the families hired artists to create them.
5. Non-Christian and non-Jewish images were also found painted in the Catacomb of Via Latina, including that of Hercules.

Resurrection of Lazarus. Early Christian fresco, c. 320–50. (Scala/Art Resource, NY)

AFTERMATH

Many of the catacombs were rediscovered starting in the 1500s. The Catacomb of Via Latina, however, is a recent find. It was discovered in 1955 during the enlargement of an apartment building in Rome. This catacomb is different from other catacombs in terms of the amount of paintings found on its walls, and it has been thought that the catacomb was created for wealthy people (Goodenough 114). It is filled with scenes from the New and Old Testaments, as well as pagan artwork.

ASK YOURSELF

1. Why do you think some of the catacombs were lost over time? Does that tell you anything about how Christians viewed or used the catacombs?
2. John 12:11 states that Jewish people were leaving their faith and joining Christ because of the resurrection of Lazarus. John 12:10 states that the Jews were going to put Lazarus to death because of this. Why would this particular miracle worry the Jewish leaders? What effects would it have on the crowds in general?

3. If you could design your own tomb in a catacomb, what images or texts would you want?

4. The Old Testament has examples of people being raised from the dead (1 Kings 17:17–24; 2 Kings 4:32–37; 2 Kings 13:21). In both cases prophets had raised them. If there are parallels to the miracles of Jesus, what does that tell you about his status in the community?

TOPICS TO CONSIDER

- Consider the role of miracles in early Christianity. Since Judaism had examples of miracle-working and resurrection, consider what else it would take for a Jewish person to join Christianity.
- Consider why everyone did not join Christianity after Jesus raised Lazarus.
- Consider the role of resurrection and miracles in modern-day Christianity. Is one more important than the other, or are both treated equally?

THE CHRISTIAN CATACOMBS

There are many Christian catacombs in Rome and in other areas surrounding the Mediterranean, and these have held the fascination of people for a very long time. Jerome, a Christian living in Bethlehem in the late 300s and early 400s CE, mentioned that as a boy he would visit these "terrifying" places. Those in Rome are the most famous and probably the most accessible since they are very popular with tourists. These catacombs are miles long, and some of them are four stories down. The catacombs have a long history, and the practice of burying bodies or cremated remains in the catacombs goes back before Christianity. However, the Christians made wide use of these tunnels that were first created when the stone tufa was excavated and used as above-ground building material. The remaining tunnels were a perfect place to store bodies until the resurrection. Many times the walls of the tunnels were carved out to create niches (called *loculi*), sometimes three high, and the bodies placed inside. The opening was then closed, and on occasion it was covered in art. The Catacomb of St. Callixtus is of prime importance for the history of Christianity because it contains the bodies of nine popes from the third century. Their tombs were rediscovered in 1849.

Further Information

Colwell, Ernest Cadman. "The Fourth Gospel and Early Christian Art." *Journal of Religion* 15, no. 2 (Apr., 1935): 191–206.

Esler, Philip Francis, and Ronald A. Piper. *Lazarus, Mary and Martha: Social-Scientific Approaches to the Gospel of John*. Minneapolis, MN: Augsberg Fortress, 2006.

Goodenough, Erwin R. "Catacomb Art." *Journal of Biblical Literature* 81, no. 2 (Jun., 1962): 113–42.

International Catacomb Society. http://www.catacombsociety.org/index.html.

Jensen, Robin Margaret. *Understanding Early Christian Art*. London: Routledge, 2000.

Lamberton, Clark D. "The Development of Christian Symbolism as Illustrated in Roman Catacomb Painting." *American Journal of Archaeology* 15, no. 4 (Oct.–Dec., 1911): 507–22.

Stevenson, James. *The Catacombs: Rediscovered Monuments of Early Christianity*. London: Thames and Hudson, 1978.

Tronzo, William. *The Via Latina Catacomb: Imitation and Discontinuity in Fourth-Century Roman Painting*. University Park: Pennsylvania State University Press, 1986.

Webb, Matilda. *The Churches and Catacombs of Early Christian Rome: A Comprehensive Guide*. Portland: Sussex Academic Press, 2001.

THE CHURCH

13. Church Offices: Apostles, Prophets, and Teachers

INTRODUCTION

Paul, in his first letter to the Corinthians, mentions that there are apostles, prophets, and teachers whom God has appointed. He spends quite a bit of time discussing the prophets. By the beginning of the second century, the offices of prophet and teacher were becoming a problem for some established churches, especially those who had permanent clergy. The *Didache,* or the *Teaching of the Twelve Apostles,* written in the early part of the second century, goes into some detail on how to tell the difference between a real teacher, prophet, or apostle and those who are false. It also discusses how a community should treat these people. It appears that the second-century Christians were trying to limit the power these traveling clergy had, while at the same time a parallel movement was occurring to consolidate the power of the bishop.

KEEP IN MIND WHILE YOU READ

1. The original Twelve Apostles were appointed by Jesus. Jesus also appointed another 70 (Luke 10:1). Unfortunately, many of their names are unknown, and it is not known where they went after Jesus sent them out.

2. Jesus gave very specific instructions to the apostles. Among other things, he stated (Matthew 10:7–15): "As you go, proclaim the good news, 'The kingdom of heaven has come near.' Cure the sick, raise the dead, cleanse the lepers, cast out demons. You received without payment; give without payment. Take no gold, or silver, or copper in your belts, no bag for your journey, or two tunics, or sandals, or a staff; for laborers deserve their food. Whatever town or village you enter, find out who in it is worthy, and stay there until you leave. As you enter the house, greet it. If the house is worthy, let your peace come upon it; but if it is not worthy, let your peace return to you. If anyone will not welcome you or listen to your words, shake off the dust from your feet as you leave that house or town. Truly I tell you, it will be more tolerable for the land of Sodom and Gomorrah on the day of judgment than for that town."

3. Eusebius of Caesarea, in *Ecclesiastical History* 3.25, states that the *Didache* was one of the rejected teachings, meaning that it should not be considered canonical and genuine.

---

1 Corinthians 12:28–14:19

And God has appointed in the church first apostles, second prophets, third teachers; then deeds of power, then gifts of healing, forms of assistance, forms of leadership, various kinds of tongues. Are all apostles? Are all prophets? Are all teachers? Do all work miracles? Do all possess gifts of healing? Do all speak in tongues? Do all interpret? But strive for the greater gifts. And I will show you a still more excellent way. If I speak in the tongues of mortals and of angels, but do not have love, I am a noisy gong or a clanging cymbal. And if I have prophetic powers, and understand all mysteries and all knowledge, and if I have all faith, so as to remove mountains, but do not have love, I am nothing. If I give away all my possessions, and if I hand over my body so that I may boast, but do not have love, I gain nothing. Love is patient; love is kind; love is not envious or boastful or arrogant or rude. It does not insist on its own way; it is not irritable or resentful; it does not rejoice in wrongdoing, but rejoices in the truth. It bears all things, believes all things, hopes all things, endures all things. Love never ends. But as for prophecies, they will come to an end; as for tongues, they will cease; as for knowledge, it will come to an end. For we know only in part, and we prophesy only in part; but when the complete comes, the partial will come to an end. When I was a child, I spoke like a child, I thought like a child, I reasoned like a child; when I became an adult, I put an end to childish ways. For now we see in a mirror, dimly, but then we will see face to face. Now I know only in part; then I will know fully, even as I have been fully known. And now faith, hope, and love abide, these three; and the greatest of these is love. Pursue love and strive for the spiritual gifts, and especially that you may prophesy. For those who speak in a tongue do not speak to other people but to God; for nobody understands them, since they are speaking mysteries in the Spirit. On the other hand, those who prophesy speak to other people for their upbuilding and encouragement and consolation. Those who speak in a tongue build up themselves, but those who prophesy build up the church. Now I would like all of you to speak in tongues, but even more to prophesy. One who prophesies is greater than one who speaks in tongues, unless someone interprets, so that the church may be built up. Now, brothers and sisters, if I come to you speaking in tongues, how will I benefit you unless I speak to you in some revelation or knowledge or prophecy or teaching? It is the same way with lifeless instruments that produce sound, such as the flute or the harp. If they do not give distinct notes, how will anyone know what is being played? And if the bugle gives an indistinct sound, who will get ready for battle? So with yourselves; if in a tongue you utter speech that is not intelligible, how will anyone know what is being said? For you will be speaking into the air. There are doubtless many different kinds of sounds in the world, and nothing is without sound. If then I do not know the meaning of a sound, I will be a foreigner to the speaker and the speaker a foreigner to me. So with yourselves; since you are eager for spiritual gifts, strive to excel in them for building up the church. Therefore, one who speaks in a tongue should pray for the power to interpret. For if I pray in a tongue, my spirit prays but my mind is unproductive. What should I do then? I will pray with the spirit, but I will pray with the mind also; I will sing praise with the spirit, but I will sing praise with the mind also.

Otherwise, if you say a blessing with the spirit, how can anyone in the position of an outsider say the "Amen" to your thanksgiving, since the outsider does not know what you are saying? For you may give thanks well enough, but the other person is not built up. I thank God that I speak in tongues more than all of you; nevertheless, in church I would rather speak five words with my mind, in order to instruct others also, than ten thousand words in a tongue.

Source: Society of Biblical Literature, eds. *Harper Collins Study Bible: New Revised Standard Version*. Rev. ed. New York: HarperCollins, 2006. All Scripture quotations appear from the *New Revised Standard Version Bible*. Division of Christian Education of the National Council of Churches of Christ in the United States of America, 1989.

Didache *11–13*

Chapter 11

Whoever then comes and teaches you all these things mentioned, receive him. But if the teacher himself is perverted and teaches another doctrine to destroy these things, do not listen to him, but if his teaching is for the increase of righteousness and knowledge of the Lord, receive him as the Lord. And concerning the apostles and prophets, act according to the ordinance of the Gospel. Let every apostle who comes to you be received as the Lord, but let him not stay more than one day, or if need be a second as well; but if he stay three days, he is a false prophet. And when an Apostle leaves let him accept nothing but bread till he reach his night's lodging; but if he asks for money, he is a false prophet. Do not test or examine any prophet who is speaking in a spirit, "for every sin shall be forgiven, but this sin shall not be forgiven." But not everyone who speaks in a spirit is a prophet, except the one who has the behavior of the Lord. From his behavior, then, the false prophet and the true prophet shall be known. And no prophet who orders a meal in a spirit shall eat of it: otherwise he is a false prophet. And every prophet who teaches the truth, who does not do what he teaches, is a false prophet. But no prophet who has been tried and is genuine, although he enacts a worldly mystery of the Church, if he does not teach others to do what he does himself, he shall be judged by you: for he has his judgment with God, for so also did the prophets of old. But whosoever shall say in a spirit "Give me money, or something else," you shall not listen to him; but if he tells you to give on behalf of others in want, let none judge him.

Chapter 12

Let everyone who "comes in the Name of the Lord" be received; but when you have tested him you shall know him, for you shall have understanding of true and false. If he who comes is a traveler, help him as much as you can, but he shall not remain with you more than two days, or, if need be, three. And if he wishes to settle among you and has a craft, let him work for his bread. But if he has no craft provide for him according to your understanding, so that no man shall live among you in idleness because he is a Christian. But if he will not do so, he is making traffic of Christ; beware of such a person.

Chapter 13

But every true prophet who wishes to settle among you is "worthy of his food." Likewise a true teacher is himself worthy, like the workman, of his food. Therefore you should take the first fruit of the produce of the winepress and of the threshing-floor and of oxen and sheep, and shall give them as the first fruits to the prophets, for they are your high priests. But if you have not a prophet, give to the poor. If you make bread, take the first fruits, and give it according to the commandment. Likewise when you open a jar of wine or oil, give the first fruits to the prophets. Of money also and clothes, and of all your possessions, take the first fruits, as it seem best to you, and give according to the commandment.

Source: *Didache*, translated by Kirsopp Lake, in *The Apostolic Fathers*, vol. 1. New York: MacMillan, 1912, 325–29.

AFTERMATH

The apostles, teachers, and prophets obviously played very important roles in the spreading and defining the Christian faith. Of these three, the apostles were the most important because they were chosen by Christ. However, by the time of Ignatius of Antioch, apostles and most prophets had disappeared from Christian communities, replaced by the bishop, the presbyter, and the deacon. Ignatius continually stressed the importance of having one bishop controlling the church. As seen from the *Didache*, the prophets and teachers in particular needed to be treated carefully because they were causing trouble for the bishops by usurping their power. The traveling apostles, prophets, and teachers were also causing trouble because they would come into local communities, spread their version of Christianity, and usually depart, leaving the local clergy to clean up the mess. Eventually these positions were phased out in order to attempt to keep the message of Christianity uniform.

ASK YOURSELF

1. What are the problems that some early Christian communities were having with these traveling clergy? Do you think these people were legitimately causing problems, or were they really spreading the truth?
2. Why is Paul so concerned with speaking in tongues and prophesying? What danger does it represent? How does one speak in tongues properly?
3. Why should an apostle stay in a community for only such a short time? Do you think that is enough time to spread the message?
4. Why would the prophets received the "first fruits"? Why are they considered to be so special?

TOPICS TO CONSIDER

- ↷ Recreate the Christian community that the *Didache* describes. Consider who in the community should be policing it and how they will go about enforcing the policy.

- ↷ The *Didache* gives firm rules on the length of stay for the apostles. The Apostle Paul traveled all over Asia Minor spreading his own brand of Christianity. Examine the life of Paul and determine how long he stayed in the various communities. Did he conform to the rules that Jesus set down and those of the *Didache*? If not, why not?

- ↷ Speaking in tongues is something that still happens in some churches. Consider the early history of this and how that impacts the speaking in tongues today. Does speaking in tongues add to the weight of the Christian message? Consider how this message impacts those who are not speaking in tongues but hearing it.

Further Information

DeWitt Burton, Ernest. "The Office of Apostle in the Early Church." *American Journal of Theology* 16, no. 4 (Oct., 1912): 561–88.

Eberts, Harry W., Jr. "Plurality and Ethnicity in Early Christian Mission." *Sociology of Religion* 58, no. 4 (Winter, 1997): 305–21.

Horrell, David. "Leadership Patterns and the Development of Ideology in Early Christianity." *Sociology of Religion* 58, no. 4 (Winter, 1997): 323–41.

Pervo, Richard I. *The Making of Paul: Constructions of the Apostle in Early Christianity.* Minneapolis, MN: Fortress Press, 2010.

Verheyden, Joseph, Korinna Zamfir, and Tobias Nicklas, eds. *Prophets and Prophecy in Jewish and Early Christian Literature.* Tübingen, Germany: Mohr Siebeck, 2010.

14. Marriage of Apostles and Priests

INTRODUCTION

There are a few instances where married apostles are mentioned in the New Testament, and it does not seem to be a problem for the early Christian communities. Peter, who became the most influential of the apostles, was married. It is mentioned in Acts 21:8–9 that Philip had four unmarried daughters, which implies that he was also married. Paul (or a disciple of Paul) states, in 1 Timothy 3:2 and 3:8, that bishops and deacons should marry only once and have control of their children. In the early 300s, the view that it was acceptable for clergy to marry began to change, and Paul, as usual, has had the most influence on the topic of marriage of the clergy. He states that unmarried people concentrate on spiritual issues while married people focus on their spouses (1 Corinthians 7:32–34). The texts below are taken from 1 Corinthians, 1 Timothy, Matthew, Clement of Alexandria, and some canons from the Council of Elvira and Nicea.

KEEP IN MIND WHILE YOU READ

1. Paul was not married. In fact, he stated that he wished that everyone would remain unmarried like he was. Clement of Alexandria (below) states that Paul was married, but it appears he was mistaken.
2. The canons issued at the Council at Elvira, Spain, probably had an effect on only the local churches in and around what is now Granada. But its principal bishop was Ossius (sometimes Hosius) of Cordoba, and Ossius presided over the great Council of Nicea in 325.
3. Some early Christians were concerned that the appearance of an unmarried, unrelated woman in the household of a clergy member would lead to problems. This implies that there were some clergy who were living with what we could call in modern terms their girlfriends.
4. Paul probably didn't write 1 Timothy. Many scholars believe that it was probably one of his disciples, mostly because of the writing style and because new issues, such as a hierarchy of church officials, appear for the first time. It was probably written between the 80s and the early 100s CE.

> **Barnabas** Barnabas was Paul's traveling companion as they spread Christianity. According to Acts 9:27, it was Barnabas who brought Paul to the original apostles in Jerusalem and vouched for his conversion to Christianity.
>
> **Cephas** The name for the Apostle Peter. *Cephas* means rock or stone.

1 Corinthians 9:1–6

Am I not free? Am I not an apostle? Have I not seen Jesus our Lord? Are you not my work in the Lord? If I am not an apostle to others, at least I am to you; for you are the seal of my apostleship in the Lord. This is my defense to those who would examine me. Do we not have the right to our food and drink? Do we not have the right to be accompanied by a believing wife, as do the other apostles and the brothers of the Lord and **Cephas**? Or is it only **Barnabas** and I who have no right to refrain from working for a living?

1 Timothy 3:1–5

The saying is sure: whoever aspires to the office of bishop desires a noble task. Now a bishop must be above reproach, married only once, temperate, sensible, respectable, hospitable, an apt teacher, not a drunkard, not violent but gentle, not quarrelsome, and not a lover of money. He must manage his own household well, keeping his children submissive and respectful in every way—for if someone does not know how to manage his own household, how can he take care of God's church?

Matthew 8:10–15

[The Parallel Text is Mark 1:28–34]

When Jesus heard him, he was amazed and said to those who followed him, "Truly I tell you, in no one in Israel have I found such faith. I tell you, many will come from east and west and will eat with Abraham and Isaac and Jacob in the kingdom of heaven, while the heirs of the kingdom will be thrown into the outer darkness, where there will be weeping and gnashing of teeth." And to the centurion Jesus said, "Go; let it be done for you according to your faith." And the servant was healed in that hour. When Jesus entered Peter's house, he saw his mother-in-law lying in bed with a fever; he touched her hand, and the fever left her, and she got up and began to serve him.

Source: Society of Biblical Literature, eds. *Harper Collins Study Bible: New Revised Standard Version.* Rev. ed. New York: HarperCollins, 2006. All Scripture quotations appear from the *New Revised Standard Version Bible.* Division of Christian Education of the National Council of Churches of Christ in the United States of America, 1989.

Clement of Alexandria, Miscellanies *3.6.52–53*

52.... . Or do they also reject the apostles? Peter and Philip had children, and Philip gave his daughters to men in marriage.

53. Even Paul did not hesitate in one letter to address his wife. The only reason why he did not take her about with him was that it would have been an inconvenience for his ministry. Accordingly he says in a letter: "Have we not a right to take about with us a wife that is a sister like the other apostles?" (1 Cor. 9:5). But the latter, in accordance with their particular ministry, devoted themselves to preaching without any distraction, and took their wives with them not as married wives, but as sisters, that they might be their fellow-ministers in dealing with housewives. It was through them that the Lord's teaching penetrated also the women's quarters without any scandal being aroused.

Source: Clement of Alexandria. *Miscellanies,* 182–202 CE. Reprinted in Oulton, John Ernest Leonard, trans. *The Library of Christian Classics.* Vol. 2, *Alexandrian Christianity: Selected Translations of Clement and Origine with Introduction and Notes.* Philadelphia: Westminster Press, 1954.

Council of Elvira, Canon 33

Bishops, presbyters, and deacons, and all other clerics having a position in the ministry, are ordered to abstain completely from their wives and not have children. Whoever, in fact, does not do this shall be expelled from the dignity of the clerical state.

Source: Council of Elvira, Canon 33, 305 CE. Reprinted in Laeuchli, Samuel. *Power and Sexuality: the Emergence of Canon Law at the Synod of Elvira.* Philadelphia: Temple University Press, 1972, 130.

Nicene Creed, Canon 3

The great **Synod** has stringently forbidden any bishop, presbyter, deacon, or any one of the clergy whatever, to have a **subintroducta** dwelling with him, except only a mother, or sister, or aunt, or such persons only as are beyond all suspicion.

> **subintroducta** An unmarried woman.
> **Synod** A church council.

Source: Nicene Creed, 325 CE. Translated by Kevin Kaatz.

AFTERMATH

The tradition of marriage among the Christian leaders changed, and some progression can be noted. Clearly, in the New Testament some apostles are married. There does not seem to be a problem with this in these early texts. Clement of Alexandria (ca. 160–215 CE) mentions, in defense of marriage, that Peter, Philip, and even Paul were all married and also does not see this as a possible controversy. However, something changes in the late 200s and early 300s. At the church Council of Elvira, Spain, in the first decade of the 300s CE, the leaders of the church forbade priests and bishops from having sex with their wives and threatened to kick them out of office if they disobeyed. Marriage was still not a problem, but sexual relations between the spouses were. Then, in 325, at the Council of Nicea, it was forbidden for any unmarried woman, other than a mother, sister, or aunt, to live with any clergy. This still did not outlaw marriage. It was again recommended at the Council of Carthage in the 390s that the married clergy abstain from all sexual relations with their wives. It wasn't until the 1100s CE that the Catholic Church expressly forbade the clergy to get married, and that tradition continues on today in the Catholic Church. The Protestant Church, using Martin Luther as an example, allows its church leaders to get married and have children.

ASK YOURSELF

1. The writings of Paul are sometimes used for opposite meanings, such as when Paul or his disciple mentions that a bishop should be married only once, yet later Christians use Paul's statement that married people focus more on worldly issues. How do you think these later Christian writers used the statements of Paul that did not agree with their own views? Do you see this happening in modern Christianity?

2. As stated above, Ossius attended both the Council of Elvira and the Council at Nicea. Do you think that Ossius played a part in the topic of marriage in the clergy? If he did, why is marriage not allowed in the canons of Elvira but allowed in the canons of Nicea?

3. The passage of Matthew states that Jesus healed the mother-in-law of Peter and that right after she was healed she got up to serve him. She is not named in the passage, but Peter is. What can this tell you about the status of women in early Christianity? Do you think this is a good example? If not, what else should be looked at to gain a good view of early Christian women?

4. The Council of Elvira allows marriage but does not allow sexual relations between the spouses. How do you think the spouses reacted to this ruling? Do you think that married couples would be able to abstain from sex, until their death, but still live as a married couple? Also, how do you think this affected the whole household?

5. Clement of Alexandria states that the wives of the apostles were like sisters and helped spread Christianity to women. Why do you think it was important that these women were to be seen as "sisters" and not wives?

TOPICS TO CONSIDER

  Trace the history of clerical celibacy up through the 1500s. Consider, at the various stages, what was happening in terms of local history that made some people deny clergy the right to marry. Also consider the power Paul's words had in this history.

  Consider marriage in general in these communities (see previous section). Consider why, for some, the clergy should not be married at all, while others thought it was acceptable to be married but not to have sex.

  In a few modern U.S. Christian communities (especially the Fundamentalist Church of Jesus Christ of Latter-Day Saints), multiple marriages are allowed for the leader, despite being against U.S. law. Consider how these groups use the biblical writings to support their views of clerical marriage.

Further Information

Brown, Peter. *The Body and Society: Men, Women, and Sexual Renunciation in Early Christianity*. New York: Columbia University Press, 1988.

Clement of Alexandria. http://www.earlychristianwritings.com/clement.html.

Frazee, Charles A. "The Origins of Clerical Celibacy in the Western Church." *Church History* 41, no. 2 (Jun., 1972): 149–67.

Heid, Stefan. *Celibacy in the Early Church: The Beginnings of Obligatory Continence for Clerics in East and West*. San Francisco: Ignatius Press, 2001.

Parish, Helen. *Clerical Celibacy in the West, c. 1100–1700*. Burlington, VT: Ashgate, 2010.

Stickler, Alphonso M., and Brian Ferme, trans. *The Case for Clerical Celibacy: Its Historical Development and Theological Foundations*. San Francisco: Ignatius Press, 1993.

15. Acceptable Readings: *Muratorian Canon*

INTRODUCTION

There is considerable debate on the formation of the official (or orthodox) books of the New Testament. While it is certain that there were early Christians writing down their thoughts on their faith and writing letters to each other, it isn't certain when the New Testament that we have today was actually formed. The official list of texts is called a canon. Marcion, a Christian who lived in the middle of the second century, had created his own list of texts that totally discounted the Old Testament as well as many of the texts that now make up the New Testament. It is thought by some scholars that other early Christian leaders, in response to Marcion, decided to make their own list of texts that Christians should read. Other scholars believe that Christians were capable of creating their own list without being influenced by Marcion. One of the earliest lists we have outside of the writings of Marcion is called the *Muratorian Canon*. It was discovered by Muratori in the library at the Columban's Monastery at Bobbio, in northern Italy. It is now at the Church of Ambrose in Milan, Italy. It was first published in 1740. The complete text is below.

KEEP IN MIND WHILE YOU READ

1. The ". . ." at the beginning of the excerpt indicates that some of the text is missing. It almost certainly discussed the Gospels of Matthew and Mark.
2. The manuscript that Muratori discovered was copied somewhere in the seventh or eighth century and is written in Latin. Internal evidence in the text seems to suggest that the original (now lost) dated to sometime in the second century and was written in Greek.
3. Pius, the bishop of Rome, is mentioned toward the end of the text. Pius was bishop from 142 to 157 CE. This possibly helps to date the original document.

Muratorian Canon

. . . those things at which he was present he placed thus. The third book of the Gospel, that according to Luke, the well-known physician Luke wrote in his own name in order after the ascension of Christ, and when Paul had associated him with himself as one studious of right. Nor did he himself see the Lord in the flesh; and he, according as he was able to accomplish it, began his narrative with the nativity of John. The fourth Gospel is that of John, one of the disciples. When his fellow-disciples and bishops entreated him, he said, "Fast ye now with me for the space of three days, and let us recount to each other whatever may be revealed to each of us." On the same night it was revealed to Andrew, one of the apostles, that John should narrate all things in his own name as they called them to mind. And hence, although different points are taught us in the several books of the Gospels, there is no difference as regards the faith of believers, inasmuch as in all of them all things are related under one imperial Spirit, which concern the Lord's nativity, His passion, His resurrection, His conversation with His disciples, and His twofold advent,—the first in the humiliation of rejection, which is now past, and the second in the glory of royal power, which is yet in the future. What marvel is it, then, that John brings forward these several things so constantly in his epistles also, saying in his own person, "What we have seen with our eyes, and heard with our ears, and our hands have handled, that have we written." For thus he professes himself to be not only the eye-witness, but also the hearer; and besides that, the historian of all the wondrous facts concerning the Lord in their order.

2. Moreover, the Acts of all the Apostles are comprised by Luke in one book, and addressed to the most excellent Theophilus, because these different events took place when he was present himself; and he shows this clearly—i.e., that the principle on which he wrote was, to give only what fell under his own notice—by the omission of the passion of Peter, and also of the journey of Paul, when he went from the city—Rome—to Spain.

3. As to the epistles of Paul, again, to those who will understand the matter, they indicate of themselves what they are, and from what place or with what object they were directed. He wrote first of all, and at considerable length, to the Corinthians, to check the schism of heresy; and then to the Galatians, to forbid circumcision; and then to the Romans on the rule of the Old Testament Scriptures, and also to show them that Christ is the first object in these;—which it is needful for us to discuss severally, as the blessed Apostle Paul, following the rule of his predecessor John, writes to no more than seven churches by name, in this order: the first to the Corinthians, the second to the Ephesians, the third to the Philippians, the fourth to the Colossians, the fifth to the Galatians, the sixth to the Thessalonians, the seventh to the Romans. Moreover, though he writes twice to the Corinthians and Thessalonians for their correction, it is yet shown—i.e., by this sevenfold writing—that there is one Church spread abroad through the whole world. And John too, indeed, in the Apocalypse, although he writes only to seven churches, yet addresses all. He wrote, besides these, one to Philemon, and one to Titus, and two to Timothy, in simple personal affection and love indeed; but yet these are hallowed in the esteem of the Catholic Church, and in the regulation of ecclesiastical discipline. There are also in circulation one to the Laodiceans, and another to the Alexandrians, forged under the name of Paul, and addressed against the heresy of Marcion; and there are also several others which cannot be received into the Catholic Church, for it is not suitable for gall to be mingled with honey.

4. The Epistle of Jude, indeed, and two belonging to the above-named John—or bearing the name of John—are reckoned among the Catholic epistles. And the book of Wisdom,

written by the friends of Solomon in his honour. We receive also the Apocalypse of John and that of Peter, though some amongst us will not have this latter read in the Church. The Pastor, moreover, did Hermas write very recently in our times in the city of Rome, while his brother bishop Pius sat in the chair of the Church of Rome. And therefore it also ought to be read; but it cannot be made public in the Church to the people, nor placed among the prophets, as their number is complete, nor among the apostles to the end of time. Of the writings of Arsinous, called also Valentinus, or of Miltiades, we receive nothing at all. Those are rejected too who wrote the new Book of Psalms for Marcion, together with Basilides and the founder of the Asian Cataphrygians.

Source: Roberts, Rev. Alexander, and James Donaldson, eds. *The Ante-Nicene Fathers: Translations of the Writings of the Fathers Down to* A.D. *325,* vol. 5. Buffalo, NY: Christian Literature Company, 1886, 603–4.

AFTERMATH

If the list that we now call the *Muratorian Canon* was known to some early Christian communities, it did not settle the debate as to what texts the Christians considered to be orthodox. At the beginning of the fourth century, Eusebius of Caesarea gives another list of canonical texts (see the section "Acceptable Readings: Eusebius of Caesarea, *Ecclesiastical History* 3.24–25"). Even at this time some Christians refused to read Revelation and Jude. The next list, considered to be the first canonical list that reflects the Christian Bible today, was written by Athanasius, the (sometime) bishop of Alexandria, Egypt. He gives his list in his *39th Festal Letter* (written around 367 CE). Another list was given in 397 by Augustine, the bishop of Hippo, North Africa, in his book titled *On Christian Doctrine*. It appears that by the end of the fourth century the Christian canon was set and was not allowed to change very much after that.

ASK YOURSELF

1. What reasons does the author of the *Muratorian Canon* give for the inclusion of these particular texts? Do you find them credible?
2. The author of the *Muratorian Canon* occasionally gives a short description of these texts. Read these particular texts (mostly the letters of Paul). Do you agree with the descriptions? If not, what are your reasons for disagreeing?
3. Although the dates of Bishop Pius of Rome are known and are used to date this text, what problems might there be with the dating?
4. The author of the *Muratorian Canon* states that there are texts that are read in some churches but not all (and therefore not considered canonical). What does this tell you about the process of picking and choosing which texts were to be read by Christians? Was it a democratic process, or do you think there were rules for the inclusion or exclusion of some texts?

TOPICS TO CONSIDER

- ෴ Recreate the list of texts from the *Muratorian Canon* and list them next to the canon that now makes up the New Testament. Consider why there are differences between the two lists.

    ∽ Today there are differences between the Catholic and the Protestant Bibles. Consider when and why these differences appeared.

    ∽ Imagine that a new text was discovered and the text claimed the author was Paul the Apostle. Consider the process that would take place to determine its authenticity. If it appeared to be authentic, consider the process that would take place to convince both Catholics and Protestants to include it in their versions of the Bible.

    ∽ Read the *Apocalypse of Peter* (http://www.gnosis.org/naghamm/apopet.html) and the *Shepherd of Hermas* (http://www.earlychristianwritings.com/shepherd.html). Consider why some early Christians rejected these texts. Also consider why they were read in some churches. What would make them popular?

Further Information

Armstrong, Jonathan J. "Victorinus of Pettau as the Author of the Canon Muratori." *Vigiliae Christianae* 62, no. 1 (2008): 1–34.

Cochrane, Eric. "Muratori: The Vocation of a Historian." *Catholic Historical Review* 51, no. 2 (Jul., 1965): 153–72.

Hahneman, Geoffrey Mark. *The Muratorian Fragment and the Development of the Canon.* Oxford: Clarendon Press, 1992.

Metzger, Bruce M. *The Canon of the New Testament: Its Origin, Development, and Significance.* Oxford: Clarendon Press, 1987.

Sundberg, Albert C. Jr. "Canon Muratori: A Fourth Century List." *Harvard Theological Review* 66 (1973): 1–41.

16. Acceptable Readings: Eusebius of Caesarea, *Ecclesiastical History*

INTRODUCTION

Eusebius, bishop of the eastern city of Caesarea between 313 and 339 CE, wrote what is considered to be the first Christian history. His book, titled *Ecclesiastical History*, starts at the creation and finishes with the story of Emperor Constantine. More important for our purposes, Eusebius gives an extensive list of writings that were considered to be canonical, or acceptable for Christians to read. One of Eusebius's goals in writing *Ecclesiastical History* was to set down a record of true Christianity so that when and if heretics appeared, the true history would be known. Like many Christian writers before him, Eusebius was worried about heretics and what could have been spurious writings that might lead Christians astray. His list is one of the earliest that we have (the *Muratorian Canon* could be earlier).

KEEP IN MIND WHILE YOU READ

1. Eusebius created this list while living in Caesarea, a city in Palestine. It is not known whether what he considers to be canonical was also considered to be canonical in other parts of the Roman Empire.
2. In modern Bibles the list of Gospels starts with Matthew, then Mark, Luke, and John. However, some ancient Christian Bibles were not in that order.
3. The criteria for a text to be considered authentic and canonical must have been part of the early Christian debate. There were Christians who read texts that were different from what their neighbors read, and at some point, someone (we don't know who) decided to regularize the list.

Eusebius of Caesarea, Ecclesiastical History *3.24–25*

Chapter 24

This extract from Clement I have inserted here for the sake of the history and for the benefit of my readers. Let us now point out the undisputed writings of this apostle. And in the first place his Gospel, which is known to all the churches under heaven, must be acknowledged as genuine. That it has with good reason been put by the ancients in the fourth place, after the other three Gospels, may be made evident in the following way. Those great and truly divine men, I mean the apostles of Christ, were purified in their life, and were adorned with every virtue of the soul, but were uncultivated in speech. They were confident indeed in their trust in the divine and wonder-working power which was granted unto them by the Savior, but they did not know how, nor did they attempt to proclaim the doctrines of their teacher in studied and artistic language, but employing only the demonstration of the divine Spirit, which worked with them, and the wonder-working power of Christ, which was displayed through them, they published the knowledge of the kingdom of heaven throughout the whole world, paying little attention to the composition of written works. And this they did because they were assisted in their ministry by one greater than man. Paul, for instance, who surpassed them all in vigor of expression and in richness of thought, committed to writing no more than the briefest epistles, although he had innumerable mysterious matters to communicate, for he had attained even unto the sights of the third heaven, had been carried to the very paradise of God, and had been deemed worthy to hear unspeakable utterances there. And the rest of the followers of our Savior, the twelve apostles, the seventy disciples, and countless others besides, were not ignorant of these things. Nevertheless, of all the disciples of the Lord, only Matthew and John have left us written memorials, and they, tradition says, were led to write only under the pressure of necessity. For Matthew, who had at first preached to the Hebrews, when he was about to go to other peoples, committed his Gospel to writing in his native tongue, and thus compensated those whom he was obliged to leave for the loss of his presence. And when Mark and Luke had already published their Gospels, they say that John, who had employed all his time in proclaiming the Gospel orally, finally proceeded to write for the following reason. The three Gospels already mentioned having come into the hands of all and into his own too, they say that he accepted them and bore witness to their truthfulness; but that there was lacking in them an account of the deeds done by Christ at the beginning of his ministry. And this indeed is true. For it is evident that the three evangelists recorded only the deeds done by the Savior for one year after the imprisonment of John the Baptist, and indicated this in the beginning of their account. For Matthew, after the forty days' fast and the temptation which followed it, indicates the chronology of his work when he says: "Now when he heard that John was delivered up he withdrew from Judea into Galilee" (Matthew 4:12). Mark likewise says: "Now after that John was delivered up Jesus came into Galilee" (Mark 1:14). And Luke, before commencing his account of the deeds of Jesus, similarly marks the time, when he says that Herod, "adding to all the evil deeds which he had done, shut up John in prison" (Luke 3:20). They say, therefore, that the apostle John, being asked to do it for this reason, gave in his Gospel an account of the period which had been omitted by the earlier evangelists, and of the deeds done by the Savior during that period; that is, of those which were done before the imprisonment of the Baptist. And this is indicated by him, they say, in the following words: "This beginning of miracles did Jesus" (John 2:11); and again when he refers to the Baptist, in the midst of the deeds of Jesus, as still baptizing in Aenon near Salim; where he states the matter clearly in the words: "For John was not yet cast into prison" (John 3:24). John accordingly, in his Gospel, records the deeds of Christ which were performed before the Baptist was cast into prison, but the other three evangelists mention the events which happened after that time. One who understands this can no longer think that the Gospels are at variance with one another, inasmuch as the Gospel according to John contains the first acts of Christ, while the others give an account of the latter part of his life. And the genealogy of our Savior according to the flesh John quite naturally omitted, because it had been already given by Matthew and Luke, and began with the doctrine of his divinity, which had, as it were, been reserved for him, as their superior, by the divine Spirit. These things may suffice, which we have said concerning the Gospel of John. The cause which led to the composition of the Gospel of Mark has been already stated by us (*Ecclesiastical History* 2:15). But as for Luke, in the beginning of his Gospel, he states himself the reasons which led him to write it. He states that since many others had more rashly undertaken to compose a narrative of the events of which he had acquired perfect knowledge, he himself, feeling the necessity of freeing us from their uncertain opinions, delivered in his own Gospel an accurate account of those events in regard to which he had learned the full truth, being aided by his intimacy and his stay with Paul and by his acquaintance with the rest of the apostles. So much for our own account of these things. But in a more fitting place we shall attempt to show by quotations from the ancients, what others have said concerning them. But of the writings of John, not only his Gospel, but also the former of his epistles, has been accepted without dispute both now and in ancient times. But the other two are disputed. In regard to the Apocalypse, the opinions of most men are still divided. But at the proper time this question likewise shall be decided from the testimony of the ancients.

Chapter 25

Since we are dealing with this subject it is proper to sum up the writings of the New Testament which have been already mentioned. First then must be put the holy quaternion of the Gospels; following them the Acts of the Apostles. After this must be reckoned the epistles of Paul; next in order the extant former epistle of John, and likewise the epistle of Peter, must be maintained. After them is to be placed, if it really seem proper, the Apocalypse of John, concerning which we shall give the different opinions at the proper time. These then belong among the accepted writings. Among the disputed writings, which are nevertheless recognized by many, are extant the so-called epistle of James and that of Jude, also the second epistle of Peter, and those that are called the second and third of John, whether they belong to the evangelist or to another person of the same name. Among the rejected writings must be reckoned also the Acts of Paul, and the so-called Shepherd, and the Apocalypse of Peter, and in addition to these the extant epistle of Barnabas, and the so-called Teachings of the Apostles; and besides, as I said, the Apocalypse of John, if it seem proper, which some, as I said, reject, but which others class with the accepted books. And among these some have placed also the Gospel according to the Hebrews, with which those of the Hebrews that have accepted Christ are especially delighted. And all these may be reckoned among the disputed books. But we have nevertheless felt compelled to give a catalogue of these also, distinguishing those works which according to ecclesiastical tradition are true and genuine and commonly accepted, from those others which, although not canonical but disputed, are yet at the same time known to most ecclesiastical writers. We have felt compelled to give this catalogue in order that we might be able to know both these works and those that are cited by the heretics under the name of the apostles, including, for instance, such books as the Gospels of Peter, of Thomas, of Matthias, or of any others besides them, and the Acts of Andrew and John and the other apostles, which no one belonging to the succession of ecclesiastical writers has deemed worthy of mention in his writings. And further, the character of the style is at variance with apostolic usage, and both the thoughts and the purpose of the things that are related in them are so completely out of accord with true orthodoxy that they clearly show themselves to be the fictions of heretics. Wherefore they are not to be placed even among the rejected writings, but are all of them to be cast aside as absurd and impious. Let us now proceed with our history.

Source: Schaff, Philip and Henry Wace, eds. *A Select Library of Nicene and Post-Nicene Fathers of the Christian Church,* vol. 1. New York: Christian Literature Company, 1890, 155–57.

AFTERMATH

When Eusebius wrote *Ecclesiastical History,* many of the texts that are now considered to be canonical were accepted by nearly all Christians. He (and others), however, questioned the authorship/validity of a few texts that are now accepted. As mentioned in the Muratorian section of this book, the canon was set by the middle to end of the fourth century by Athanasius, the bishop of Alexandria, Egypt, in his *39th Festal Letter,* written around 367 CE (link given below). While Eusebius rejects writings such as the *Teachings of the Twelve Apostles* and the *Shepherd,* Athanasius states that while they are not canonical, they can be read by early Christians. It is difficult to say why Eusebius believed they should be rejected writings, while Athanasius believed they could be read by Christian communities. It could have been a regional difference between Caesarea in Palestine and Alexandria, Egypt. Regardless, by the end of the fourth century the canon was essentially set, and there were to be no new texts added.

ASK YOURSELF

1. Why do you think that Eusebius spent so much time talking about the apostles at the beginning of chapter 24? What is he trying to prove?
2. Who decides what is canonical and what isn't? Is Eusebius trying to be the person who decides what Christians should read, or is he leaving it up to someone else to make the authorized list? What determines a canonical text for Eusebius?
3. Compare the list of Eusebius with modern Bibles today. What texts are considered to be canonical now but were questioned during the time of Eusebius? What later made these questionable texts acceptable?
4. Eusebius states (3:24), "One who understands this can no longer think that the Gospels are at variance with one another." Examine his argument for this statement. Do you agree with his conclusion?

TOPICS TO CONSIDER

- Compare the list of canonical writings of the *Muratorian Canon* and that given by Eusebius. Consider the similarities and differences. Why are there differences?
- Create a small group and decide what is canonical and what is not. Consider what rules would have to be created and what you will do if some disagree on a particular text.

    > Read Hebrews, James, Jude, 2 Peter, and 2 and 3 John in any Bible. Eusebius notes that these texts were disputed, but today they are recognized as being canonical. Consider why some Christians in the ancient world rejected these particular writings. What exactly about them would have been objectionable?

    > Eusebius gives a large number of pseudo-acts and gospels toward the end of chapter 25. Read the *Gospel of Thomas* or the *Gospel of Peter* (links given below), and consider how these gospels are different from the Acts of the Apostles. Consider why these gospels were rejected by early (and modern) Christians.

UNACCEPTABLE READINGS?

Some Christians were reading texts that Eusebius and others considered unacceptable. While there is no one reason that makes a text unacceptable, usually it involves the mention of secret knowledge. In the *Apocalypse of Peter*, Christ twice tells Peter to cover his eyes and to tell him what he saw. The first time Peter sees nothing, but the second time he sees "a new light greater than the light of day" and that this light fell upon Christ. What he saw, however, was to be kept a secret. For other texts like the *Acts of Paul* (also known as the *Acts of Paul and Thecla*), it was known that the author was not Paul. Tertullian, living in the middle of the second century, states that a presbyter had written it and attached the name of the Apostle Paul to it. The *Gospel According to the Hebrews* (or just *Hebrews*), which was considered to be acceptable soon after the time of Eusebius, was disputed. The author was thought to be Paul, but the language and topic are different from Paul's other writings. The authorship is now attributed to one of Paul's disciples.

Further Information

Athanasius. *Festal Letter 39.* http://www.ccel.org/ccel/schaff/npnf204.xxv.iii.iii.xxv.html.

Brakke, David. "Canon Formation and Social Conflict in Fourth-Century Egypt: Athanasius of Alexandria's Thirty-Ninth 'Festal Letter.'" *Harvard Theological Review* 87, no. 4 (Oct., 1994): 395–419.

Ehrman, Bart D. *Forged: Writing in the Name of God—Why the Bible's Authors Are Not Who We Think They Are.* New York: HarperCollins, 2011.

Ehrman, Bart D. "The New Testament Canon of Didymus the Blind." *Vigiliae Christianae* 37, no. 1 (Mar., 1983): 1–21.

Gospel of Peter. http://www.earlychristianwritings.com/text/gospelpeter.html.

Gospel of Thomas. http://www.gnosis.org/naghamm/gthlamb.html.

Metzger, Bruce M. *The Canon of the New Testament: Its Origin, Development, and Significance.* Oxford: Clarendon Press, 1987.

Patzia, Arthur G. *The Making of the New Testament: Origin, Collection, Text & Canon.* Downers Grove, IL: InterVarsity Press, 1995.

Von Campenhausen, Hans. *The Formation of the Christian Bible.* Philadelphia: Fortress, 1972.

Wallace, Daniel B., ed. *Revisiting the Corruption of the New Testament: Manuscript, Patristic, and Apocryphal Evidence.* Grand Rapids, MI: Kregel, 2011.

17. CATACOMBS OF ROME

INTRODUCTION

The catacombs can tell us quite a bit about the early Christians. Some of the most important artwork from early Christianity comes from the catacombs. These were underground tunnels where Christians would bury their dead, usually (but not always) in niches in the walls. The earliest paintings in the catacombs can be dated to the 200s CE, which also dates to the beginning of the first Christian catacombs. Many times artwork would be painted on the walls or ceilings near the burial plots, usually with no writing. The scenes, however, would have been very familiar to Christians. Many times these scenes are from the Old Testament, but the ones below are all from the New Testament. In the ancient world, catacombs were dark and sometimes scary places. Jerome, a Catholic from the fourth century, wrote that on Sundays he and his friends would go into the catacombs. He mentioned the niches and "the horror of the blackness."

KEEP IN MIND WHILE YOU READ

1. The scenes from the early Christian catacombs were taken from both the Old and the New Testaments.
2. It used to be thought that the catacombs were places where Christians would flee in times of persecution. Now that is not thought to be the case, primarily because the catacombs would not be big enough to support large populations of people.
3. The paintings given on the next page were taken from Rome, but there are other places that have Christian catacombs, including Naples.

Jonah thrown to the whale. Early Christian fresco, mid 3rd century. (Scala/Art Resource, NY)

Christ and the Samaritan Woman at the Well. Early Christian fresco, 4th century. (Scala/Art Resource, NY)

AFTERMATH

Christians continued to bury their dead in the catacombs around Rome until at least the early 400s CE. After this period the catacombs were nearly forgotten, although not completely. In the 700s there were written guides for people who wanted to visit the catacombs. Scholarly interest in the catacombs started in the 1500s, when people began to venture down into the tunnels and map them. The Catholic Church, recognizing their importance, started to buy the land to protect these areas, and many of the objects found in the catacombs are now in the Vatican Museum. Many of these catacombs can be visited today.

ASK YOURSELF

1. Who do you think painted these scenes? Do they look like professional artwork?
2. It is understandable why someone would want a Lazarus scene painted near or over their gravesite. But why would someone want a painting of the Samaritan woman at the well, or the story of Jesus healing the bleeding woman? What message do you think is being presented? Do you think these were painted for a man or a woman?
3. Why do you think the early Christians wanted artwork at their gravesites, as opposed to something written?
4. How did these early paintings (and sculptures) from the catacombs affect later artwork? Do you think they had any impact?
5. As stated above, many of the paintings were taken from scenes in the Hebrew Bible. What can this tell you about the use of these writings by the early Christians?

TOPICS TO CONSIDER

- ☞ Christ is pictured as beardless in this representation (as well as in other catacomb paintings). Reexamine how he is portrayed in early Christian artwork and how he is portrayed in modern artwork. Consider why there is a difference.
- ☞ Consider the role that funerary artwork plays today and the possible connections it has to early Christian artwork.
- ☞ Consider how early Christian artwork was influenced by Roman artwork.
- ☞ Examine the artwork from one of the catacombs and categorize it. Consider whether there were trends, or whether the artwork was created without connection to what had come previously.

Further Information

Grabar, Andre. *Christian Iconography: A Study of Its Origins.* Princeton, NJ: Princeton University Press, 1968.

International Catacomb Society. "Visiting the Catacombs." http://www.catacombsociety. org/visiting_Christian.html.

Kirschbaum, Engelbert, and John Murray, trans. *The Tombs of St Peter & St Paul.* 1st ed. New York: St. Martin's Press, 1959.

Mancinelli, Fabrizio. *The Catacombs of Rome and the Origins of Christianity.* Florence: Scala, 1981.

Portella, Ivana Della. *Subterranean Rome.* Cologne, Germany: Könemann, 2000.

Webb, Matilda. *The Churches and Catacombs of Early Christian Rome: A Comprehensive Guide.* Brighton, England: Sussex Academic Press, 2001.

18. The Nicene Creed

INTRODUCTION

The Council of Nicea took place in 325 CE in the city of Nicea (modern-day Turkey). This council was the most important council in Christian history. It met just a few years after the Roman Empire had its first Christian emperor, Constantine. Emperor Constantine took an active interest in Christianity because he believed the Christian God had given him a victory over Maxentius. After the victory, Constantine became the emperor in the western half of the Roman Empire, which encompassed England, France, Spain, Italy, and some places in central Europe. In 324 CE, Constantine became the sole emperor when he defeated Licinius, the emperor of the east. Constantine was genuinely shocked when he learned that not all Christians got along with each other. This was especially the case between two rival Christian groups—the Arians and what would later be called the Nicenes. The Arians were named after Arius, who believed that God had always existed and that the Son came after. They also believed that Christ was the true son of God but that God created him. The Nicenes believed that God, Christ, and the Holy Spirit had always existed from the beginning.

While the differences were subtle, the fighting was not. Ultimately, Constantine called together various clergy from throughout the Roman Empire, and in many cases the government paid for their transportation. The meeting became known as the first ecumenical Council of Nicea. It is referred to as an ecumenical council because bishops from the western and eastern sides of the Roman Empire were invited to attend. There had been previous councils, but these were smaller and mostly dealt with local issues. When the 300 (or so) bishops came together in Nicea to discuss the two forms of Christianity, most bishops believed that God, the Son, and the Holy Spirit had always existed. This belief did not come without conflict. We are not sure who wrote the actual Nicene Creed, but we do know that Bishop Eusebius of Caesarea created the prototype. Eusebius of Caesarea originally backed Arius and his ideas, but after he was temporarily excommunicated, Eusebius of Caesarea decided that Arius was wrong. His early prototype was open to interpretation, and some at the council believed that the Arians could take advantage of this and further their cause, so the council rewrote part of it to stress the one nature that God and Christ shared. A vote was taken, and the new version was accepted by nearly all who were present. There were five bishops present who refused to accept this new document. The council also took a vote on the anathemas against Arius. Some bishops, like Eusebius of Nicomedia, stated that the council had misinterpreted the beliefs of Arius, and he (and some others) accepted the creed but refused to sign the anathemas.

The main motivations of the Nicene Creed were threefold: to create one belief for all Christians to follow, to stress the oneness of Christ with God (and the Holy Spirit), and to curse Arius, his supporters, and their beliefs. There were many variations of Christian belief, even from the beginning of the religion, and these differences led to constant conflict in the Christian community. Constantine witnessed this firsthand. He wanted to support the God who had helped him, and this council, he believed, was the way to do that. The council had hoped to crush the growing Arian movement, and to do this they also tacked on a list of curses at the end of the document to make sure that the ideas of Arius would not be accepted. The anathemas made it clear that if one did not believe that Christ and God were one nature, then one was not part of the orthodox faith. After the council was finished, Emperor Constantine sent its findings out to various bishops who could not attend. The bishops themselves also took copies of the Nicene Creed back to their churches to spread the new-formulated faith.

KEEP IN MIND WHILE YOU READ

1. While Emperor Constantine was a Christian, it is possible that he was not as knowledgeable on the details of the faith.
2. The text of the Nicene Creed was written in Greek, even though some of the bishops who attended were from the Latin-speaking west. Many educated people were bilingual.
3. That the word used for "one nature" (*homoousius*) was the source of much controversy during and after the council. Many bishops did not like the term because it didn't have a biblical backing. It was also a problem because there was not an adequate translation in Latin for many of the western bishops.

The Nicene Creed

We believe in one God, the Father Almighty, Creator of all things seen and not seen,

And in one Lord Jesus Christ, the Son of God, begotten from the Father, the Only Begotten,

That is to say, from the nature of the Father, God from God, Light from light, True God from true God, begotten, not made, one nature (*homoousius*) with God,

Through whom all things were made, things in heaven and on earth,

Who because of us men, and because of our salvation, came down and became flesh,

and took human form, suffered, and rose on the third day,

Went up into the heavens, will come to judge the living and the dead, and in the Holy Spirit.

homoousius "One nature," in reference to God and Christ.

Those saying that there was a time when he was not, and before he was born he was not in existence, and that he came to be out of nothing, or who claim that the Son of God is of another **hypostasis** or nature, or is created, or is changeable or alterable,

These the Holy Catholic and Apostolic church anathematizes.

Source: The Nicene Creed, 325. Translation by Kevin Kaatz, 2012.

> **hypostasis** A Greek word which has many meanings, including "person" and "substance." It caused many theological difficulties because of its many definitions.
> **Those saying** The Arians.

AFTERMATH

Arius and some of his supporters were sent into exile to keep them from spreading their ideas further. A few months after this, Eusebius of Nicomedia was also sent into exile because of his refusal to sign the anathemas. After a few years both Arius and Eusebius of Nicomedia were recalled from exile by Emperor Constantine when they were asked to explain their beliefs. Both professed to follow the new Nicene Creed, but in reality that was not the case. Emperor Constantine either was naïve or sincerely believed that Arius and Eusebius of Nicomedia had actually changed their ideas. After their recall Christianity became more divided between the two camps. After the death of Constantine, his three sons, Constantius II, Constans, and Constantine II, divided up the empire between them: Constantius II took control of the eastern part, which included Nicomedia. While Constantius II was a Christian, he believed in the Arian form of Christianity, and it was through his efforts (and those of Eusebius of Nicomedia) that Arian bishops were installed in many eastern cities. Despite his effort, it became a minor movement in the Roman Empire in the 380s CE.

ASK YOURSELF

1. Why did Constantine become involved in this case in the first place? Do modern political leaders insert themselves into religious politics? If yes, in what ways?
2. Knowing that the Nicene Creed was originally written in Greek, how do you think this alters the contents as it is being translated into other languages?
3. How does the Nicene Creed, written in 325 CE, affect modern Christians today?
4. How successful was the Nicene Creed in suppressing the Arian form of Christianity?
5. Why do you think the Nicene Creed stressed the humanity of Jesus? What would modern Christianity be like without this statement?

TOPICS TO CONSIDER

- ➤ The Baptism of Constantine has been portrayed by many painters through the ages. One example can be found here: http://www.artrenewal.org/pages/artwork.php?artworkid=12128. Notice that the bishop who baptizes the emperor is Bishop Sylvester, not Eusebius of Nicomedia. Consider why later artists would portray his baptism is such a manner.

      ↔ Emperor Constantine's foray into Christian politics changed the dynamics of the religion. It became the preferred religion as opposed to an outlawed religion. Consider how this affected the everyday life of Christians in the Roman Empire.

THE TRUE BAPTISM OF EMPEROR CONSTANTINE

The Council of Nicea was called to settle the issue between the two competing forms of Christianity. It was seen as a triumph of Nicene Christianity when Arius and his friends were cursed and sent into exile. However, when Emperor Constantine began to feel ill in 337 CE, he decided that he should be baptized before his death. At this time it was not unusual to wait until one was gravely ill to be baptized. He made his way to Nicomedia and was finally baptized by none other than Eusebius of Nicomedia, the Arian bishop of that city. However, if the accounts of his death and baptism are examined, many early Christians could not get themselves to admit that Constantine died an Arian. Eusebius of Caesarea mentioned his baptism, but not who performed it. It was Jerome, in the late fourth century, who finally admitted that the great Constantine, defender of Nicene Christianity, allowed himself to be baptized by an Arian. Later artists (as noted above) either believed a false account that stated that Constantine had been baptized by the Nicene bishop Sylvester of Rome or didn't know of the passage from Jerome.

Further Information

Armstrong, Gregory T. "Church and State Relations: The Changes Wrought by Constantine." *Journal of Bible and Religion* 32, no. 1 (Jan., 1964): 1–7.

Beatrice, Pier Franco. "The Word 'Homoousios' from Hellenism to Christianity." *Church History* 71, no. 2 (Jun., 2002): 243–72.

Davis, Leo Donald. *The First Seven Ecumenical Councils (325–787): Their History and Theology*. Collegeville, MN: Liturgical Press, 1983.

The Fourth Century Christianity website. http://www.fourthcentury.com/.

The Imperial Index: The Rulers of the Roman Empire. http://www.roman-emperors.org/impindex.htm.

Pohlsander, Hans A. *The Emperor Constantine*. New York: Routledge, 1996.

Skarsaune, Oskar. "A Neglected Detail in the Creed of Nicaea (325)." *Vigiliae Christianae* 41, no. 1 (Mar., 1987): 34–54.

Ulrich, Jörg. "Nicaea and the West." *Vigiliae Christianae* 51, no. 1 (Mar., 1997): 10–24.

Williams, Rowan. *Arius: Heresy and Tradition*. Rev. ed. Grand Rapids, MI: Eerdmans, 2002.

19. The Canons from the Council of Nicea (325 ce)

INTRODUCTION

After the Council of Nicea finished the Nicene Creed (see previous text), the bishops then decided to create a list of laws (or canons) for Christians to follow. This was not the first time that church councils had made lists of rules, but Nicea was an ecumenical council, meaning that bishops from all over came to take part. These canons were meant to cover all Christians, everywhere. There were many topics that the council covered, and many of them reflect the problems that were occurring in the church. All of the canons are included below.

KEEP IN MIND WHILE YOU READ

1. Although the council has been called ecumenical, the reality is that the vast majority of bishops were from the eastern side of the empire. Even the bishop of Rome was too elderly to attend, but he sent representatives.
2. Many of the following canons were created because of controversies in the early church.
3. Canons 10, 11, and 14 were created because of the Great Persecution (303–313 ce). Many clergy (and laypeople) decided to turn over the holy writings and to denounce Christ. Once the persecution was over, the lapsed wanted to return to their former positions.
4. Emperor Constantine called for the council and was present for most of the proceedings.

castrated To have the genitals removed. Sometimes only the testes were cut off.

laver Baptism.

subintroducta A woman who was a disciple, but her presence could lead to something immoral.

The Canons from the Council of Nicea

Canon 1

If anyone in sickness has been subjected by physicians to a surgical operation, or if he has been **castrated** by barbarians, let him remain among the clergy; but, if any one in sound health has castrated himself, it behooves that such an one, if [already] enrolled among the clergy, should cease [from his ministry], and that from henceforth no such person should be promoted. But, as it is evident that this is said of those who willfully do the thing and presume to castrate themselves, so if any have been made eunuchs by barbarians, or by their masters, and should otherwise be found worthy, such men the Canon admits to the clergy.

Canon 2

Forasmuch as, either from necessity, or through the urgency of individuals, many things have been done contrary to the Ecclesiastical canon, so that men just converted from heathenism to the faith, and who have been instructed but a little while, are straightway brought to the spiritual **laver,** and as soon as they have been baptized, are advanced to the episcopate or the presbyterate, it has seemed right to us that for the time to come no such thing shall be done. For to the catechumen himself there is need of time and of a longer trial after baptism. For the apostolical saying is clear, "Not a novice; lest, being lifted up with pride, he fall into condemnation and the snare of the devil." But if, as time goes on, any sensual sin should be found out about the person, and he should be convicted by two or three witnesses, let him cease from the clerical office. And whoever shall transgress these [enactments] will imperil his own clerical position, as a person who presumes to disobey the great Synod.

Canon 3

The great Synod has stringently forbidden any bishop, presbyter, deacon, or any one of the clergy whatever, to have a **subintroducta** dwelling with him, except only a mother, or sister, or aunt, or such persons only as are beyond all suspicion.

Canon 4

It is by all means proper that a bishop should be appointed by all the bishops in the province; but should this be difficult, either on account of urgent necessity or because of distance, three at least should meet together, and the suffrages of the absent [bishops] also being given and communicated in writing, then the ordination should take place. But in every province the ratification of what is done should be left to the Metropolitan.

Canon 5

Concerning those, whether of the clergy or of the laity, who have been excommunicated in the several provinces, let the provision of the canon be observed by the bishops which provides that persons cast out by some be not readmitted by others. Nevertheless, inquiry should be made whether they have been excommunicated through captiousness, or contentiousness, or any such like ungracious disposition in the bishop. And, that this matter may have due investigation, it is decreed that in every province synods shall be held twice a year, in order that when all the bishops of the province are assembled together, such questions may by them be thoroughly examined, that so those who have confessedly offended against their bishop, may be seen by all to be for just cause excommunicated, until it shall seem fit to a general meeting of the bishops to pronounce a milder sentence upon them. And let these synods be held, the one before Lent, (that the pure Gift may be offered to God after all bitterness has been put away), and let the second be held about autumn.

Canon 6

Let the ancient customs in Egypt, Libya and **Pentapolis** prevail, that the Bishop of Alexandria have jurisdiction in all these, since the like is customary for the Bishop of Rome also. Likewise in Antioch and the other provinces, let the Churches retain their privileges. And this is to be universally understood, that if anyone be made bishop without the consent of the Metropolitan, the great Synod has declared that such a man ought not to be a bishop. If, however, two or three bishops shall from natural love of contradiction, oppose the common suffrage of the rest, it being reasonable and in accordance with the ecclesiastical law, then let the choice of the majority prevail.

> **Pentapolis** The five major cities in Libya.

Canon 7

Since custom and ancient tradition have prevailed that the Bishop of Aelia [i.e., Jerusalem] should be honored, let him, saving its due dignity to the Metropolis, have the next place of honor.

Canon 8

Concerning those who call themselves Cathari, if they come over to the Catholic and Apostolic Church, the great and holy Synod decrees that they who are ordained shall continue as they are in the clergy. But it is before all things necessary that they should profess in writing that they will observe and follow the dogmas of the Catholic and Apostolic Church; in particular that they will communicate with persons who have been twice married, and with those who having lapsed in persecution have had a period [of penance] laid upon them, and a time

Chorepiscopus A clergy member who was one step below the bishop.
Licinius The Roman co-emperor in the east. He ruled from 308 to 324. He coruled with Constantine starting in 306.

[of restoration] fixed so that in all things they will follow the dogmas of the Catholic Church. Wheresoever, then, whether in villages or in cities, all of the ordained are found to be of these only, let them remain in the clergy, and in the same rank in which they are found. But if they come over where there is a bishop or presbyter of the Catholic Church, it is manifest that the Bishop of the Church must have the bishop's dignity; and he who was named bishop by those who are called Cathari shall have the rank of presbyter, unless it shall seem fit to the Bishop to admit him to partake in the honor of the title. Or, if this should not be satisfactory, then shall the bishop provide for him a place as **Chorepiscopus,** or presbyter, in order that he may be evidently seen to be of the clergy, and that there may not be two bishops in the city.

Canon 9

If any presbyters have been advanced without examination, or if upon examination they have made confession of crime, and men acting in violation of the canon have laid hands upon them, notwithstanding their confession, such the canon does not admit; for the Catholic Church requires that [only] which is blameless.

Canon 10

If any who have lapsed have been ordained through the ignorance, or even with the previous knowledge of the ordainers, this shall not prejudice the canon of the Church; for when they are discovered they shall be deposed.

Canon 11

Concerning those who have fallen without compulsion, without the spoiling of their property, without danger or the like, as happened during the tyranny of **Licinius,** the Synod declares that, though they have deserved no clemency, they shall be dealt with mercifully. As many as were communicants, if they heartily repent, shall pass three years among the hearers; for seven years they shall be prostrators; and for two years they shall communicate with the people in prayers, but without oblation.

Canon 12

As many as were called by grace, and displayed the first zeal, having cast aside their military girdles, but afterwards returned, like dogs, to their own vomit, (so that some spent money and by means of gifts regained their military stations); let these, after they have passed the space of three years as hearers, be for ten years prostrators. But in all these cases it is necessary to examine well into their purpose and what their repentance appears to be like. For as many as give evidence of their conversions by deeds, and not pretense, with fear, and tears, and perseverance, and good works, when they have fulfilled their appointed time as hearers, may properly communicate in prayers; and after that the bishop may determine yet more favorably concerning them. But those who take [the matter] with indifference, and who think the form of [not] entering the Church is sufficient for their conversion, must fulfill the whole time.

Canon 13

Concerning the departing, the ancient canonical law is still to be maintained, to wit, that, if any man be at the point of death, he must not be deprived of the last and most indispensable Viaticum. But, if any one should be restored to health again who has received the communion when his life was despaired of, let him remain among those who communicate in prayers only. But in general, and in the case of any dying person whatsoever asking to receive the Eucharist, let the Bishop, after examination made, give it him.

Canon 14

Concerning catechumens who have lapsed, the holy and great Synod has decreed that, after they have passed three years only as hearers, they shall pray with the catechumens.

Canon 15

On account of the great disturbance and discords that occur, it is decreed that the custom prevailing in certain places contrary to the Canon, must wholly be done away; so that neither bishop, presbyter, nor deacon shall pass from city to city. And if any one, after this decree of the holy and great Synod, shall attempt any such thing, or continue in any such course, his proceedings shall be utterly void, and he shall be restored to the Church for which he was ordained bishop or presbyter.

Canon 16

Neither presbyters, nor deacons, nor any others enrolled among the clergy, who, not having the fear of God before their eyes, nor regarding the ecclesiastical Canon, shall recklessly remove from their own church, should by any means to be received by another church; but every constraint should be applied to restore them to their own parishes; and, if they will not go, they must be excommunicated. And if anyone shall dare surreptitiously to carry off and in his own Church ordain a man belonging to another, without the consent of his own proper bishop, from whom although he was enrolled in the clergy list he has seceded, let the ordination be void.

Canon 17

Forasmuch as many enrolled among the Clergy, following covetousness and lust of gain, have forgotten the divine Scripture, which says, "He has not given his money upon usury," and in lending money ask the hundredth of the sum [as monthly interest], the holy and great Synod thinks it just that if after this decree anyone be found to receive usury, whether he accomplish it by secret transaction or otherwise, as by demanding the whole and one half, or by using any other contrivance whatever for filthy lucre's sake, he shall be deposed from the clergy and his name stricken from the list.

Canon 18

It has come to the knowledge of the holy and great Synod that, in some districts and cities, the deacons administer the Eucharist to the presbyters, whereas neither canon nor custom permits that they who have no right to offer should give the Body of Christ to them that do offer. And this also has been made known, that certain deacons now touch the Eucharist even before the bishops. Let all such practices be utterly done away, and let the deacons remain within their own bounds, knowing that they are the ministers of the bishop and the inferiors of the presbyters. Let them receive the Eucharist according to their order, after the presbyters, and let either the bishop or the presbyter administer to them. Furthermore, let not the deacons sit among the presbyters, for that is contrary to canon and order. And if, after this decree, any one shall refuse to obey, let him be deposed from the diaconate.

Canon 19

Concerning the Paulianists who have flown for refuge to the Catholic Church, it has been decreed that they must by all means be rebaptized; and if any of them who in past time have been numbered among their clergy should be found blameless and without reproach, let them be rebaptized and ordained by the Bishop of the Catholic Church; but if the examination should discover them to be unfit, they ought to be deposed. Likewise in the case of their deaconesses, and generally in the case of those who have been enrolled among their clergy, let the same form be observed. And we mean by deaconesses such as have assumed the habit, but who, since they have no imposition of hands, are to be numbered only among the laity.

Canon 20

Forasmuch as there are certain persons who kneel on the Lord's Day and in the days of Pentecost, therefore, to the intent that all things may be uniformly observed everywhere (in every parish), it seems good to the holy Synod that prayer be made to God standing.

Source: Schaff, Philip, and Henry Wace, eds. *A Select Library of Nicene and Post-Nicene Fathers of the Christian Church,* vol. 14. New York: Charles Scribner's Sons, 1900, 8–42.

AFTERMATH

The Council of Nicea was held to stop dissent in the early church, especially the schism between the Arians and the Nicenes. Canon 6, which deals with the bishop of Alexandria, did not solve the Arian problem in Egypt. Athanasius became bishop of Alexandria in 328 and remained its bishop until 373 CE. He had many problems with Arius (the founder of Arianism), and later with the Arian bishop Eusebius of Nicomedia, who later became bishop of Constantinople. Athanasius was sent into exile many times for his refusal to accept the Arians into communion. However, the council dealt with numerous other difficulties. While the bishops tried hard to find solutions, a few issues continued to plague the church, mentioned in canons 15 and 16, which state the rules for moving from one church to another. Moving to another city to become bishop occurred many times after the canon was enacted, especially in times of conflict within local churches.

ASK YOURSELF

1. Why do you think the very first canon from the Council of Nicea concerns self-castration? Why do you think the bishops made the distinction between those who castrated themselves and those who were castrated?
2. Canon 2 is about people who have advanced too fast in the church hierarchy. Why do you think this would be a problem? What are some of the dangers of advancing too quickly?
3. Canon 6 states that the superior bishop in the major cities must be included in the creation of new bishops. It also states that if there are arguments, then the majority should be able to choose the new bishop. Do you think the process worked?
4. Do you think the decisions by the bishops indicate that democratic principles were found in the early church? Be sure to take into account the presence of Emperor Constantine during the proceedings.
5. Is there a related theme to these canons? If so, why? If not, why not?

TOPICS TO CONSIDER

> ☙ While it is not known how many bishops were present during the council, it appears that they decided, as a block, to create these canons. Recreate the counterarguments to these canons.

- ☙ Consider the religious practices of the Cathari and Paulinists (canons 8 and 19). Consider how dissent in the early church affected the decisions of the council.

- ☙ Form a group and imagine that most of you are bishops, with one person being the emperor and two being the secretaries. Form 10 canons for your church. Have the secretaries (independent of each other) keep track of the conversations that take place, as well as a log of the deliberations on which rules should be the official canons. Consider how this exercise may be a reflection of what happened in Nicea, in 325 CE.

Further Information

Armstrong, Gregory T. "Church and State Relations: The Changes Wrought by Constantine." *Journal of Bible and Religion* 32, no. 1 (Jan., 1964): 1–7.

Chadwick, Henry. "Faith and Order at the Council of Nicaea: A Note on the Background of the Sixth Canon." *Harvard Theological Review* 53, no. 3 (Jul., 1960): 171–95.

Davis, Leo Donald. *The First Seven Ecumenical Councils (325–787): Their History and Theology,* Theology and Life Series 21. Collegeville, MN: Liturgical Press, 1983.

Drake, H. A. "Constantine and Consensus." *Church History* 64, no. 1 (Mar., 1995): 1–15.

Grant, Robert M. "Religion and Politics at the Council at Nicaea." *Journal of Religion* 55, no. 1 (Jan., 1975): 1–12.

Ulrich, Jörg. "Nicaea and the West." *Vigiliae Christianae* 51, no. 1 (Mar., 1997): 10–24.

EARLY CHRISTIAN WOMEN

20. MENSTRUATION

INTRODUCTION

A menstruating woman had always been considered to be ritually impure in Judaic law. The monthly cycle meant that she would be sequestered for seven days after the flow of blood stopped, and on the eighth day she would have to bring a sacrifice to the temple. The texts of the New Testament do not discuss the subject of menstruation. But the Synoptic Gospels (Matthew, Mark, and Luke) each tell the story of a woman who had a hemorrhage for 12 years. According to their accounts, she was considered to be impure as well. Although the food restrictions were dropped when Jewish people joined Christianity, it appears that at least some of the restrictions on menstruating women continued. We can see this from one of the letters of Dionysius (see below) as well as some comments by Jerome, a Catholic living in Bethlehem in the late fourth and early fifth centuries. The following texts are from Leviticus 15:19–33, Mark 5:25–34, and Dionysius, *Epistle to Bishop Basilides,* Canon II.

KEEP IN MIND WHILE YOU READ

1. Non-Christian Roman society also had some interesting ideas about women who were menstruating. Pliny the Elder, in his *Natural History* 28.23, states that, among other things, if a woman who is menstruating walks naked around a field, the bugs that damage the crops will fall to the ground and if she touches ivy during this period, it will die.
2. Dionysius, sometimes referred to Dionysius the Great, was the bishop of Alexandria, Egypt, from 247 until his death in 264. Unfortunately, many of his writings have been lost.
3. The woman described in the passage from Mark is not menstruating but has a medical problem that has caused her to lose blood for 12 years. It is possible that the author (and the authors of Matthew and Luke) ties her hemorrhage to Leviticus 15:25, which states that if a woman has a discharge outside of her normal time, she is to be considered ritually impure.

Leviticus 15:19–33

When a woman has a discharge of blood that is her regular discharge from her body, she shall be in her impurity for seven days, and whoever touches her shall be unclean until the evening. Everything upon which she lies during her impurity shall be unclean; everything also upon which she sits shall be unclean. Whoever touches her bed shall wash his clothes, and bathe in water, and be unclean until the evening. Whoever touches anything upon which she sits shall wash his clothes, and bathe in water, and be unclean until the evening; whether it is the bed or anything upon which she sits, when he touches it he shall be unclean until the evening. If any man lies with her, and her impurity falls on him, he shall be unclean seven days; and every bed on which he lies shall be unclean. If a woman has a discharge of blood for many days, not at the time of her impurity, or if she has a discharge beyond the time of her impurity, all the days of the discharge she shall continue in uncleanness; as in the days of her impurity, she shall be unclean. Every bed on which she lies during all the days of her discharge shall be treated as the bed of her impurity; and everything on which she sits shall be unclean, as in the uncleanness of her impurity. Whoever touches these things shall be unclean, and shall wash his clothes, and bathe in water, and be unclean until the evening. If she is cleansed of her discharge, she shall count seven days, and after that she shall be clean. On the eighth day she shall take two turtledoves or two pigeons and bring them to the priest to the entrance of the tent of meeting. The priest shall offer one for a sin offering and the other for a burnt offering; and the priest shall make atonement on her behalf before the LORD for her unclean discharge. Thus you shall keep the people of Israel separate from their uncleanness, so that they do not die in their uncleanness by defiling my tabernacle that is in their midst. This is the ritual for those who have a discharge: for him who has an emission of semen, becoming unclean thereby, for her who is in the infirmity of her period, for anyone, male or female, who has a discharge, and for the man who lies with a woman who is unclean.

Mark 5:25–34

Now there was a woman who had been suffering from hemorrhages for twelve years. She had endured much under many physicians, and had spent all that she had; and she was no better, but rather grew worse. She had heard about Jesus, and came up behind him in the crowd and touched his cloak, for she said, "If I but touch his clothes, I will be made well." Immediately her hemorrhage stopped; and she felt in her body that she was healed of her disease. Immediately aware that power had gone forth from him, Jesus turned about in the crowd and said, "Who touched my clothes?" And his disciples said to him, "You see the crowd pressing in on you; how can you say, 'Who touched me?'" He looked all around to see who had done it. But the woman, knowing what had happened to her, came in fear and trembling, fell down before him, and told him the whole truth. He said to her, "Daughter, your faith has made you well; go in peace, and be healed of your disease."

Source: Society of Biblical Literature, eds. *Harper Collins Study Bible: New Revised Standard Version*. Rev. ed. New York: HarperCollins, 2006. All Scripture quotations appear from the *New Revised Standard Version Bible*. Division of Christian Education of the National Council of Churches of Christ in the United States of America, 1989.

Dionysius, Epistle to Bishop Basilides, *Canon II*

The question touching women in the time of their separation, whether it is proper for them when in such a condition to enter the house of God, I consider a superfluous inquiry. For I do not think that, if they are believing and pious women, they will themselves be rash enough in such a condition either to approach the holy table or to touch the body and blood of the Lord. Certainly the woman who had the issue of blood of twelve years' standing did not touch the Lord Himself, but only the hem of His garment, with a view to her cure (Mark 5:25–34). For to pray, however a person may be situated, and to remember the Lord, in whatever condition a person may be, and to offer up petitions for the obtaining of help, are exercises altogether blameless. But the individual who is not perfectly pure both in soul and in body, shall be interdicted from approaching the holy of holies.

Source: Roberts, Rev. Alexander, and James Donaldson, eds. *The Ante-Nicene Fathers: Translations of the Writings of the Fathers Down to A.D. 325,* vol. 6. Buffalo, NY: Christian Literature Company, 1886, 96.

AFTERMATH

Christians, even though they had broken away from Judaism and had left behind the food restrictions, appear to have kept some of the ideas of ritual impurity of menstruating women. As seen, Dionysius in the middle of the 200s CE, assumes that no menstruating Christian woman would dare approach the altar and/or take communion. Jerome (347–420 CE) wrote, in his *Commentary on Zacharia,* chapter 3: "Nothing is more filthy, unclean than a menstruant; whatever she will have touched, she makes it unclean, and still of whose filth is cleansed by the baptism of Christ, through the cleansing of sins" (Herbert 97). But not all early Christian writers felt this way. John Chrysostom (347–407 CE), in his *Homily on Matthew,* states (*Homily* 31.1–2) that the woman had been hiding herself for 12 years because she thought she was held under Jewish law. But Chrysostom states that she did not know the true opinion of Jesus; otherwise, she would not have tried to secretly touch the hem of his garment. He implies that belief in Christ meant that the Jewish purity laws concerning menstruation no longer held.

ASK YOURSELF

1. The Synoptic parallels to Mark (Matthew 9:20–22 and Luke 8:43–48) are close to what is found in Mark. There are differences, however. The account in Matthew is shorter, and there is a textual difference in Luke. In Luke 8:46, the text states, "But Jesus said, 'Someone touched me; for I noticed that power had gone out from me.'" If Mark is the earliest Gospel, then how can you account for the shortness of the story in Matthew and the speech change of Jesus? If we only had either Matthew or Luke, would that alter our understanding of this story?
2. Why is a menstruating woman considered to be unclean, at least according to Leviticus? If you are a woman, how do you feel about this? If you are a Jewish woman, do you abide by this particular purity rule?
3. The text from Leviticus also discusses semen emission, stating that it is also unclean. Why is this considered to be unclean? Is the uncleanliness different from that of a menstruating woman?

TOPICS TO CONSIDER

- ❧ Read, in its entirety, the sections of Jerome and John Chrysostom mentioned. Clearly they have differing views of menstruating women. Consider why there is a difference between these two church fathers. Also consider their views on women in general.
- ❧ Consider the views of modern Christianity on the purity of women during their menstrual cycle, especially the views of the Orthodox, Catholic, and some Protestant groups. Are the women in these different Christian religions allowed to take part in all the religious festivals?
- ❧ The woman described in the passage from Mark decided to touch the clothing of Jesus while she was in a crowd of people. Jesus then asked who had touched his clothes. Consider the state of medicine and healing during the first century, especially in terms of women's health.

THE TABOO OF MENSTRUATION

Many civilizations had (and still have) a taboo against women who are menstruating. As Phipps has pointed out, early Hindu and Persian societies had strict penalties against menstruating women who touched anyone. In ancient India, for example, she could be beaten, and in both ancient India and ancient Persia, if a menstruating woman touched bedding or clothing, it would have to be cleaned. The menstruating woman would also have to sleep in a special room and abstain from sexual intercourse (Phipps 299). These restrictions almost certainly carried down to Judaism and made their way into Christian teachings. The fact that a woman menstruates is the main reason women are not allowed to become priests in the Catholic Church today. This is despite the view of other early Christians who rejected the purity laws of Judaism and did not see menstruation as a bar to approaching the altar.

Further Information

Chrysostom, John. *Homily 31 on Matthew.* http://www.newadvent.org/fathers/200131. htm.

Dionysius, *Letters.* http://www.ccel.org/ccel/schaff/anf06.html.

Fonrobert, Charlotte. *Menstrual Purity: Rabbinic and Christian Reconstructions of Biblical Gender.* Stanford, CA: Stanford University Press, 2000.

Herbert, Judith A., Anne-Marie Korte, and Judith Ann Johnson. *Wholly Woman, Holy Blood: A Feminist Critique of Purity and Impurity.* Harrisburg, PA: Trinity Press, International, 2003.

Phipps, William E. "The Menstrual Taboo in the Judeo-Christian Tradition." *Journal of Religion and Health* 19, no. 4 (Winter, 1980): 298–303.

Pliny the Elder. *The Natural History* 28.23. http://www.perseus.tufts.edu/hopper/text?doc= Perseus:text:1999.02.0137.

Selvidge, Marla J. "Mark 5:25–34 and Leviticus 15:19–20: A Reaction to Restrictive Purity Regulations." *Journal of Biblical Literature* 103, no. 4 (Dec., 1984): 619–23.

21. WOMEN MARTYRS

INTRODUCTION

Men were not the only ones who were killed by the Roman state for disobeying the order to renounce their faith. There are also many examples of women who were killed for believing in Christ. One of the most moving of these martyrdoms is the execution of Perpetua and Felicitas. These women were from Carthage, North Africa, and were killed in the early 200s during a persecution under the Roman emperor Septimius Severus, who ruled from 193 to 211. Like other martyrdoms, their execution was carried out in an amphitheater in front of a crowd. Also like other martyrdoms, Perpetua, Felicitas, and other Christians who were killed in this account were attacked by wild animals. After being attacked by a cow, Perpetua then led the sword of the gladiator assigned to kill her to her own throat. The text below starts at last chapter of the martyrdom.

KEEP IN MIND WHILE YOU READ

1. Early scholars believed that Tertullian had either written or edited the *Passion*. But the general consensus now is that he did not write it, and in many cases, the *Passion of Perpetua and Felicitas* is now published separately from the writings of Tertullian. Chapter 1 states that part of the martyrdom was written by Perpetua herself.
2. Some scholars believe that Perpetua and Felicitas may have been Montanists (see the section "Women Prophets").
3. Martyrdom was something that many Christians desired, and this is clear from this particular martyrdom. Some church leaders tried to discourage this particular wish because it made the Christians look too fanatical.
4. According to chapter 1, Perpetua had an infant son who was still nursing when she was taken into custody.
5. Felicitas was eight months pregnant when she was taken in by the authorities. As described in chapter 5, it was forbidden to execute a pregnant woman. She and her friends prayed that she would give birth early. This is what happened, and she gave birth to a little girl. The baby was given away to a woman who raised her as her own daughter, and Felicitas was then able to fulfill her wish to be a martyr.

Ceres The daughter of Saturn and who was also associated with agriculture.

Saturn A god of agriculture.

scourges Whips.

their victory Another term for "their martyrdom."

venatores People who whipped the Christians as they were led into the amphitheater. Usually they were employed to entertain the audience with their hunting skills.

Passion of Perpetua and Felicitas 6

. . . The day of **their victory** shone forth, and they proceeded from the prison into the amphitheater, as if to an assembly, joyous and of brilliant countenances; if perchance shrinking, it was with joy, and not with fear. Perpetua followed with placid look, and with step and gait as a matron of Christ, beloved of God; casting down the luster of her eyes from the gaze of all. Moreover, Felicitas, rejoicing that she had safely brought forth, so that she might fight with the wild beasts; from the blood and from the midwife to the gladiator, to wash after childbirth with a second baptism. And when they were brought to the gate, and were constrained to put on the clothing—the men, that of the priests of **Saturn**, and the women, that of those who were consecrated to **Ceres**—that noble-minded woman resisted even to the end with constancy. For she said, "We have come thus far of our own accord, for this reason, that our liberty might not be restrained. For this reason we have yielded our minds, that we might not do any such thing as this: we have agreed on this with you." Injustice acknowledged the justice; the tribune yielded to their being brought as simply as they were. Perpetua sang psalms, already treading under foot the head of the Egyptian; Revocatus, and Saturninus, and Saturus uttered threats against the gazing people about this martyrdom. When they came within sight of Hilarianus, by gesture and nod, they began to say to Hilarianus, "You judge us," say they, "but God will judge you." At this the people, exasperated, demanded that they should be tormented with **scourges** as they passed along the rank of the **venatores**. And they indeed rejoiced that they should have incurred any one of their Lord's passions.

2. But He who had said, "Ask, and you shall receive," (John 16.24) gave to them when they asked, that death which each one had wished for. For when at any time they had been discoursing among themselves about their wish in respect of their martyrdom, Saturninus indeed had professed that he wished that he might be thrown to all the beasts; doubtless that he might wear a more glorious crown. Therefore in the beginning of the exhibition he and Revocatus made trial of the leopard, and moreover upon the scaffold they were harassed by the bear. Saturus, however, held nothing in greater abomination than a bear; but he imagined that he would be put an end to with one bite of a leopard. Therefore, when a wild boar was supplied, it was the huntsman rather who had supplied that boar who was gored by that same beast, and died the day after the shows. Saturus only was drawn out; and when he had been bound on the floor near to a bear, the bear would not come forth from his den. And so Saturus for the second time is recalled unhurt.

3. Moreover, for the young women the devil prepared a very fierce cow, provided especially for that purpose contrary to custom, rivaling their sex also in that of the beasts. And so, stripped and clothed with nets, they were led forth. The populace shuddered as they saw one young woman of delicate frame, and another with breasts still dropping from her recent childbirth. So, being recalled, they are unbound. Perpetua is first led in. She was tossed, and fell on her loins; and when she saw her tunic torn from her side, she drew it over her as a veil for her middle, rather mindful of her modesty than her suffering. Then she was called for again, and bound up her disheveled hair; for it was not becoming for a martyr to suffer with disheveled hair, lest she should appear to be mourning in her glory. So she rose up; and when she saw Felicitas crushed, she approached and gave her her hand, and lifted her up. And both of them stood together; and the brutality of the populace being appeased, they were recalled to

the Sanavivarian gate. Then Perpetua was received by a certain one who was still a catechumen, Rusticus by name, who kept close to her; and she, as if aroused from sleep, so deeply had she been in the Spirit and in an ecstasy, began to look round her, and to say to the amazement of all, "I cannot tell when we are to be led out to that cow." And when she had heard what had already happened, she did not believe it until she had perceived certain signs of injury in her body and in her dress, and had recognized the catechumen. Afterwards causing that catechumen and the brother to approach, she addressed them, saying, "Stand fast in the faith, and love one another, all of you, and be not offended at my sufferings."

4. The same Saturus at the other entrance exhorted the soldier Pudens, saying, "Assuredly here I am, as I have promised and foretold, for up to this moment I have felt no beast. And now believe with your whole heart. Lo, I am going forth to that beast, and I shall be destroyed with one bite of the leopard." And immediately at the conclusion of the exhibition he was thrown to the leopard; and with one bite of his he was bathed with such a quantity of blood, that the people shouted out to him as he was returning, the testimony of his second baptism, "Saved and washed, saved and washed." Manifestly he was assuredly saved who had been glorified in such a spectacle. Then to the soldier Pudens he said, "Farewell, and be mindful of my faith; and let not these things disturb, but confirm you." And at the same time he asked for a little ring from his finger, and returned it to him bathed in his wound, leaving to him an inherited token and the memory of his blood. And then lifeless he is cast down with the rest, to be slaughtered in the usual place. And when the populace called for them into the midst, that as the sword penetrated into their body they might make their eyes partners in the murder, they rose up of their own accord, and transferred themselves whither the people wished; but they first kissed one another, that they might consummate their martyrdom with the kiss of peace. The rest indeed, immoveable and in silence, received the sword-thrust; much more Saturus, who also had first ascended the ladder, and first gave up his spirit, for he also was waiting for Perpetua. But Perpetua, that she might taste some pain, being pierced between the ribs, cried out loudly, and she herself placed the wavering right hand of the youthful gladiator to her throat. Possibly such a woman could not have been slain unless she herself had willed it, because she was feared by the impure spirit. Most brave and blessed martyrs! Truly called and chosen unto the glory of our Lord Jesus Christ, whom whoever magnifies, and honors, and adores, assuredly ought to read these examples for the edification of the Church, not less than the ancient ones, so that new virtues also may testify that one and the same Holy Spirit is always operating even until now, and God the Father **Omnipotent,** and His Son Jesus Christ our Lord, whose is the glory and infinite power for ever and ever. Amen.

> **Omnipotent** All powerful.

Source: Roberts, Rev. Alexander, and James Donaldson, eds. *The Ante-Nicene Fathers: Translations of the Writings of the Fathers Down to A.D. 325,* vol. 3. Buffalo, NY: Christian Literature Company, 1903, 704–6.

AFTERMATH

Accounts of the martyrdoms were read by or told to early Christians, and the martyrs were used as examples for those who were facing their own persecutions. Special status was granted to the martyrs, and sometimes they were seen as intercessors. People would pray to them in hopes that the martyrs would have direct access to Christ. As can be seen from this martyrdom, some Christians actively sought this out. This desire, however, became a cause of concern among the clergy. There was a concerted drive to try to convince possible martyrs, both male and female, to not be so excited to be executed. When the official Christian persecution ended with the rise of Emperor Constantine, martyrdom stopped being an issue.

ASK YOURSELF

1. Many ancient Christians were willing to die for their faith. Would you be willing to do the same? Why or why not?
2. Why is the martyrdom considered to be a "victory"? What is it a victory over? Why would people like Perpetua and Felicitas pray for death?
3. What do you think is the point of the *Passion of Perpetua and Felicitas*? In other words, why would Tertullian include (or possibly write) this martyrdom? What lessons are Christians supposed to be learning by reading this text?
4. Men are certainly mentioned in this martyrdom, but the women are the focus. Does it matter that the focus is on women? Do you think the martyrdom of women makes the account more appealing to women?
5. Why do you think a wild cow was used against the women? Do you think it has any symbolism to the Romans?
6. Are people of other religions willing to die for their faith? If so, are the reasons the same today as for the ancient Christians?

TOPICS TO CONSIDER

    ∾ Read the entire passion and list the accusations that were being used against these women. Consider how they vary from accusations made against men.

    ∾ It was stated that Perpetua even guided the sword to her own throat. Modern Christianity rarely has a martyr. Consider how Christianity would deal with a martyr today. Do you think the martyrs would receive special status like the ancient martyrs?

    ∾ Consider how the family members of the martyred Christians would have felt. Sometimes family members are described in the martyr texts, and in this one in particular, Perpetua's father and brother are mentioned.

OTHER WOMEN MARTYRS

Women as well as men were martyred. As in the case with Felicitas, sometimes the martyrdom would be delayed in the case of pregnancy. But usually women were treated no differently than men. The martyrdom of Perpetua and Felicitas is the most famous of the female martyrdoms, but there were many others. In Thessalonika, Greece, in 304, a number of women were put to death because of their faith. Their account is titled "The Martyrdom of Saints Agape, Irene, and Chione at Salonki," and it occurred during the Great Persecution. The women had tried to flee the city but were brought back. Some of them were found guilty of treason because they refused to worship the emperor, and their penalty was to be burned alive. Some, including Irene, were deemed to be too young and were put into prison. However, Irene was once again brought before the prefect; he tried to humiliate her at a brothel, and still she refused to worship the emperor. Irene then signed a statement saying she was Christian. and that led to her, too, being burned alive. Another woman named Crispina (as told in the *Martyrdom of Crispina*) was also killed in the same year as Irene and her friends. She also refused to worship the emperor or follow the Roman gods. Unlike Irene, Crispina was beheaded for her beliefs.

⮞ Before they were killed, the martyrs sometimes had visions. Read the entire story of the *Passion of Perpetua and Felicitas* and consider the visions that Perpetua had before her death. What was the meaning of these visions? What do the visions mean to those who would be reading the story?

Further Information

Castelli, Elizabeth. *Martyrdom and Memory: Early Christian Culture Making.* New York: Columbia University Press, 2004.

Halporn, J. W. "Literary History and Generic Expectations in the Passio and Acta Perpetuae." *Vigiliae Christianae* 45, no. 3 (Sep., 1991): 223–41.

Klawiter, Frederick C. "The Role of Martyrdom and Persecution in Developing the Priestly Authority of Women in Early Christianity: A Case Study of Montanism." *Church History.* 49, no. 3 (Sep., 1980): 251–61.

Lefkowitz, Mary R. "The Motivations for St. Perpetua's Martyrdom." *Journal of the American Academy of Religion* 44, no. 3 (Sep., 1976): 417–21.

Musurillo, Herbert Anthony, ed. *The Acts of the Christian Martyrs: Texts, Translations, and Introduction.* Oxford: Oxford University Press, 1972.

The Passion of the Holy Martyrs Perpetua and Felicitas. http://www.ccel.org/ccel/schaff/anf03.vi.vi.ii.html.

Pettersen, Alvyn. "Perpetua: Prisoner of Conscience." *Vigiliae Christianae* 41, no. 2 (Jun., 1987): 139–53.

Shaw, Brent D. "The Passion of Perpetua." *Past & Present,* no. 139 (May, 1993): 3–45.

Street, Gail. *Redeemed Bodies: Women Martyrs in Early Christianity.* Louisville, KY: John Knox Press, 2009.

Wypustek, Andrzej. "Magic, Montanism, Perpetua, and the Severan Persecution." *Vigiliae Christianae* 51, no. 3 (Aug., 1997): 276–97.

22. Women as Deaconesses

INTRODUCTION

Women played a vitally important role in early Christianity. Paul's letters make this very clear: without the support of women, Paul would have had a hard time spreading his version of Christianity. Despite their important contribution, their role is seen to be limited by Jesus in his act of appointing 12 male disciples. This tradition of not appointing women to the upper levels of clergy still continues today in some Christian groups, especially the Catholic Church. Paul, however, states that women held offices in the church, especially that of deaconess. Phoebe (Romans 16:1–2), Lydia (Acts 16:14–15), and Priscilla (Acts 18; Romans 16:3–4) were deaconesses. Sometimes it is difficult to tell what the responsibilities of the deaconesses were. Phoebe in particular is called a deacon and not a deaconess (see text below). Her role in unclear, except that she was wealthy and used her money to help Paul. Priscilla and her husband, Aquila, were tent makers who accompanied Paul on some of his travels. Together they helped spread Christianity (Acts 18:26). The office of deaconess seems to be an eastern adaptation, but there is evidence that there were female deacons in the west (Eisen 182–85, although some evidence is later than our period). With women holding the office of deaconesses it was natural that some women wanted to become priests. There were female priests in the first four centuries of Christianity, but they were in groups that were then and now considered to be heretical. See Rossi and Otranto (84–86) for specific examples. The texts below are Romans 16, 1 Timothy 2:5–15, and the *Didascalia*.

KEEP IN MIND WHILE YOU READ

1. The *Didascalia* was written sometime in the early 200s, possibly in Syria. It describes what is going on in eastern Christianity and may not describe what is happening in churches outside of the east (or even outside of Syria).

2. The full title of the *Didascalia* is the *Catholic Teaching of the Twelve Apostles and Holy Disciples of Our Savior*. The original language it was written in was Greek, but very little of that survives today. A Syriac translation survives, and that is the basis for the English translation.

3. The women described in the following passages are being described by men, not by women. There could possibly be a difference between what women were really doing and what men described them as doing.
4. Paul stated that Andronicus *and* Junia were "prominent among the apostles" (Romans 6:7). This seems to infer that Junia was an apostle, although it could also be interpreted to mean that the original apostles knew of Andronicus and Junia and that they might have been helping the apostles like Prisca and Phoebe were helping Paul.
5. While I have chosen to use the *New Revised Standard Version* (NRSV) translation of the Bible, the text found in this edition sometimes does not match the Greek. This is especially the case where the text of the NRSV mentions "and the brothers and sisters who are with them": the words "and sisters" are not in the original Greek. The editors of the NRSV had adopted inclusionary language. See also (among many) Matthew 5:47, Romans 1:13, Romans 7:1.

Romans 16:1–16

Cenchreae The eastern seaport of Corinth.

the church in their house Because practicing Christianity was illegal, Christians originally met in private houses.

holy kiss This was a common way for Christians to greet each other. It is still done in some modern churches.

who were in prison with me Paul mentions his imprisonments in 2 Corinthians 6:5, 11:23, Galatians 3:23, and Philemon 1:10 (among others).

I commend to you our sister Phoebe, a deacon (*diakonon*) of the church at **Cenchreae,** so that you may welcome her in the Lord as is fitting for the saints, and help her in whatever she may require from you, for she has been a benefactor of many and of myself as well. Greet Prisca and Aquila, who work with me in Christ Jesus, and who risked their necks for my life, to whom not only I give thanks, but also all the churches of the Gentiles.

Greet also **the church in their house**. Greet my beloved Epaenetus, who was the first convert in Asia for Christ. Greet Mary, who has worked very hard among you. Greet Andronicus and Junia, my relatives **who were in prison with me**; they are prominent among the apostles, and they were in Christ before I was. Greet Ampliatus, my beloved in the Lord. Greet Urbanus, our co-worker in Christ, and my beloved Stachys. Greet Apelles, who is approved in Christ. Greet those who belong to the family of Aristobulus. Greet my relative Herodion. Greet those in the Lord who belong to the family of Narcissus. Greet those workers in the Lord, Tryphaena and Tryphosa. Greet the beloved Persis, who has worked hard in the Lord. Greet Rufus, chosen in the Lord; and greet his mother—a mother to me also. Greet Asyncritus, Phlegon, Hermes, Patrobas, Hermas, and the brothers and sisters who are with them. Greet Philologus, Julia, Nereus and his sister, and Olympas, and all the saints who are with them. Greet one another with a **holy kiss**. All the churches of Christ greet you.

1 Timothy 2:5–15

For there is one God; there is also one mediator between God and humankind, Christ Jesus, himself human, who gave himself a ransom for all—this was attested at the right time. For this I was appointed a herald and an apostle (I am telling the truth, I am not lying), a teacher of the Gentiles in faith and truth. I desire, then, that in every place the men should pray, lifting up holy hands without anger or argument; also that the women should dress themselves modestly and decently in suitable clothing, not with their hair braided, or with gold, pearls, or expensive clothes, but with good works, as is proper for women who profess reverence for God. Let a woman learn in silence with full submission. I permit no woman to teach or to have authority over a man; she is to keep silent. For Adam was formed first, then Eve; and Adam was not deceived, but the woman was deceived and became a transgressor. Yet she will be saved through childbearing, provided they continue in faith and love and holiness, with modesty.

> **men should pray, lifting up holy hands** Christians did not pray with their hands together, touching, in front of them. They put their hands up in the air, over the head, with the palms forward.

Source: Society of Biblical Literature, eds. *Harper Collins Study Bible: New Revised Standard Version*. Rev. ed. New York: HarperCollins, 2006. All Scripture quotations appear from the *New Revised Standard Version Bible*. Division of Christian Education of the National Council of Churches of Christ in the United States of America, 1989.

Didascalia *16*

Wherefore, O bishop, appoint workers of righteousness as helpers who may co-operate with you for salvation. You shall choose and appoint as deacons from those that please you out of all the people: a man for the performance of the most things that are required, but a woman for the ministry of women. For there are houses where you cannot send a (male) deacon to the women, on account of the heathen, but you may send a deaconess. Also, because in many other matters, the office of a woman deacon is required. In the first place, when women go down into the water (i.e., get baptized), those who go down into the water should be anointed by a deaconess with the oil of anointing; and where there is no woman at hand, and especially no deaconess, he who baptizes must of necessity anoint her who is being baptized. But where there is a woman, and especially a deaconess, it is not fitting that women should be seen by men: but with the imposition of hand you anoint the head only. As of old the priests and kings were anointed in Israel, do in same manner, with the imposition of hand, anoint the head of those who receive baptism, whether of men or of women; and afterwards—whether you baptize, or you command the deacons or presbyters to baptize—let a woman deacon, as we have already said, anoint the women. But let a man pronounce over them the invocation of the divine Names in the water. And when she who is being baptized has come up from the water, let the deaconess receive her, and teach and instruct her how the seal of baptism ought to be (kept) unbroken in purity and holiness. For this cause we say that the ministry of a woman deacon is especially needful and important. For our Lord and Savior also was ministered unto by women ministers, *Mary Magdalene, and Mary the daughter of James and mother of Jose, and the mother of the sons of Zebedee* (Matthew 27:56), with other women beside. And you have need of the ministry of a deaconess for many things; for a deaconess is required to go into the houses of the heathen where there are believing women, and to visit those who are sick, and to minister to them in that of which they have need, and to bathe those who have begun to recover from sickness.

And let the deacons imitate the bishops in their conversation: let them even be laboring more than he. And let them *not love filthy lucre* (1 Timothy 3:8); but let them be diligent in the ministry. And in proportion to the number of the congregation of the people of the

Church, so let the deacons be, so that they may be able to take knowledge (of each) and refresh all, so that for the aged women who are infirm, and for brethren and sisters who are in sickness—for every one they may provide the ministry which is proper for him.

But let a woman rather be devoted to the ministry of women, and a male deacon to the ministry of men. And let him be ready to obey and to submit himself to the command of the bishop. And let him labor and toil in every place where he is sent to minister or to speak of some matter to anyone, for it is appropriate that each one to know his office and to be diligent in executing it. And let you (bishop and deacon) be of one counsel and of one purpose, and one soul dwelling in two bodies. And know what the ministry is, according as our Lord and Savior said in the Gospel: *Whoever among you who desires to be chief, let him be your servant: even as the Son of Man came not to be ministered to, but to minister, and to give his life a ransom for many* (Matthew 20:26–28). So also you the deacons ought to do, if it falls to you to lay down your life for your brethren in the ministry which is due to them. For neither did our Lord and Savior Himself disdain (to be) ministering to us, as it is written in Isaiah: *To justify the righteous, who has performed well a service for many* (Isa 53.11). If then the Lord of heaven and earth *performed a service* for us, and bore and endured everything for us, how much more must we to do the like for our brethren, that we may imitate Him, for we are imitators of Him, and hold the place of Christ. And again in the Gospel you find it written how our Lord *girded a linen cloth about his loins and cast water into a wash-basin,* while we reclined (at supper), and drew nigh *and washed the feet of* us all *and wiped them with the cloth* (John 13.4–12). Now this He did that He might show us (an example of) charity and brotherly love, that we also should do in like manner one to another. If then our Lord did thus, will you, deacons, hesitate to do the like for them that are sick and infirm, you who are workmen of the truth, and bear the likeness of Christ? Therefore minister with love, and neither murmur nor hesitate; otherwise you will have ministered as it were for men's sake and not for the sake of God, and you will receive your reward according to your ministry in the day of judgment. Therefore it is required of you, deacons, that you visit all who are in need, and inform the bishop of those who are in distress; and you shall be his soul and his mind, and in all things you shall be taking trouble and be obedient to him.

Source: *Didascalia Apostolorum*. Introduction by Richard Hugh Connolly. Oxford: Clarendon Press, 1929, 146–50. Used by permission of Wipf and Stock Publishers. www.wipfandstock.com.

AFTERMATH

Late in the fourth century the office of the deaconess became more common, at least in the east. John Chrysostom (347–407) wrote a treatise called the *Homilies* (30 and 31) on Romans 16, where he specifically praises the women from Paul's letters. In the west there is some evidence of women deaconesses, but it is very sparse and dates to the late 400s or early 500s. A series of church councils, starting in the 300s, severely limited or excluded women from holding church offices. In 325 the Council of Nicea issued a list of canons, or laws, and Canon 19 states that there was a group of Christians named Paulinists who wanted to join the Catholic Church. Canon 19 mentions that this group had deaconesses and that they were laity, not clergy. In the second half of the 300s the church Council of Laodicea met and issued Canon 44, which stated that women could not approach the altar. In 441, at the First Council of Orange, the clergy issued Canon 25, which stated that women could not hold clerical office (Rossi 83). In modern times, Pope Paul VI in 1976 issued the *Declaration on the Question of Admission of Women to the Ministerial Priesthood* (web link below). In it he firmly denies that women should become priests or deaconesses.

ASK YOURSELF

1. In many Christian churches, women are not allowed to become deaconesses and priests, and the rule is justified using biblical texts, especially the one from Paul that forbids women to talk in church. If you are Catholic, how do you feel about this position? Do you think that women are unsuited to hold a priestly office?

2. What do you think of the author of 1 Timothy's statement: "Let a woman learn in silence with full submission. I permit no woman to teach or to have authority over a man; she is to keep silent"? Do you think this statement would have been different if it had been written by a woman?

3. Examine the statements about women in Paul's writings and compare them to those made by the author of 1 Timothy. If the author of 1 Timothy was a disciple of Paul, how can you account for the differences in opinion? Why do you think that the opinion of 1 Timothy became the position of the Catholic Church today, and not the opinion of Paul?

4. What would early Christianity have been like if the women described by Paul had decided not to help him? Do you think he would have been able to travel around what is modern-day Turkey without their help? Do you think that Christianity would have spread as quickly as it did if these women had rejected Paul?

5. Do you agree with the translators of the *New Revised Standard Version* in using inclusive language, which is different from the Greek?

TOPICS TO CONSIDER

> ⤳ Consider the role that women played in the early church, especially as described by the *Didascalia*. Consider the limits that the church put on women, and consider why men put limits on them.

> ⤳ Read Pope Paul VI's "Declaration on the Question of Admission of Women to the Ministerial Priesthood," issued in 1976. Consider how this declaration was influenced by early Christian belief. Also consider how the New Testament has been used in comparison to the texts given above.

> ⤳ At the General Convention in 1976 the Episcopal Church of the United States voted to allow women as bishops, priests, and deacons, while the Anglican Church of England allowed women to become priests in 1992 but does not yet allow them to become bishops. Consider the differences of opinion on this matter between the Catholics and the Episcopalian/Anglican communities.

Further Information

Didascalia Apostolorum. http://www.bombaxo.com/didascalia.html.
Eisen, Ute E. *Women Officeholders in Early Christianity: Epigraphical and Literary Studies.* Collegeville, MN: Liturgical Press, 2000.

Pope Paul VI. "Declaration on the Question of Admission of Women to the Ministerial Priesthood." http://www.papalencyclicals.net/Paul06/p6interi.htm

Rossi, Mary Ann, and Giorgio Otranto. "Priesthood, Precedent, and Prejudice: On Recovering the Women Priests of Early Christianity." *Journal of Feminist Studies in Religion* 7, no. 1 (Spring, 1991): 73–94.

Torjesen, Karen J. *When Women Were Priests: Women's Leadership in the Early Church and the Scandal of Their Subordination in the Rise of Christianity.* San Francisco: HarperSanFrancisco, 1993.

Witherington, Ben III. *Women and the Genesis of Christianity.* Cambridge: Cambridge University Press, 1990.

23. VIRGINITY

INTRODUCTION

A virgin is a female who has never had sexual intercourse. After having sex, a woman could then abstain and she would be celibate. In the Roman Empire, during the time of Emperor Augustus (ruled 31 BCE–14 CE), women had to have a certain number of children before they could choose to become celibate. Emperor Constantine, who became the first Christian emperor, started to relax those laws, mostly because by the 300s CE, virginity had become popular among Christian women. The Apostle Paul had written about marriage and stated that people should remain unmarried, unless they could not control their sexual urges. This began a movement in Christianity where women could forgo sexual activity so that they could be totally devoted to their religion. Many early male Christians wrote about the goodness of virginity but also about the restrictions that virgins had to abide by in order to remain virgins for Christ. Unfortunately, we don't have much information on what women themselves had to say about this.

Overall, being a virgin was considered to be a good thing, and there were many rules that virgins had to follow to keep their special status. Cyprian, a bishop of Carthage, North Africa, from 249 to 258 CE, wrote *On the Dress of Virgins,* possibly right after he became bishop. In it he discusses the way a virgin should look. As will be seen, Cyprian was against all forms of jewelry, makeup, or any type of hairstyle. I have included selections from the book and have included the biblical verses within the text.

KEEP IN MIND WHILE YOU READ

1. Cyprian came from a wealthy non-Christian family. He was highly educated and well known in Carthage for his public-speaking ability. He became a priest in 248 CE and early the next year was made bishop.
2. Cyprian was bishop of Carthage during the Emperor Decius's persecution in 250 CE (the Decian persecution). This was an empire-wide persecution that affected many Christians. Cyprian was still bishop when Emperor Valerian also started a persecution against Christians. Cyprian was exiled and in 258 CE was beheaded.

3. Cyprian knew the writings of Tertullian, who lived in Carthage and died sometime in the second decade of the third century. Tertullian wrote a book titled *On the Dress of Women*, which Cyprian had read. It was probably this book that inspired him to write *On the Dress of Virgins*.

Cyprian, On the Dress of Virgins, *selections*

(1) Discipline, the safeguard of hope, the bond of faith, the guide of the way of salvation, the stimulus and nourishment of good dispositions, the teacher of virtue, causes us to abide always in Christ, and to live continually for God, and to attain to the heavenly promises and to the divine rewards. To follow her is wholesome, and to turn away from her and neglect her is deadly. The Holy Spirit says in the Psalms, "Keep discipline, lest perchance the Lord be angry, and you perish from the right way, when His wrath is quickly kindled against you (Psalms 2:12)." And again: "But to the ungodly God says: "Why do you preach my laws, and take my covenant into your mouth, whereas you hate discipline, and have cast my words behind you (Psalms 1:17)?" And again we read: "He who casts away discipline is miserable (Wisdom 3:11)." And from Solomon we have received the mandates of wisdom, warning us: "My son, do not despise the discipline of the Lord, nor faint when you are rebuked by Him: for the Lord loves who he corrects (Proverbs 3:11)." But if God rebukes whom He loves, and rebukes him for the very purpose of amending him, brethren also, and especially priests, do not hate, but love those whom they rebuke, that they may mend them, since God, predicted by Jeremiah, pointed to our times when he said, "And I will give you shepherds according to my heart: and they shall feed you with the food of discipline (Jeremiah 3:15)."...

(3) My address is now to virgins, whose glory, as it is more eminent, excites the greater interest. This is the flower of the ecclesiastical seed, the grace and ornament of spiritual endowment, a joyous disposition, the wholesome and uncorrupted work of praise and honor, God's image answering to the holiness of the Lord, the more illustrious portion of Christ's flock. The glorious fruitfulness of Mother Church rejoices by their means, and in them abundantly flourishes; and in proportion as a copious virginity is added to her number, so much the more it increases the joy of the Mother. To these I speak, these I exhort with affection rather than with power; not that I would claim—last and least, and very conscious of my lowliness as I am—any right to censure, but because, being unceasingly careful even to solicitude, I fear more from the onset of Satan...

5. But if continency follows Christ, and virginity is destined for the kingdom of God, what have they to do with earthly dress, and with ornaments, wherewith while they are striving to please men they offend God? Not considering that it is declared, "They who please men are put to confusion, because God has despised them (Psalms 53:5);" and that Paul also has gloriously and sublimely uttered, "If I yet pleased men, I should not be the servant of Christ (Galatians 1:10)." But continence and modesty consist not alone in purity of the flesh, but also in seemliness, as well as in modesty of dress and adornment; so that, according to the apostle, she who is unmarried may be holy both in body and in spirit. Paul instructs and teaches us, saying, "He that is unmarried cares for the things of the Lord, how he may please God: but he who has contracted marriage cares for the things which are of this world, how he may please his wife. So both the virgin and the unmarried woman consider those things which are the Lord's, that they may be holy both in body and spirit

(1 Corinthians 7:32)." A virgin ought not only to be so, but also to be perceived and believed to be so: no one on seeing a virgin should be in any doubt as to whether she is one. Perfectness should show itself equal in all things; nor should the dress of the body discredit the good of the mind. Why should she walk out adorned? Why with dressed hair, as if she either had or sought for a husband? Rather let her dread to please if she is a virgin; and let her not invite her own risk, if she is keeping herself for better and divine things. Those who do not have a husband whom they profess they please, should persevere, sound and pure, not only in body, but also in spirit. For it is not right that a virgin should have her hair braided for the appearance of her beauty, or boast of her flesh and of its beauty, when she has no struggle greater than that against her flesh, and no contest more obstinate than that of conquering and subduing the body. . .

12. The characteristics of ornaments, and of garments, and the allurements of beauty, are not fitting for any but prostitutes and immodest women; and the dress of none is more precious than of those whose modesty is lowly. Thus in the Holy Scriptures, by which the Lord wished us to be both instructed and admonished, the harlot city is described more beautifully arrayed and adorned, and with her ornaments; and the rather on account of those very ornaments about to perish. "And there came," it is said, "one of the seven angels, which had the seven phials, and talked with me, saying, Come here, I will show you the judgment of the great whore, who sits upon many waters, with whom the kings of the earth have committed fornication. And he carried me away in spirit; and I saw a woman sit upon a beast, and that woman was arrayed in a purple and scarlet mantle, and was adorned with gold, and precious stones, and pearls, having a golden cup in her hand, full of curses, and filthiness, and fornication of the whole earth (Revelation 17:1–4)." Let chaste and modest virgins avoid the dress of the unchaste, the manners of the immodest, the ensigns of brothels, the ornaments of harlots. . .

15. And indeed in that very matter, for the sake of the fear which faith suggests to me, for the sake of the love which brotherhood requires, I think that not virgins only and widows, but married women also, and all of the sex alike, should be admonished, that the work of God and His fashioning and formation ought in no manner to be adulterated, either with the application of yellow color, or with black dust or rouge, or with any kind of medicament which can corrupt the native lineaments. God says, "Let us make man in our image and likeness (Genesis 1:26);" and does anyone dare to alter and to change what God has made? They are laying hands on God when they try to re-form that which He formed, and to transfigure it, not knowing that everything which comes into being is God's work, everything that is changed is the devil's. If any artist, in painting, were to delineate in envious coloring the countenance and likeness and bodily appearance of anyone; and the likeness being now painted and completed, another person were to lay hands on it, as if, when it was already formed and already painted, he, being more skilled, could amend it, a serious wrong and a just cause of indignation would seem natural to the former artist. And do you think yourself likely with impunity to commit a boldness of such wicked temerity, an offence to God the creator? For although you may not be immodest among men, and are not unchaste with your seducing dyes, yet when those things which belong to God are corrupted and violated, you are engaged in a worse adultery. That you think yourself to be adorned, that you think your hair to be dressed, is an assault upon the divine work, is a prevarication of the truth …

17. Are you not afraid, I entreat you, being such as you are, that when the day of resurrection comes, your Maker may not recognize you again, and may turn you away when you come to His rewards and promises, and may exclude you, rebuking you with the vigor of a Censor and Judge, and say: "This is not my work, nor is this our image. You have polluted

your skin with a false medicament, you have changed your hair with an adulterous color, your face is violently taken possession of by a lie, your figure is corrupted, your countenance is another's. You cannot see God, since your eyes are not those which God made, but those which the devil has spoiled. You have followed him, you have imitated the red and painted eyes of the serpent. As you are adorned in the fashion of your enemy, with him also you shall burn by and by." Are not these, I beg, matters to be reflected on by God's servants? Are they not always to be dreaded day and night? Let married women see to it, in what respect they are flattering themselves concerning the solace of their husbands with the desire of pleasing them, and while they put them forward indeed as their excuse, they make them partners in the association of guilty consent. Virgins, assuredly, to whom this address is intended to appeal, who have adorned themselves with arts of this kind, I should think ought not to be counted among virgins, but, like infected sheep and diseased cattle, to be driven from the holy and pure flock of virginity, lest by living together they should pollute the rest with their contagion; lest they ruin others even as they have perished themselves. . .

21. Therefore hear me, O virgins, as a parent; hear, I beseech you, one who fears while he warns; hear one who is faithfully consulting for your advantage and your profit. Be such as God the Creator made you; be such as the hand of your Father ordained you. Let your countenance remain in you incorrupt, your neck unadorned, your figure simple; let not wounds be made in your ears, nor let the precious chain of bracelets and necklaces circle your arms or your neck; let your feet be free from golden bands, your hair stained with no dye, your eyes worthy of beholding God. Let your baths be performed with women, among whom your bathing is modest. Let the shameless feasts and lascivious banquets of marriages be avoided, the contagion of which is perilous. Overcome dress, since you are a virgin; overcome gold, since you overcome the flesh and the world. It is not consistent to be unable to be conquered by the greater, and to be found no match for the less. Straight and narrow is the way which leads to life; hard and difficult is the track which tends to glory. By this pathway the martyrs progress, the virgins pass, the just of all kinds advance. Avoid the broad and roomy ways. There are deadly snares and death-bringing pleasures; there the devil flatters, that he may deceive; smiles, that he may do mischief; entices, that he may slay. The first fruit for the martyrs is a hundred-fold; the second is yours, sixty-fold. As with the martyrs there is no thought of the flesh and of the world, no small, and trifling, and delicate encounter; so also in you, whose reward is second in grace, let there be the strength in endurance next to theirs. The ascent to great things is not easy. What toil we suffer, what labor, when we endeavor to ascend the hills and the tops of mountains! What, then, that we may ascend to heaven? If you look to the reward of the promise, your labor is less. Immortality is given to the persevering, eternal life is set before them; the Lord promises a kingdom. . .

24. Every one of which things, O good virgins, you ought to observe, to love, to fulfill, who giving yourselves to God and Christ, are advancing in both the higher and better part to the Lord, to whom you have dedicated yourselves. You that are advanced in years, suggest a teaching to the younger. You that are younger, give a stimulus to your equals. Stir one another up with mutual exhortations; provoke to glory by rival proofs of virtue. Endure bravely, go on spiritually, attain happily. Only remember us at that time, when virginity shall begin to be rewarded in you.

Source: Roberts, Rev. Alexander, and James Donaldson, eds. *The Ante-Nicene Fathers: Translations of the Writings of the Fathers Down to A.D. 325*, vol. 5. Buffalo, NY: Christian Literature Company, 1886, 430–36.

AFTERMATH

Unfortunately it is not known whether the virgins in Carthage accepted the advice of Cyprian. If he wrote this right after becoming bishop, then any order in the church would have been disrupted by the Decian persecution, and then following it the Valerian persecution, during which Cyprian lost his life. However, the idea of women joining the church and remaining virgins for Christ became a very popular way for women to live their lives, especially in the fourth century. By the end of that century we have many writings about some famous virgins (such as Macrina, Melania the Younger, and Olympias). It is not completely clear why some women renounced sex and marriage and joined the church as virgins. It is possible that some wanted to escape the hold that men would have had on them if they had gotten married. As Castelli points out (68–69), John Chrysostom (bishop of Constantinople from 398 to 407 CE) also wrote a book called *On Virginity*, in which he discusses the problems that come with being married and the way virgins avoid these by not marrying. Virgins also had a special position in the church, which married women did not hold. It is not clear also what made virginity was so popular starting in the 300s. After Constantine, when it was legal to practice Christianity, martyrdoms had stopped, and some think that virginity, as an example of perfection, rose to replace martyrdom.

ASK YOURSELF

1. Cyprian, in chapter 3, states that the glory of virgins "excites the greater interest." What do you think he means by that? Why are virgins special? Why does he write a whole treatise on this topic?
2. Cyprian states that he does not have the right to censure women for their behavior. Do you agree with this statement? Do you think he is writing this out of "affection"?
3. How would Christian women in the third century react to this? What could this letter tell you about the status of these virgins in the Christian community? Do you think that the position of a Christian virgin was something that many women would have wanted?
4. In chapter 12 Cyprian seems to move beyond discussing virgins into discussing the dress and appearance of women in general. He states that jewelry, fancy clothes, and makeup are only for "prostitutes and immodest women." How do you feel about that statement if you are female? How do you feel about that statement if you are a male?
5. Cyprian uses Revelation 17:1–4 to show another example of a bad woman. Cyprian left out the last bit of verse 4. Read this verse and think about why he didn't include it. Does it change the meaning from what he is trying to convey?

TOPICS TO CONSIDER

- ❧ Cyprian uses Psalms 53:5 and Galatians 1:10 to prove that virgins should not wear makeup or jewelry. Consider how Cyprian makes use of these particular verses to demonstrate his point. Also, consider why Cyprian made use of the Old Testament so much in this book.
- ❧ Consider the topic of virginity today, both in Christianity as well as in public opinion. Is virginity something that is honored? If not, discuss how it is viewed today and compare it to how it was viewed by Cyprian.

- ❧ Read the entire *On the Dress of Virgins* (see website below). Copy out the biblical verses that Cyprian uses to encourage virgins to look plain. Consider any pattern you might see in these verses. Select a few of them and consider how other Christians, both before and after the time of Cyprian, were using the exact same passages. Are they being used in a similar way? If not, why not?

- ❧ As stated, Cyprian was inspired to write this book after reading Tertullian's *On the Dress of Women*. Read Tertullian's work (see website below), and consider how Cyprian used Tertullian. Remember to look at the uses of the Old and New Testaments, as well as the arguments that they use.

- ❧ Cyprian's text (and Tertullian's) was obviously written by a man. Consider how the history of virgins for Christ would have been composed if it had been written by a woman. Rewrite this text from the viewpoint of a woman. Consider too the role of Cyprian and Tertullian in their community and how this affected their views.

VIRGINS IN ANTIQUITY

Virgins were important to Roman society, especially the Vestal Virgins. These were women who maintained the sacred fire of Vesta, the goddess of the hearth, in her temple in the Roman Forum. It was an important and powerful role in Roman culture and lasted up through the time of Emperor Theodosius, when he outlawed paganism around 391 CE. The girls who would be the Vestal Virgins were chosen between the ages of 6 and 10, and once they joined, it was required that they remain as Vestal Virgins for 30 years. After this period they were allowed to leave, and, if they wanted, they could marry. There were serious punishments if these women broke their vow of chastity. The penalty was almost always death, or if they allowed the sacred flame to extinguish, they would be whipped. In Greek society, some of the more famous virgins were the Pythia at the Delphic Oracle. These priestesses were the ones responsible for speaking for Apollo when questions were brought to the caves at Delphi. Virginity also played an important role in the divine. Mary, the Mother of Jesus, is seen as a virgin. In Greek religion, Athena and Artemis were virgin goddesses.

Further Information

Chrysostom, John. *On Virginity.* In *John Chrysostom: "On Virginity," "Against Marriage,"* edited by Elizabeth Clark, translated by Sally Rieger Shore. Lewiston, NY: Edwin Mellon Press, 1989.

Cyprian. *On the Dress of Virgins.* http://www.ccel.org/ccel/schaff/anf05.iv.v.ii.html

Deming, Will. *Paul on Marriage and Celibacy: The Hellenistic Background of 1 Corinthians 7.* 2nd ed. Grand Rapids, MI: Eerdmans, 2004.

Kraemer, Ross S. "The Conversion of Women to Ascetic Forms of Christianity." *Signs* 6, no. 2, Studies in Change (Winter, 1980): 298–307.

Launderville, Dale. *Celibacy in the Ancient World: Its Ideal and Practice in Pre-Hellenistic Israel, Mesopotamia, and Greece.* Collegeville, MN: Liturgical Press, 2010.

McNamara, Jo Ann. "Sexual Equality and the Cult of Virginity in Early Christian Thought." *Feminist Studies* 3, no. 3/4 (Spring–Summer, 1976): 145–58.

Methuen, Charlotte. "The "Virgin Widow": A Problematic Social Role for the Early Church?" *Harvard Theological Review* 90, no. 3 (Jul., 1997): 285–98.

Tertullian. *On the Dress of Women.* http://www.ccel.org/ccel/schaff/anf04.html.

24. WOMEN PROPHETS

INTRODUCTION

There were many Christian groups throughout the history of early Christianity. One group that started in what is now Turkey was the Montanists (middle of the second century). The leader of the group was Montanus, who was a prophet. As we have seen, the early church had three types of leaders: the prophet, the teacher, and the apostle. The interesting thing about the Montanists is that they had women who were also prophets; the two most famous are Priscilla and Maximilla. These two women were targets for many writers who disagreed with Montanism because they were prophets. When a prophet prophesied, they would usually go into a trance and speak the words of God. The Montanists did the same, and they usually spoke in tongues (which was fairly common in other Christian groups as well). Their belief was that the prophets of Montanism were directly channeling the voice of God or the Holy Spirit while doing this. Maximilla called herself the "Word, the Spirit and the Power" (Epiphanius, *Panarion,* as noted in Klawiter 252). Priscilla had a dream where Christ came to her as a woman and made revelations to her (Klawiter 253).

Another feature in Montanism was the high regard it had for martyrs. Christian martyrs were common, and it appears that the Montanists had large numbers of people killed for their beliefs. Usually, martyrdom strengthens the faith of those left behind, and this was also true for the Montanists. Some, like Butler and Klawiter, believe that the famous *Passion of Perpetua and Felicitas* was written by someone belonging to the New Prophecy (257). The texts below are Hippolytus, *Refutation against Heresies,* and Eusebius of Caesarea, *Church History.*

KEEP IN MIND WHILE YOU READ

1. While they are generally called Montanists or Phrygians, the people who practiced this form of Christianity called themselves *pneumatikoi,* or those filled with the spirit (*pneumos* is a Greek word for spirit). They called their religion the New Prophecy.
2. Some scholars think that Tertullian, the bishop of Carthage, North Africa, converted to a form of Montanism toward the end of his life. Augustine, who was active in the late 300s and early 400s, believed Tertullian to be a heretic.

3. Hippolytus was the bishop of Rome sometime in the early 200s, and at the same time there was another bishop. This obviously caused problems, and in 235 he was sent into exile and died one year later, in 236. *The Refutation against Heresies* was his most important book.
4. Eusebius also discusses the Montanists in his *Church History* 5.16–19.

Hippolytus, Refutation against Heresies *8.12*

Noetians A Christian group who believed in God, Jesus, and the Holy Spirit but believed they did not all exist at the same time. Thus, when Jesus was born, there was no God or Holy Spirit. This meant they believed that God was actually crucified on the cross.

Phrygians People who are named after the place they originated, in central Turkey.

But there are others who themselves are even more heretical in nature (than the foregoing), and are **Phrygians** by birth. These have been rendered victims of error from being previously captivated by (two) wretched women, called a certain Priscilla and Maximilla, whom they supposed prophetesses. And they assert that into these the Paraclete Spirit had departed; and antecedently to them, they in like manner consider Montanus as a prophet. And being in possession of an infinite number of their books, (the Phrygians) are overrun with delusion; and they do not judge whatever statements are made by them, according to (the criterion of) reason; nor do they give heed unto those who are competent to decide; but they are heedlessly swept onwards, by the reliance which they place on these people. And they allege that they have learned something more through these, than from law, and prophets, and the Gospels. But they magnify these wretched women above the Apostles and every gift of Grace, so that some of them presume to assert that there is in them a something superior to Christ. These acknowledge God to be the Father of the universe, and Creator of all things, similarly with the Church, and (receive) as many things as the Gospel testifies concerning Christ. They introduce, however, the novelties of fasts, and feasts, and meals of parched food, and meals of radishes, alleging that they have been instructed by women. And some of these assent to the heresy of the **Noetians,** and affirm that the Father himself is the Son, and that this (one) came under generation, and suffering, and death. Concerning these I shall again offer an explanation, after a more minute manner; for the heresy of these has been an occasion of evils to many. We therefore are of opinion, that the statements made concerning these (heretics) are sufficient, when we shall have briefly proved to all that the majority of their books are silly, and their attempts (at reasoning) weak, and worthy of no consideration. But it is not necessary for those who possess a sound mind to pay attention (either to their volumes or their arguments).

Source: Roberts, Rev. Alexander, and James Donaldson, eds. *The Ante-Nicene Fathers: Translations of the Writings of the Fathers Down to A.D. 325,* vol. 5. Buffalo, NY: Christian Literature Company, 1886, 123–24.

Eusebius, Church History *5.16.1–22*

Against the so-called Phrygian heresy, the power which always contends for the truth raised up a strong and invincible weapon, Apolinarius of Hierapolis, whom we have mentioned before, and with him many other men of ability, by whom abundant material for our history has been left. A certain one of these, in the beginning of his work against them, first intimates that he had contended with them in oral controversies. He commences his work in this manner: "Having for a very long and sufficient time, beloved Avircius Marcellus, been urged by you to write a treatise against the heresy of those who are called after Miltiades, I have hesitated until the present time, not through lack of ability to refute the falsehood or bear testimony for the truth, but from fear and apprehension that I might seem to some to be making additions to the doctrines or precepts of the Gospel of the New Testament, which it is impossible for one who has chosen to live according to the Gospel, either to increase or to diminish. But being recently in Ancyra in Galatia, I found the church there greatly agitated by this novelty, not prophecy, as they call it, but rather false prophecy, as will be shown. Therefore, to the best of our ability, with the Lord's help, we disputed in the church many days concerning these and other matters separately brought forward by them, so that the church rejoiced and was strengthened in the truth, and those of the opposite side were for the time confounded, and the adversaries were grieved. The presbyters in the place, our fellow-presbyter Zoticus of Otrous also being present, requested us to leave a record of what had been said against the opposers of the truth. We did not do this, but we promised to write it out as soon as the Lord permitted us, and to send it to them speedily."

Having said this with other things, in the beginning of his work, he proceeds to state the cause of the above-mentioned heresy as follows: "Their opposition and their recent heresy which has separated them from the Church arose on the following account. There is said to be a certain village called Ardabau in that part of Mysia, which borders upon Phrygia. There first, they say, when Gratus was **proconsul** of Asia, a recent convert, Montanus by name, through his unquenchable desire for leadership, gave **the adversary** opportunity against him. And he became beside himself, and being suddenly in a sort of frenzy and ecstasy, he raved, and began to babble and utter strange things, prophesying in a manner contrary to the constant custom of the Church handed down by tradition from the beginning. Some of those who heard his spurious utterances at that time were indignant, and they rebuked him as one that was possessed, and that was under the control of a demon, and was led by a deceitful spirit, and was distracting the multitude; and they forbade him to talk, remembering the distinction drawn by the Lord and his warning to guard watchfully against the coming of false prophets (Matthew 7:15). But others imagining themselves possessed of the Holy Spirit and of a prophetic gift, were elated and not a little puffed up; and forgetting the distinction of the Lord, they challenged the mad and insidious and seducing spirit, and were cheated and deceived by him. In consequence of this, he could no longer be held in check, so as to keep silence. Thus by artifice, or rather by such a system of wicked craft, the devil, devising destruction for the disobedient, and being unworthily honored by them, secretly excited and inflamed their understandings which had already become estranged from the true faith. And he also stirred up two women, and filled them with the false spirit, so that they talked wildly and unreasonably and strangely, like the person already mentioned. And the spirit pronounced them blessed as they rejoiced and gloried in him, and puffed them up by the magnitude of his promises. But sometimes he rebuked them openly in a wise and faithful manner, that he might seem to be a reprover. But those of the Phrygians that were deceived were few in number. "And the arrogant spirit taught them to revile the entire universal Church under heaven, because the spirit of false

> **the adversary** The devil.
> **proconsul** A governor of a Roman province.

prophecy received neither honor from it nor entrance into it. For the faithful in Asia met often in many places throughout Asia to consider this matter, and examined the novel utterances and pronounced them profane, and rejected the heresy, and thus these persons were expelled from the Church and debarred from communion."

Having related these things at the outset, and continued the refutation of their delusion through his entire work, in the second book he speaks as follows of their end: "Since, therefore, they called us slayers of the prophets because we did not receive their loquacious prophets, who, they say, are those that the Lord promised to send to the people (Matthew 23:34), let them answer as in God's presence: Who is there, friends, of these who began to talk, from Montanus and the women down, that was persecuted by the Jews, or slain by lawless men? None. Or has any of them been seized and crucified for the Name? Truly not. Or has one of these women ever been scourged in the synagogues of the Jews, or stoned? No; never anywhere. But by another kind of death Montanus and Maximilla are said to have died. For the report is that, incited by the spirit of frenzy, they both hung themselves; not at the same time, but at the time which common report gives for the death of each. And thus they died, and ended their lives like **the traitor Judas**. So also, as general report says, that remarkable person, the first steward, as it were, of their so-called prophecy, one Theodotus—who, as if at sometime taken up and received into heaven, fell into trances, and entrusted himself to the deceitful spirit—was pitched like a ring, and died miserably. They say that these things happened in this manner. But as we did not see them, O friend, we do not pretend to know. Perhaps in such a manner, perhaps not, Montanus and Theodotus and the above-mentioned woman died." He says again in the same book that the holy bishops of that time attempted to refute the spirit in Maximilla, but were prevented by others who plainly co-operated with the spirit. He writes as follows: "And let not the spirit, in the same work of Asterius Urbanus, say through Maximilla, 'I am driven away from the sheep like a wolf. I am not a wolf. I am word and spirit and power.' But let him show clearly and prove the power in the spirit. And by the spirit let him compel those to confess him who were then present for the purpose of proving and reasoning with the talkative spirit,—those eminent men and bishops, Zoticus, from the village Comana, and Julian, from Apamea, whose mouths the followers of Themiso muzzled, refusing to permit the false and seductive spirit to be refuted by them." Again in the same work, after saying other things in refutation of the false prophecies of Maximilla, he indicates the time when he wrote these accounts, and mentions her predictions in which she prophesied wars and anarchy. Their falsehood he censures in the following manner: "And has not this been shown clearly to be false? For it is to-day more than thirteen years since the woman died, and there has been neither a partial nor general war in the world; but rather, through the mercy of God, continued peace even to the Christians." These things are taken from the second book. I will add also short extracts from the third book, in which he speaks thus against their boasts that many of them had suffered martyrdom: "When therefore they are at a loss, being refuted in all that they say, they try to take refuge in their martyrs, alleging that they have many martyrs, and that this is sure evidence of the power of the so-called prophetic spirit that is with them. But this, as it appears, is entirely fallacious. For some of the heresies have a great many martyrs; but surely we shall not on that account agree with them or confess that they hold the truth. And first, indeed, those called Marcionites, from the heresy of Marcion, say that they have

> **the traitor Judas** Judas was one of the Twelve Disciples. He betrayed Jesus, and according to Matthew 27:5, he repented of what he had done and then hanged himself.

a multitude of martyrs for Christ; yet they do not confess Christ himself in truth." A little farther on he continues: "When those called to martyrdom from the Church for the truth of the faith have met with any of the so-called martyrs of the Phrygian heresy, they have separated from them, and died without any fellowship with them, because they did not wish to give their assent to the spirit of Montanus and the women. And that this is true and took place in our own time in **Apamea on the Mæander,** among those who suffered martyrdom with Gaius and Alexander of **Eumenia,** is well known."

> **Apamea on the Mæander** A city in Phrygia.
> **Eumenia** A town north of Apamea.

Source: Wace, Henry, and Philip Schaff, eds. *A Select Library of Nicene and Post-Nicene Fathers of the Christian Church,* vol. 1. Oxford: Parker, 1890, 229–33.

AFTERMATH

Soon after Montanist Christianity spread throughout Turkey, church councils were held to denounce it. The biggest criticism was the use of prophecy. Some Christians did not believe that Montanus, and especially Maximilla and Priscilla, spoke with the voice of God or the Holy Spirit and therefore were heretics. By 177 CE, news of the new form of Christianity reached Rome, and the bishop of Rome excommunicated the whole group. Despite this, Tertullian possibly joined them in the first decade of the 200s. If he did not join this group, he certainly defended some of its positions. Unfortunately, it isn't known how long the New Prophecy managed to attract new members. Augustine, another North African bishop, wrote in his *On Heresies* (chapter 86) that there existed a group of Tertullianists that could possibly be the remnants of the Montanists. Augustine states that the group had given up their basilica to the Catholics. It is possible that the Montanists lasted up through the 500s CE.

ASK YOURSELF

1. What is the main grievance that Hippolytus had with the Montanists? Do you think this is a legitimate cause for concern? Is his complaint the same as that of other people who wrote against them?
2. Eusebius leaves out some material from his primary source. Why do you think he did this? Can you guess what this material might have said?
3. Apolinarius of Hierapolis states that both Montanus and Maximilla both hanged themselves. He compares this to the suicide of Judas. Why do you think this was an important point to make? Do you think that this is really what happened to them? If not, why would the anonymous author make this claim?
4. Why do you think that having martyrs was an important point for the Montanists? What did the martyrs do that increased their power?

TOPICS TO CONSIDER

- ↝ Prophecy was extremely important to the Montanists. For many other Christian groups, prophecy was also still important, but the role of prophets was steadily being reduced. The great prophets for early Christians were those from the Old Testament. Consider the role of prophecy in the non-Montanist groups and discuss why many Christians thought that Montanist prophecy was controlled by the devil.

- ❧ The role of prophecy is downplayed or rejected in many modern Christian groups. Consider how some of these groups would react to a prophet today, especially one that claimed to speak the word of God.
- ❧ Female prophets were extremely rare in early Christianity. Consider how the gender of the prophet would have affected the reception of the message. Also consider how male dominance of Christianity affected women and their role in the church. Is Christianity still a male-dominated religion?

Further Information

Butler, Rex D. *The New Prophecy and "New Visions": Evidence of Montanism in the Passion of Perpetua and Felicitas*. Washington, DC: Catholic University of America Press, 2006.

Denzey, Nicola. "What Did the Montanists Read?" *Harvard Theological Review* 94, no. 4 (Oct., 2001): 427–48.

Klawiter, Frederick C. "The Role of Martyrdom and Persecution in Developing the Priestly Authority of Women in Early Christianity: A Case Study of Montanism." *Church History* 49, no. 3 (Sep., 1980): 251–61.

Tabbernee, William. *Fake Prophecy and Polluted Sacraments*. Leiden, the Netherlands: Brill, 2007.

Trevett, Christine. *Montanism: Gender, Authority and the New Prophecy*. Cambridge: Cambridge University Press, 1996.

Wypustek, Andrzej. "Magic, Montanism, Perpetua, and the Severan Persecution." *Vigiliae Christianae* 51, no. 3 (Aug., 1997): 276–97.

25. RULES FOR WIDOWS

INTRODUCTION

Roman law made it mandatory for people to marry, and in the case of widows, according to the *Lex Julia* (Ulpian Fragment, section 14), or the Julian law, they could remain unmarried for one year if they were under the age of 50. This was later changed to two years. These laws were designed primarily with inheritance in mind. There are some similarities found in biblical texts. The author of 1 Timothy states that young widows should remarry. The biblical texts also mention the duty of caring for widows along with that of caring for strangers and orphans (Exodus 22:21–22; Deuteronomy 10:18–19; Jeremiah 7:6; James 1:27 [although here the author is only concerned with widows and orphans], and 1 Timothy 5:3–16). The text of 1 Timothy gives guidelines for the community to decide who is actually a widow who should be helped. Helping widows was also a common duty mentioned by later writers, especially in the *Shepherd of Hermas* (see 8:3; 38:10; 58:10, among others). As important members in the early church, widows went from being taken care of to caring for others and having important roles to fill. As shown in the *Didascalia Apostolorum* (below), widows are very active in their communities, so much so that the *Didascalia* sets rules for them. It may be that they were usurping the bishop's role in some cases. The texts below are 1 Timothy 5:3–16 and sections of chapter 15 from the *Didascalia*.

KEEP IN MIND WHILE YOU READ

1. Some scholars believe that 1 Timothy was written not by Paul but by one of his disciples, possibly two to three generations after Paul. This is because of the changes in vocabulary found in some of Paul's letters. However, not all believe this. They believe that Paul could have easily used different vocabulary because the situation was different.

2. The *Didascalia* dates from the early 200s CE. According to chapter 24, however, the following were the reasons for its writing: "When therefore the whole Church was in peril of falling into heresy, we, all the twelve Apostles came together to Jerusalem and took thought what should be done. And *it seemed good to us, being all of one accord* (Acts 15.25), to write this Catholic *Didascalia* for the confirming of you all.

And we have established and set down therein that you worship God Almighty and Jesus Christ and the Holy Spirit; that you employ the holy Scriptures, and believe in the resurrection of the dead; and that you make use of all His creatures with thanksgiving (cf. 1 Tim 4.3); and that men should marry . . ."

3. The full title of the *Didascalia* is given in a Syriac manuscript. It reads: "Catholic Teaching of the Twelve Apostles and Holy Disciples of our Savior." The word *catholic* means "universal."

1 Timothy 5:3–16

Do not speak harshly to an older man, but speak to him as to a father, to younger men as brothers, to older women as mothers, to younger women as sisters—with absolute purity. Honor widows who are really widows. If a widow has children or grandchildren, they should first learn their religious duty to their own family and make some repayment to their parents; for this is pleasing in God's sight. The real widow, left alone, has set her hope on God and continues in **supplications** and prayers night and day; but the widow who lives for pleasure is dead even while she lives. Give these commands as well, so that they may be above reproach. And whoever does not provide for relatives, and especially for family members, has denied the faith and is worse than an unbeliever.

> **supplications** Prayers or petitions.

Let a widow be put on the list if she is not less than sixty years old and has been married only once; she must be well attested for her good works, as one who has brought up children, shown hospitality, washed the saints' feet, helped the afflicted, and devoted herself to doing good in every way. But refuse to put younger widows on the list; for when their sensual desires alienate them from Christ, they want to marry, and so they incur condemnation for having violated their first pledge. Besides that, they learn to be idle, gadding about from house to house; and they are not merely idle, but also gossips and busybodies, saying what they should not say. So I would have younger widows marry, bear children, and manage their households, so as to give the adversary no occasion to revile us. For some have already turned away to follow Satan. If any believing woman has relatives who are really widows, let her assist them; let the church not be burdened, so that it can assist those who are real widows.

Source: Society of Biblical Literature, eds. *Harper Collins Study Bible: New Revised Standard Version.* Rev. ed. New York: HarperCollins, 2006. All Scripture quotations appear from the *New Revised Standard Version Bible.* Division of Christian Education of the National Council of Churches of Christ in the United States of America, 1989.

Didascalia *15, selections*

Every widow therefore ought to be meek and quiet and gentle. And let her also be without malice and without anger; and let her not be talkative or clamorous, or forward in tongue, or quarrelsome. And when she sees anything unseemly done, or hears it, let her be as though she saw and heard it not, for a widow should have no other care save to be praying for those who give, and for the whole Church. And when she is asked a question by anyone, let her not straightway give an answer, except only concerning righteousness and faith in God; but let her send them that desire to be instructed to the rulers. And to those who question them let them (the widows) make answer only in refutation of idols and concerning the unity of God. But concerning punishment and reward, and the kingdom of the name of Christ, and His dispensation, neither a widow nor a layman ought to speak; for when they speak without the knowledge of doctrine, they will bring blasphemy upon the word. For our Lord likened the word of His tidings to mustard (Matthew 13:31); but mustard, unless it be skillfully tempered, is bitter and sharp to those who use it. Wherefore our Lord said in the Gospel, to widows and to all the laity: "Do not cast your pearls before swine, lest they trample upon them and turn against you and maul you" (Matthew 7:6). For when the Gentiles who are being instructed hear the word of God not fittingly spoken, as it ought to be, unto edification of eternal life—and all the more in that it is spoken to them by a woman—how that our Lord clothed Himself in a body, and concerning the passion of Christ: they will mock and scoff, instead of applauding the word of doctrine; and she shall incur a heavy judgment for sin.

It is neither right nor necessary therefore that women should be teachers, and especially concerning the name of Christ and the redemption of His passion. For you have not been appointed to this, O women, and especially widows, that you should teach, but that you should pray and entreat the Lord God. For he the Lord God, Jesus Christ our Teacher, sent us the Twelve to instruct the People and the Gentiles; and there were with us women disciples, Mary Magdalene and Mary the daughter of James and the other Mary; but He did not send them to instruct the people with us. For if it were required that women should teach, our Master Himself would have commanded these to give instruction with us. But let a widow know that she is the altar of God; and let her sit ever at home, and not stray or run about among the houses of the faithful to receive. For the altar of God never strays or runs about anywhere, but is fixed in one place.

A widow must not therefore stray or run about among the houses. For those who are **gadabouts** and without shame cannot be still even in their houses, for they are no widows, but wallets, and they care for nothing else but to be making ready to receive. And because they are gossips and chatterers and murmurers, they stir up quarrels; and they are bold and shameless. Now they that are such are unworthy of Him who called them; for neither in the common assembly of rest of the Sunday, when they have come, are such women or men watchful, but they either fall asleep or prate about some other matter: so that through them others also are taken captive by the enemy Satan, who suffers not such persons to be watchful unto the Lord. And they who are such, coming in empty to the Church, go out more empty still, since they hearken not to that which is spoken or read to receive it with the ears of their hearts. Such persons, then, are like those of whom Isaiah said: "Hearing, you shall hear and shall not understand; and seeing, you shall see, and shall not see. For the heart of this people is dull, and with their ears, they hear heavily, and their eyes they have shut: lest at any time they should see with their eyes, and hear with their ears" (Isaiah 6.9–10). So in like manner the ears of such widows' hearts are stopped, because they will not sit beneath the roof of their houses and pray and entreat the Lord, but are impatient to be running after gain; and by their chattering they execute the desires of the Enemy. Now such a widow does not conform to the altar of Christ; for it is written in the Gospel: "If two shall agree together, and shall ask concerning anything at all, it shall be given them

> **gadabouts** People who move around either aimlessly or move around for pleasure.

(Matthew 18.19). And if they shall say to a mountain that it be removed and fall into the sea, it shall so be done.

Now we see that there are widows who esteem the matter as one of traffic, and receive greedily; and instead of doing good (works) and giving to the bishop for the entertainment of strangers and the refreshment of those in distress, they lend out on bitter usury; and they care only for Mammon, whose god is their purse and their belly: "for where their treasure is, there is also their heart" (Matthew 6:21). For she who is in the habit of roaming abroad and running about to receive takes no thought for good works, but serves **Mammon** and ministers to filthy **lucre**. And she cannot please God, nor is she obedient to His ministry, so as to be constantly praying and making intercession, because her mind is quite taken captive by the greed of avarice. And when she stands up to pray, she remembers where she may go to receive somewhat; or else that she has forgotten to tell some matter to her friends. And when she stands (in prayer), her mind is not upon her prayer, but upon that thought which has occurred to her mind. Now the prayer of such a one is not heard in regard to anything. But she soon interrupts her prayer by reason of the distraction of her mind; for she does not offer prayer to God with all her heart, but goes off with the thought suggested by the Enemy, and talks with her friends about some unprofitable matter. For she knows not how she has believed, or of what order she has been accounted worthy.

lucre Money.
Mammon Wealth, usually used negatively.

But a widow who wishes to please God sits at home and meditates upon the Lord day and night, and without ceasing at all times offers intercession and prays with purity before the Lord (1 Timothy 5:5). And she receives whatever she asks, because her whole mind is set upon this. For her mind is not greedy to receive, nor has she much desire to make large expenses; nor does her eye wander, that she should see aught and desire it, and her mind be withdrawn; nor does she hear evil words to give heed to them, because she does not go forth and run about abroad. Therefore her prayer suffers no hindrance from anything; and thus her quietness and tranquility and modesty are acceptable before God, and whatever she asks of God, she presently receives her request. For such a widow, not loving money or filthy lucre, and not avaricious nor greedy, but constant in prayer, and meek and unperturbed, and modest and reverent, sits at home and works at (her) wool, that she may provide somewhat for those who are in distress, or that she may make a return to others, so that she receive nothing from them. For she thinks of that widow of whom our Lord gave testimony in the Gospel, who came and cast into the treasury two mites, which is one dinar: whom when our Lord and Teacher, the trier of hearts, saw, He said to us: "O my disciples, this poor widow cast in more alms than anyone; for everyone cast in of that which was superfluous to him: but this, of all that she possessed she laid her up treasure" (Mark 12.42–4).

Widows ought then to be modest, and obedient to the bishops and the deacons, and to reverence and respect and fear the bishop as God. And let them not act after their own will, nor desire to do anything apart from that which is commanded them, or without counsel to speak with any one by way of making answer, or to go to anyone to eat or drink, or to fast with anyone, or to receive nothing of anyone, or to lay hand on and pray over anyone without the command of the bishop or the deacon. But if she does what that is not commanded her, let her be rebuked for having acted without discipline. For where do you know, O woman, from whom do you receive, or from what ministry are you nourished, or for whom you fast, or upon whom you lay your hand? For you do not know that concerning every one of these you will render an account to the Lord in the day of judgment, seeing that you do their works? But you, O widow who are without discipline, see your fellow widows or your brethren in sickness, and have no care to fast and pray over your members, and to lay hand upon them and to visit them, but pretend to be not in health, or not at leisure; but to others, who are in sins or are gone forth from the Church, because they give much, you are ready and glad to go and to visit them. You then who are such should be ashamed; for you wish to be wiser and to know better, not only than the men, but even than the presbyters and the bishops. Know then, sisters, that whatever the pastors with the deacons command you, and you obey them, you obey God; and with whomsoever you communicate by the command of the bishop, you are without blame before God; and so is every brother of the laity who obeys the bishop and submits to him: for they (the bishops) are to render an account for all. But if you obey not the mind of the bishops and deacons, they indeed will be quit of your offences, but you shall render an account of all that you do of your own will, whether men or women . . .

That a woman should baptize, or that one should be baptized by a woman, we do not counsel, for it is a transgression of the commandment, and a great peril to her who baptizes and to him who is baptized. For if it were lawful to be baptized by a woman, our Lord and Teacher Himself would have been baptized by Mary His mother, whereas He was baptized by John, like others of the people. Do not therefore imperil yourselves, brethren and sisters, by acting beside the law of the Gospel . . . Do you therefore admonish and rebuke those (widows) who are undisciplined and likewise exhort and encourage and help forward those who conduct themselves rightly. And let widows keep themselves from cursing, for they have been appointed to bless. Wherefore, do not let the bishop, nor a presbyter, nor a deacon, nor a widow utter a curse out of their mouth, "that they may not inherit a curse but a blessing" (1 Peter 3:9). And let this also be your care, O bishop, that not even one of the laity utter from his mouth a curse: for you have the care of all.

Source: *Didascalia Apostolorum*. Introduction by Richard Hugh Connolly. Oxford: Clarendon Press, 1929, 138–45. Used by permission of Wipf and Stock Publishers. www. wipfandstock.com.

AFTERMATH

Christian groups continued to care for widows for many centuries. Eusebius of Caesarea, in his *Ecclesiastical History* (6.43.11), states that there were 1,500 widows and poor people in the care of the church in Rome. This is quite a large number, and if it is any indication of other churches, there were many widows who needed support. The author of 1 Timothy had given rules on who could be considered for aid, and it may have been an attempt to limit the financial burden this might have caused the churches.

The topic of widowhood was very popular among the late fourth-century Christian writers. Ambrose, bishop of Milan (374–397), wrote a treatise titled *Concerning Widows* sometime around 377 CE, soon after writing his *Concerning Virgins*. In it, Ambrose tries to convince a widow that she shouldn't remarry. He uses many examples from both the Old and the New Testaments. Chrysostom, a bishop of Constantinople from 398 to 404, wrote *A Letter to a Young Widow*. Chrysostom tells this woman that it is an honor to be a widow, despite all the pain she has gone through with losing her spouse. While most of the letter is a touching message about her grief, the message is that Chrysostom encourages her not to remarry.

The fourth century also contains accounts of wealthy widows who traveled to various holy places and donated their money to various Christian causes. A woman named Macrina traveled from Rome to the deserts of Egypt to see the famous monk Anthony. Jerome, a priest living in Bethlehem, also benefited greatly from the rich widow Paula and her virgin daughter Eustochion. These women help set up two monasteries; Paula and Eustochion ran the women's monastery while Jerome ran the male monastery.

ASK YOURSELF

1. Why do you think the author of 1 Timothy puts so much stress on taking care of "real" widows who are over a certain age? What is the problem with widows who are younger? Also, Paul states that people should not remarry if they cannot control themselves. Why does the author of 1 Timothy differ?

2. The author of 1 Timothy states that some women "have already turned away to follow Satan." What do you think he means by this? What would make the women leave the Christian community described by 1 Timothy?

3. Read the entirety of chapter 15 of the *Didascalia* (see web link below). The sections that were not included in this book were sometimes areas in which the author had repeated himself. Examine these sections along with the sections that were given above. Why would the author repeat material?

4. From reading both passages, what exactly are the complaints being made against the widows? Do you think these are legitimate complaints?

5. All of the widows described in these passages are female. Why do you think the passages do not mention widowers? Do you think they would also need special care or protection as given by the church?

6. What are the roles of widows, at least according to these passages? Do you think they liked the roles that were placed on them, and would they have been satisfied? If you were one of these widows, how would you react?

TOPICS TO CONSIDER

- Although the early Christians were many times Roman citizens, they followed their own rules within their own communities. Consider the differences between Roman law and Jewish/Christian belief on the roles of widows in society. Why did the Christians treat their widows differently?

- Examine the state of widowhood in modern Christianity. Consider how widows are officially treated now and how they were officially treated in antiquity. Also consider how the ancient view has affected the modern view.

- Consider how widows in Judaism and early Christianity first became seen as a group that needed some type of special care or protection.

- Rewrite 1 Timothy from the viewpoint of a woman. Consider how a female author would have treated widows any differently.

- The *Didascalia* discussed many aspects of the early Christian community. Consider why a whole section of the *Didascalia* was dedicated just to widows and their roles and restrictions in Christian society.

Further Information

Ambrose. *The Treatise Concerning Widows.* http://www.ccel.org/ccel/schaff/npnf210.iv.viii.ii.html.

Bassler, Jouette M. "The Widows' Tale: A Fresh Look at 1 Tim 5:3–16." *Journal of Biblical Literature* 103, no. 1 (Mar., 1984): 23–41.

Calder, W. M. "Early-Christian Epitaphs from Phrygia." *Anatolian Studies* 5 (1955): 25–38.

Chrysostom, John. *Letter to a Young Widow.* http://www.ccel.org/ccel/schaff/npnf109.vi.iii.html.

Didascalia Apostolorum. http://www.bombaxo.com/didascalia.html.

Methuen, Charlotte. "The 'Virgin Widow': A Problematic Social Role for the Early Church?" *Harvard Theological Review* 90, no. 3 (Jul., 1997): 285–98.

Methuen, Charlotte. "Widows, Bishops and the Struggle for Authority in the Didascalia Apostolorum," *Journal of Ecclesiastical History* 46 (1995): 197–213.

Thurston, Bonnie Bowman. *The Widows: A Women's Ministry in the Early Church.* Minneapolis, MN: Fortress, 1989.

Yarbrough, Anne. "Christianization in the Fourth Century: The Example of Roman Women." *Church History* 45, no. 2 (Jun., 1976): 149–65.

CONFLICTS OF THE EARLY CHURCH

26. EPISTLE OF BARNABAS

INTRODUCTION

Christianity is an offshoot of Judaism. Nearly all of the early followers were Jews. When the followers of Christ began to break away from their fellow Jews, they did not want to leave the Old Testament behind. Barnabas was an early Christian who traveled with Paul and attempted to convert both Jews and Gentiles to Christianity. In the beginning, Barnabas was the leader, but as Paul became more confident in his ability to teach, Paul took over. Barnabas was also known for his disagreement with Paul over eating with the Gentile converts (that is, those who were not Jewish). It isn't clear who wrote this *Epistle of Barnabas*. The date normally assigned to this letter ranges from 70 to 135 CE. Tradition states that it was this Barnabas, the very friend of Paul. However, many scholars believe this to be unlikely. Regardless of the authorship, the importance of this letter cannot be overstated. It contains much information about early Christians. More important, the letter shows that the Old Testament is full of prophecies of Christ. If indeed Christianity was the fulfillment of the promises of the Old Testament, early Christians needed to retain ownership of these writings. One way of doing this was to show that Christ had been foretold in the Old Testament. The *Epistle of Barnabas* is an excellent example of this trend in some early Christian writings. The following excerpt is primarily about the cross of Christ. As will be seen, the author recounts various places in the Old Testament which seem to indicate the presence of Christian baptism and the cross of Jesus.

KEEP IN MIND WHILE YOU READ

1. Outside of the biblical texts, there are many instances of letters being written and then ascribed to people found in both the Old and New Testaments. This also occurs within the Bible, especially with a number of letters that are usually ascribed to Paul but are now believed to have been written by his disciples.
2. Barnabas (or whoever the author is) uses many examples of finding Christ in the Old Testament. This was one method of coopting the Old Testament and made it very relevant to early Christians.

3. There are a few places where Barnabas is mentioned in the New Testament (Acts 9:27; 11:22–26; 15:26–40; Galatians 2:13; and [among others] 1 Corinthians 9:6). He was probably more important in the beginning, with Paul being his companion in their missionary journeys. Later, Paul overshadows him.
4. It is traditionally believed that the *Epistle of Barnabas* was written in Egypt, primarily because another early Christian, Clement of Alexandria, makes the first mention of this text.

Epistle of Barnabas 11–12

Chapter 11

Let us further inquire whether the Lord took any care to foreshadow the water (of baptism) and the cross. Concerning the water, indeed, it is written, in reference to the Israelites, that they should not receive that baptism which leads to the remission of sins, but should procure another for themselves. The prophet therefore declares, "Be astonished, O heaven, and let the earth tremble at this, because this people has committed two great evils: they have forsaken Me, a living fountain, and have hewn out for themselves broken cisterns. Is my holy hill Zion a desolate rock? For you shall be as the fledglings of a bird, which fly away when the nest is removed" (for a similar text, see Isaiah 16:1–2). And again the prophet says, "I will go before you and make level the mountains, and will break the brazen gates, and bruise in pieces the iron bars; and I will give you the secret, hidden, invisible treasures, that they may know that I am the Lord God" (Isaiah 45:2–3). And "He shall dwell in a lofty cave of the strong rock" (Isaiah 33:16). Furthermore, what says He in reference to the Son? "His water is sure; you shall see the King in His glory, and your soul shall meditate on the fear of the Lord" (Isaiah 33:16–18). And again He says in another prophet, "The man who does these things shall be like a tree planted by the courses of waters, which shall yield its fruit in due season; and his leaf shall not fade, and all that he does shall prosper. Not so are the ungodly, not so, but even as chaff, which the wind sweeps away from the face of the earth. Therefore the ungodly shall not stand in judgment, nor sinners in the counsel of the just; for the Lord knows the way of the righteous, but the way of the ungodly shall perish" (Psalms 1:3–6). Note how He has described at once both the water and the cross. For these words imply, Blessed are they who, placing their trust in the cross, have gone down into the water; for, says He, they shall receive their reward in due time: then He declares, I will recompense them. But now He says, "Their leaves shall not fade." This means that every word which proceeds out of your mouth in faith and love shall tend to bring conversion and hope to many. Again, another prophet says, "And the land of Jacob shall be extolled above every land." (Zephaniah 3:19). This means the vessel of His Spirit, which He shall glorify. Further, what says He? "And there was a river flowing on the right, and from it arose beautiful trees; and whosoever shall eat of them shall live forever" (Ezekiel 47:12). This means, that we indeed descend into the water full of sins and defilement, but come up, bearing fruit in our heart, having the fear (of God) and trust in Jesus in our spirit. "And whosoever shall eat of these shall live forever," This means: Whosoever, He declares, shall hear you speaking, and believe, shall live forever.

Chapter 12

In like manner He points to the cross of Christ in another prophet, who says, "And when shall these things be accomplished? And the Lord says, When a tree shall be bent down, and again arise, and when blood shall flow out of wood" (source unknown). Here again you have an intimation concerning the cross, and Him who should be crucified. Yet again He speaks of this in Moses, when Israel was attacked by strangers. And that He might remind them, when assailed, that it was on account of their sins they were delivered to death, the Spirit speaks to the heart of Moses, that he should make a figure of the cross, and of Him about to suffer thereon; for unless they put their trust in Him, they shall be overcome forever. Moses therefore placed one weapon above another in the midst of the hill, and standing upon it, so as to be higher than all the people, he stretched forth his hands, and thus again Israel acquired the mastery. But when again he let down his hands, they were again destroyed. For what reason? That they might know that they could not be saved unless they put their trust in Him. And in another prophet He declares, "All day long I have stretched forth My hands to an unbelieving people, and one that gainsays My righteous way" (Isaiah 65:2). And again Moses makes a type of Jesus, (signifying) that it was necessary for Him to suffer, (and also) that He would be the author of life (to others), whom they believed to have destroyed on the cross when Israel was failing. For since transgression was committed by Eve through means of the serpent, (the Lord) brought it to pass that every (kind of) serpents bit them, and they died, that He might convince them, that on account of their transgression they were given over to the straits of death. Moreover Moses, when he commanded, "You shall not have any graven or molten (image) for your God," (Deuteronomy 27:15) did so that he might reveal a type of Jesus. Moses then makes a brazen serpent, and places it upon a beam, and by proclamation assembles the people. When, therefore, they were come together, they sought Moses so that he would offer sacrifice in their behalf, and pray for their recovery. And Moses spoke unto them, saying, "When any one of you is bitten, let him come to the serpent placed on the pole; and let him hope and believe, that even though dead, it is able to give him life, and immediately he shall be restored" (Numbers 21:9). And they did so. You have in this also (an indication of) the glory of Jesus; for in Him and to Him are all things. What, again, says Moses to Jesus (Joshua) the son of Nave, when he gave him this name, as being a prophet, with this view only, that all the people might hear that the Father would reveal all things concerning His Son Jesus to the son of Nave? This name then being given him when he sent him to spy out the land, he said, "Take a book into your hands, and write what the Lord declares, that the Son of God will in the last days cut off from the roots all the house of Amalek" (Exodus 17:14). See again: Jesus who was manifested, both by type and in the flesh, is not the Son of man, but the Son of God. Since, therefore, they were to say that Christ was the son of David, fearing and understanding the error of the wicked, he says, "The Lord said to my Lord, Sit at My right hand, until I make your enemies your footstool." (Psalms 110:1). And again, Isaiah says, "The Lord said to Christ, my Lord, whose right hand I have held, that the nations should yield obedience before Him; and I will break in pieces the strength of kings" (see Isaiah 45:1). See how David calls Him Lord and the Son of God.

Source: Roberts, Rev. Alexander, and James Donaldson, eds. *The Ante-Nicene Fathers: Translations of the Writings of the Fathers Down to A.D. 325,* vol. 1. Buffalo, NY: Christian Literature Company, 1885, 144–45.

AFTERMATH

The Old Testament was very important to the early Christians and in fact was the only scripture they had until the writings of the apostles. When the writings of Paul, the Gospels, and the rest of the writings of the apostles had become sacred, there were debates whether to include the Hebrew writings among the texts that Christians should be reading. This is especially apparent in the writings of Marcion. In reaction to Marcion (and others), early Christians had to develop new ways of keeping the Old Testament a part of Christianity. The writings of Barnabas, with his insistence that the coming of Christ was foretold, made sure that the writings of the Old Testament were kept as part of the readings by the Christians.

ASK YOURSELF

1. If Barnabas did not write this letter, why would someone write it in his name? What evidence exists that this could have been written by Paul's companion?
2. Why would Barnabas be interested in finding evidence for Jesus in the Old Testament? What benefit would that have had for him and his readers?
3. Do you find the examples given by Barnabas believable? What factors affect your belief or disbelief?
4. Some of the biblical quotes given in the text of Barnabas do not quite match the *New Revised Standard Version* translation. In some cases the text is similar but not a direct match. How can you account for these differences?

TOPICS TO CONSIDER

- Consider how the ancient Jewish population felt with the wholesale takeover of their sacred texts by the Christians. Not only did the Christians use the Old Testament, they also changed the meaning to fit their new belief. How do modern Jewish people feel about this? How do Christians today explain their usage of the Old Testament as their own religious text?
- Consider the modern Christian use of the Old Testament. Is finding Christ in the Old Testament still important?
- Read the rest of the *Epistle of Barnabas* and consider his other examples of finding Christ in the Old Testament. Consider how the author uses these verses to prove his point that Christ was foretold. How do Jewish people use these very same quotes?

Further Information

Barnard, L. W. "The Date of the *Epistle of Barnabas:* A Document of Early Egyptian Christianity." *Journal of Egyptian Archaeology* 44 (Dec., 1958): 101–7.

Barnard, L. W. "The *Epistle of Barnabas:* A Paschal Homily?" *Vigiliae Christianae* 15, no. 1 (Mar., 1961): 8–22.

Becker, Jurgen. *Paul: Apostle to the Gentiles.* Louisville, KY: John Knox Press, 1993.

Epistle of Barnabas. http://www.ccel.org/ccel/schaff/anf01.vi.ii.i.html.

Paget, James Carleton. *The* Epistle of Barnabas: *Outlook and Background.* Tübingen: J.C.B. Mohr, December 1994.

Paget, James Carleton. "Paul and the *Epistle of Barnabas.*" *Novum Testamentum* 38, Fasc. 4 (Oct., 1996): 359–81.

27. Ignatius, Anti-Judaism: Excerpts from His *Letter to the Philadelphians* and *Magnesians*

INTRODUCTION

Ignatius, bishop in the late first century in the city of Antioch, is an important witness to the growth of Christianity. His city had been important to the Christian movement since its beginning. It isn't known exactly when Ignatius became the bishop, but it is certain that he died as a martyr sometime during the reign of the Roman emperor Trajan (98–117 CE). Like Paul the Apostle, Ignatius was ordered to Rome to stand trial for being Christian, and on his forced journey, he wrote numerous letters to church authorities in Asia Minor and Rome. Ignatius covered many topics in his letters, from the authority of the bishop, to the presence of heretics, to, more important for our purposes, the continued presence of Judaism in early Christian communities. Although Christianity was an offshoot of Judaism, by the middle/end of the first century there was a concerted push by the Christians to separate themselves from the Jews, even though Jesus and all of the early disciples were Jewish. One reason for the break was that early Christians blamed the Jews for the crucifixion. The two excerpts below are from Ignatius's letters to Christians in the cities of Philadelphia and Magnesia. In both, Ignatius mentions the dangers of Judaism.

KEEP IN MIND WHILE YOU READ

1. People who believed in Christ and retained some of their Jewish roots are called Jewish Christians. There were many of these Jewish Christian groups in the first and second centuries.
2. Ignatius mentions many early groups that did not hold the same beliefs as he did. The New Testament is filled with examples of groups who did not agree with Paul or the other early disciples. Many times these disagreements were over the fundamental question of the identity of Jesus. Other disagreements were over the relationship between Judaism and Christianity. The disputes mentioned by Ignatius are very similar to the problems found in the New Testament.
3. Even though Ignatius rejects Jewish beliefs being injected into Christianity, he does not hesitate to make use of the Old Testament. Like other early Christians, he believed that the Old Testament now belonged to the Christians.

4. The manuscript tradition of the letters of Ignatius is confusing, primarily because so much has been added to the original letters. Some manuscripts belong to the Short Recension family (containing the shorter versions of his letters), while others belong to the Long Recension family. The longer version is generally thought to have been included sometime in the late fourth century, so it cannot be part of the original collection of letters. I have decided to include both versions below.

To the Philadelphians

circumcised The removal of the foreskin from the penis. Genesis 17:10 states the circumcision of every male, on the eighth day after birth, would seal the covenant between God and his people. The Apostle Paul, in the Christian Bible, argues that males who want to become Christian would not need to be circumcised first.

Ebionite The Ebionites were an early Jewish Christian sect.

Jews who killed Christ This was a common charge against the Jews. Unfortunately, this belief still accounts for some anti-Semitic feelings.

prince of this world The Devil, or Satan.

Simon Magus The story of Simon is found in Acts 8:9–24. After being baptized, he then offered money to the apostles so that he could buy the power of bringing down the Holy Spirit (from this we get the word *simony*). He was rejected. He is usually referred to as Simon the Magician.

Short Version, Chapter 6: But if anyone preach the Jewish law to you, do not listen to him. For it is better to listen to Christian doctrine from a man who has been **circumcised,** than to Judaism from one uncircumcised. But if either of them do not speak concerning Jesus Christ, they are in my judgment but as monuments and sepulchers of the dead, upon which are written only the names of men. Therefore flee the wicked devices and snares of the **prince of this world,** lest at any time being conquered by his works, and you grow weak in your love. But be all joined together with an undivided heart. And I thank my God that I have a good conscience in respect to you, and that no one has it in his power to boast, either privately or publicly, that I have burdened anyone, either a lot or a little. And I wish for all among whom I have spoken, that they may not possess that for a testimony against them.

Longer Version: If anyone preaches the one God of the law and the prophets, but denies Christ to be the Son of God, he is a liar, even as also is his father the devil, and is a Jew falsely so called, being possessed of mere carnal circumcision. If anyone confesses Christ Jesus the Lord, but denies the God of the law and of the prophets, saying that the Father of Christ is not the Maker of heaven and earth, he has not continued in the truth any more than his father the devil, and is a disciple of **Simon Magus,** not of the Holy Spirit. If anyone says there is one God, and also confesses Christ Jesus, but thinks the Lord to be a mere man, and not the only-begotten God, and Wisdom, and the Word of God, and deems Him to consist merely of a soul and body, such an one is a serpent, that preaches deceit and error for the destruction of men. And such a man is poor in understanding, even as by name he is an **Ebionite.** If anyone confesses the truths mentioned, but calls lawful wedlock, and the procreation of children, destruction and pollution, or deems certain kinds of food abominable, such an one has the apostate dragon dwelling within him. If anyone confesses the Father, and the Son, and the Holy Ghost, and praises the creation, but calls the incarnation merely an appearance, and is ashamed of the passion, such a one has denied the faith, no less than the **Jews who killed Christ.** If anyone confesses these things, and that God the Word did dwell in a human body, being within it as the Word, even as the soul also is in the body, because it was God that inhabited it, and not a human soul, but affirms that unlawful unions are a good thing, and places the highest happiness in pleasure, as does the man who is falsely called a **Nicolaitan,** this person can neither be a lover of God, nor a lover of Christ, but is a corrupter of his own flesh, and therefore void of the Holy Spirit, and a stranger to Christ. All such persons are but monuments and sepulchres of the dead, upon which are written only the names of dead men. Flee, therefore, the wicked devices and snares of the spirit which now works in the children of this world, lest at any time being overcome, you grow weak in your love. But be joined together with an undivided heart and a willing mind, "being of one accord and of one judgment," (Philippians 2:2) being always of the same opinion about the same things, both when you are at ease and in danger, both in sorrow and in joy. I thank God, through Jesus Christ, that I have a good conscience in respect to you, and that no one has it in his power to boast, either privately or publicly, that I have burdened anyone either in much or in little. And I wish for all among whom I have spoken, that they may not possess that for a testimony against them.

> **Nicolaitan** A Christian group. Among other things, they were accused of practicing adultery.

To the Magnesians

Shorter Version, Chapter 8: Do not be deceived with strange doctrines, nor with old fables, which are unprofitable. For if we still live according to the Jewish law, we acknowledge that we have not received grace. For the divinest prophets lived according to Christ Jesus. On this account also they were persecuted, being inspired by His grace to fully convince the unbelieving that there is one God, who has manifested Himself by Jesus Christ His Son, who is His eternal Word, not proceeding forth from silence, and who in all things pleased Him that sent Him.

Longer Version, Chapter 8: Do not be deceived with strange doctrines, "nor give heed to fables and endless genealogies," (1 Timothy 1:4) and things in which the Jews make their boast. "Old things are passed away: behold, all things have become new" (2 Corinthians 5:17). For if we still live according to the Jewish law, and the circumcision of the flesh, we deny that we have received grace. For the holiest prophets lived according to Jesus Christ. On this account also they were persecuted, being inspired by grace to fully convince the unbelieving that there is one God, the Almighty, who has manifested Himself by Jesus Christ His Son, who is His Word, not spoken, but essential. For He is not the voice of an articulate utterance, but a substance begotten by divine power, who has in all things pleased Him that sent Him.

Shorter Version, Chapter 9: If, therefore, those who were brought up in the ancient order of things have come to the possession of a new hope, no longer observing the Sabbath, but living in the observance of the Lord's Day, on which also our life has sprung up again by Him and by His death—whom some deny, by which mystery we have obtained faith, and therefore endure, that we may be found the disciples of Jesus Christ, our only Master—how shall we be able to live apart from Him, whose disciples the prophets themselves in the Spirit did wait for Him as their Teacher? And therefore He whom they rightly waited for, being come, raised them from the dead.

Longer Version, Chapter 9: If, then, those who were conversant with the ancient Scriptures came to newness of hope, expecting the coming of Christ, as the Lord teaches us when He says, "If you had believed Moses, you would have believed Me, for he wrote of Me" (John 5:46), and again, "Your father Abraham rejoiced to see My day, and he saw it, and was glad; for before Abraham was, I am" (John 8:56 and 58); how shall we be able to live without Him? The prophets were His servants, and foresaw Him by the Spirit, and waited for Him as their Teacher, and expected Him as their Lord and Savior, saying, "He will come and save us." (Isaiah 35:4). Let us therefore no longer keep the Sabbath after the Jewish manner, and rejoice in days of idleness; for "he that does not work, let him not eat" (2 Thessalonians 3:10). For the [holy] oracles say, "By the sweat of your face shall you eat your bread" (Genesis 3:19). But let every one of you keep the Sabbath after a spiritual manner, rejoicing in meditation on the law, not in relaxation of the body, admiring the workmanship of God, and not eating things prepared the day before, nor using lukewarm drinks, and walking within a prescribed space, nor finding delight in dancing and plaudits which have no sense in them. And after the observance of the Sabbath, let every friend of Christ keep the Lord's Day as a festival, the resurrection-day, the queen and chief of all the days [of the week]. Looking forward to this, the prophet declared, "To the end, for the eighth day," on which our life both sprang up again, and the victory over death was obtained in Christ, whom the children of perdition, the enemies of the Savior, deny, "whose god is their belly, who mind earthly things," (Philemon 3: 18–19) who are "lovers of pleasure, and not lovers of God, having a form of godliness, but denying the power thereof" (2 Timothy 3:4). These make merchandise of Christ, corrupting His word, and giving up Jesus to sale: they are corrupters of women, and covetous of other men's possessions, swallowing up wealth insatiably; from whom you may be delivered by the mercy of God through our Lord Jesus Christ!

Shorter Version, Chapter 10: Let us not, therefore, be insensible to His kindness; for were He to reward us according to our works, we should cease to be. Therefore, having become His disciples, let us learn to live according to the principles of Christianity. For whosoever is called by any other name besides this, is not of God. Lay aside, therefore, the evil, the old, the sour leaven, and be changed into the new leaven, which is Jesus Christ. Be salted in Him, lest anyone among you should be corrupted, since by your savior you shall be convicted. It is absurd to profess Christ Jesus, and to Judaize. For Christianity did not embrace Judaism, but Judaism Christianity, that so every tongue which believeth might be gathered together to God.

Longer Version, Chapter 10: Let us not, therefore, be insensible to His kindness; for were He to reward us according to our works, we should cease to be. For "if you, Lord, shall mark iniquities, O Lord, who shall stand?" (Psalms 130:3). Let us therefore prove ourselves worthy of that name which we have received. For whoever is called by any other name besides this, he is not of God; for he has not received the prophecy which speaks concerning us: "The people shall be called by a new name, which the Lord shall name them, and shall be a holy people" (Isaiah 62:2 and 62:12), and this was first fulfilled in Syria; for "the disciples were called Christians at Antioch," (Acts 11:26) when Paul and Peter were laying the foundations of the Church. Lay aside, therefore, the evil, the old, the corrupt leaven, and be changed into the new leaven of grace. Abide in Christ, that the stranger may not have dominion over you. It is absurd to speak of Jesus Christ with the tongue, and to cherish in the mind a Judaism which has now come to an end. For where there is Christianity there cannot be Judaism. For Christ is one, in whom every nation that believes, and every tongue that confesses, is gathered unto God. And those that were of a stony heart have become the children of Abraham, the friend of God; and in his seed all those have been blessed who were ordained to eternal life in Christ.

Source: Roberts, Rev. Alexander, and James Donaldson, eds. *The Ante-Nicene Fathers: Translations of the Writings of the Fathers Down to A.D. 325,* vol. 1. Buffalo, NY: Christian Literature Company, 1885, 63, 82.

AFTERMATH

Ignatius was martyred in Rome sometime during the reign of Emperor Trajan (98–117 CE). His letters were collected by Polycarp, the bishop of Smyrna, who was also a martyr and died in the middle of the second century. Ignatius's letters were popular enough to be actively collected after his death. We know that Eusebius, bishop of Caesarea, had a collection of Ignatius's letters in the early 300s CE (*Ecclesiastical History* 3.36). Ignatius's anti-Jewish feelings played a part in the almost total separation of the Jews and the Christians by the end of the second century.

ASK YOURSELF

1. How does Judaism affect modern Christianity today? Do Jews and Christians get along with each other?
2. The United States is a big supporter of the modern state of Israel. How does the history of early Christianity/Judaism affect this relationship?
3. Can a Christian be a Jewish Christian today? How would the faith of such a person differ from a person who believes in Christianity or in Judaism?

TOPICS TO CONSIDER

- Those of the Jewish faith have a long history of persecution by the Christians. Split into two groups and have one side be Christian and the other Jewish. List the reasons for persecution and defend them if you are on the Christian side.
- Consider how the message of Ignatius was influenced by his upcoming martyrdom.
- Consider how the letters of Ignatius would have been received by early Christian communities. Would his anti-Jewish message have been received favorably? If so, why? If not, why not?
- Compare the Shorter Recension with the Longer Recension. Consider why someone would insert this extra material into the original letters of Ignatius. If you were only given the Longer Recension, how would this impact your understanding of Ignatius?

JEWISH CHRISTIANS

The first Christians were Jews (including Jesus), and when some of the early apostles, including Paul, wanted to bring Gentiles into the new faith, there was resistance. The main problems for the Jewish-leaning Christians were that the Gentiles did not have to undergo circumcision or keep some of the dietary restrictions. This led to tension between the two groups. Paul's struggle circled around how to keep both groups happy. Many of the new Christians (called Jewish Christians) also kept some of their Jewish rites even after their conversion and this led people like Ignatius to warn them to separate, as in his statement "It is absurd to profess Christ Jesus, and to Judaize." More tension developed between the two groups when in the late 60s CE there was a revolt of the Jewish population against the Romans. When Jerusalem fell in 70 CE, the Romans expelled both the Jews and the Christians from the city. The synagogue was important for Jesus and the first Christians, but after the revolt, Christians stopped using the synagogue and tried to break away from their Jewish roots. The tension can be seen not only in Ignatius but in other early Christians such as Irenaeus and Eusebius of Caesarea. Jewish Christian communities disappeared sometime in the 400s.

Further Information

Barnard, L. W. "The Background of St. Ignatius of Antioch." *Vigiliae Christianae* 17, no. 4 (Dec., 1963): 193–206.

Brent, Allen. *Ignatius of Antioch: A Martyr Bishop and the Origin of the Episcopacy*. New York: T&T Clark International, 2009.

Brown, Charles Thomas. *The Gospel and Ignatius of Antioch,* Studies in Biblical Literature, vol. 12. New York: Peter Lang, 2000.

Cohen, Shayou J. D. "Judaism without Circumcision and 'Judaism' without 'Circumcision' in Ignatius." *Harvard Theological Review* 95, no. 4 (Oct., 2002): 395–415.

Davies, Stevan L. "The Predicament of Ignatius of Antioch." *Vigiliae Christianae* 30, no. 3 (Sep., 1976): 175–80.

Donahue, Paul J. "Jewish Christianity in the Letters of Ignatius of Antioch." *Vigiliae Christianae* 32, no. 2 (Jun., 1978): 81–93.

Hannah, Jack W. "The Setting of the Ignatian Long Recension." *Journal of Biblical Literature* 79, no. 3 (Sep., 1960): 221–38.

Ignatius. *Letters* (audio). http://www.youtube.com/view_play_list?p=CEA5BBE5A9094A43.

Ignatius. *Letters* (text). http://www.ccel.org/ccel/schaff/anf01.v.html.

Robinson, Thomas A. *Ignatius of Antioch and the Parting of the Ways: Early Jewish-Christian Relations*. Peabody, MA: Hendrickson, 2009.

28. Justin Martyr, *Dialogue with Trypho, a Jew*

INTRODUCTION

It isn't clear when Justin Martyr wrote the *Dialogue with Trypho,* but the probable date is the late 140s CE, and it is the oldest known apology, or defense of Christianity, written against the Jews (Quasten 202). Justin was certainly not the first Christian to write against the Jews, but he had an impact on the relationship between the two groups. Justin was not a fan of Judaism. He believed that the Jews had made a serious mistake in not following the teachings of Jesus, and his *Dialogue with Trypho* was his attempt to teach the Jewish population the proper religion. It appears that Justin met Trypho the Jew as he was walking with some friends. Justin wrote down the following dialogue after the fact.

The following section of the *Dialogue* starts with chapter 10. Trypho had asked Justin to discuss philosophy in general, and Justin relates his journey to becoming a Christian. He told Trypho that he had joined a few philosophical groups, but none of them, in his opinion, led to the knowledge of God. Justin had met, on another walk, an old man who, after a series of philosophical questions, led him to become Christian. At the end of this story, Trypho tells Justin it would be better for him to follow the Jewish faith instead of Christianity. Justin forgives him for being wrong, and the two of them, along with friends, sit down to discuss Christianity. Chapters 1, 10, and 11 are included below.

KEEP IN MIND WHILE YOU READ

1. By the time of Justin's death (165 CE), it had been nearly a century since Christians had broken away from Judaism and had wholesale taken over the Old Testament.
2. The debate is taking place in Greece. In chapter 2, Trypho mentioned that he had escaped the Jewish revolt against the Romans, which took place between 132 and 136 CE. This revolt was led by Bar Kochba and was put down after the Romans sent in a large military force into Jerusalem. As punishment for revolting, the Romans barred the Jews from Jerusalem. The Romans, who still thought of the Christians as a Jewish sect, also barred them from Jerusalem.
3. Justin was martyred (killed for his faith) around 165 CE by being whipped and beheaded after he refused to worship the Roman gods. This is how he got his name.

Justin Martyr, Dialogue with Trypho, a Jew

Chapter 1

While I was going about one morning in the walks of the Xystus, a certain man, with others in his company, having met me, and said, "Hail, O philosopher!" And immediately after saying this, he turned round and walked along with me; his friends likewise followed him. And I in turn having addressed him, said, "What is there important?" And he replied, "I was instructed," says he "by Corinthus the Socratic in Argos, that I ought not to despise or treat with indifference those who array themselves **in this dress** but to show them all kindness, and to associate with them, as perhaps some advantage would spring from the intercourse either to some such man or to myself. It is good, moreover, for both, if either the one or the other be benefited. On this account, therefore, whenever I see any one in such costume, I gladly approach him, and now, for the same reason, have I willingly accosted you; and these accompany me, in the expectation of hearing for themselves something profitable from you." "But who are you, most excellent man?" So I replied to him in jest. Then he told me frankly both his name and his family. "Trypho," says he, "I am called; and I am a Hebrew of the circumcision, and having escaped from the war lately carried on there I am spending my days in Greece, and chiefly at Corinth." "And in what," said I, "would you be profited by philosophy so much as by your own lawgiver and the prophets?" "Why not?" he replied. "Do not the philosophers turn every discourse on God? And do not questions continually arise to them about His unity and providence? Is not this truly the duty of philosophy, to investigate the Deity?" "Assuredly," said I, "so we too have believed. But the most have not taken thought of this whether there be one or more gods, and whether they have a regard for each one of us or no, as if this knowledge contributed nothing to our happiness; nay, they moreover attempt to persuade us that God takes care of the universe with its genera and species, but not of me and you, and each individually, since otherwise we would surely not need to pray to Him night and day. But it is not difficult to understand the upshot of this; for fearlessness and license in speaking result to such as maintain these opinions, doing and saying whatever they choose, neither dreading punishment nor hoping for any benefit from God. For how could they? They affirm that the same things shall always happen; and, further, that I and you shall again live in like manner, having become neither better men nor worse. But there are some others, who, having supposed the soul to be immortal and immaterial, believe that though they have committed evil they will not suffer punishment (for that which is immaterial is insensible), and that the soul, in consequence of its immortality, needs nothing from God." And he, smiling gently, said, "Tell us your opinion of these matters, and what idea you entertain respecting God, and what your philosophy is."

> **in this dress** The cloak of a philosopher that Justin was wearing.

Chapter 10

And when they ceased, I again addressed them thus:—"Is there any other matter, my friends, in which we are blamed than this, that we live not after the law, and are not circumcised in the flesh as your forefathers were, and do not observe sabbaths as you do? Are our lives and customs also slandered among you? And I ask this: have you also believed concerning us, that **we eat men; and that after the feast, having extinguished the lights, we engage in promiscuous concubinage**? Or do you condemn us in this alone, that we adhere to such tenets, and believe in an opinion, untrue, as you think?" "This is what we are amazed at," said Trypho, "but those things about which the multitude speak are not worthy of belief; for they are most repugnant to human nature. Moreover, I am aware that your precepts in the **so-called Gospel** are so wonderful and so great, that I suspect no one can keep them; for I have carefully read them. But this is what we are most at a loss about: that you, professing to be pious, and supposing yourselves better than others, are not in any particular separated from them, and do not alter your mode of living from the nations, in that you observe no festivals or sabbaths, **and do not have the rite of circumcision;** and further, resting your hopes on a man that was crucified, you yet expect to obtain some good thing from God, while you do not obey His commandments. Have you not read, that that soul shall be cut off from his people who shall not have been circumcised on the eighth day? And this has been ordained for strangers and for slaves equally. But you, despising this covenant rashly, reject the consequent duties, and attempt to persuade yourselves that you know God, when, however, you perform none of those things which they do who fear God. If, therefore, you can defend yourself on these points, and make it manifest in what way you hope for anything whatsoever, even though you do not observe the law, this we would very gladly hear from you, and we shall make other similar investigations."

and do not have the rite of circumcision Circumcision was a rite of passage for the Jewish men whereby the foreskin of the penis was removed. Paul the Apostle made a strong case in his letters that men who wanted to become Christian did not need to be circumcised first.

so-called Gospel The word *gospel* means "good news." Trypho is probably referring to all of the Gospels. Trypho does not believe that the message in the Gospel is true.

we eat men; and that after the feast, having extinguished the lights, we engage in promiscuous concubinage These were very common charges against the Christians. Part of the reason for these charges is the misunderstanding around the words of Jesus during the Last Supper and especially found in John 6:50–56: "Very truly, I tell you, unless you eat the flesh of the Son of Man and drink his blood, you have no life in you."

Chapter 11

"There will be no other God, O Trypho, nor was there from eternity any other existing" (I thus addressed him), "but He who made and disposed this entire universe. Nor do we think that there is one God for us, another for you, but that He alone is God who led your fathers out from Egypt with a strong hand and a high arm. Nor have we trusted in any other (for there is no other), but in Him in whom you also have trusted, the God of Abraham, and of Isaac, and of Jacob. But we do not trust through Moses or through the law;

for then we would do the same as yourselves. But now, for I have read that there shall be a final law, and a covenant, the chiefest of all, which it is now incumbent on all men to observe, as many as are seeking after the inheritance of God. For the law promulgated on Horeb is now old, and belongs to yourselves alone; but this is for all universally. Now, law placed against law has abrogated that which is before it, and a covenant which comes after in like manner has put an end to the previous one; and an eternal and final law—namely, Christ—has been given to us, and the covenant is trustworthy, after which there shall be no law, no commandment, no ordinance. Have you not read this which Isaiah says: "Listen to Me, listen to Me, my people; and, you kings, listen to Me: for a law shall go forth from Me, and My judgment shall be for a light to the nations. My righteousness approaches swiftly, and My salvation shall go forth, and nations shall trust in My arm?" (**Isaiah 51:4–5**). And by Jeremiah, concerning this same new covenant, He thus speaks: "Behold, the days come, says the Lord, that I will make a new covenant with the house of Israel and with the house of Judah; not according to the covenant which I made with their fathers, in the day that I took them by the hand, to bring them out of the land of Egypt" (**Jeremiah 31:31–32**). If, therefore, God proclaimed a new covenant which was to be instituted, and this for a light of the nations, we see and are persuaded that men approach God, leaving their idols and other unrighteousness, through the name of Him who was crucified, Jesus Christ, and abide by their confession even unto death, and maintain piety. Moreover, by the works and by the attendant miracles, it is possible for all to understand that He is the new law, and the new covenant, and the expectation of those who out of every people wait for the good things of God. For the true spiritual Israel, and descendants of Judah, Jacob, Isaac, and Abraham (who in uncircumcision was approved of and blessed by God on account of his faith, and called the father of many nations), are we who have been led to God through this crucified Christ, as shall be demonstrated while we proceed.

> **Isaiah 51:4–5** and **Jeremiah 31:31–32** Justin uses the Hebrew scripture against Trypho to show that even the Hebrew prophets believed that Christ would come to bring a new law.

Source: Roberts, Rev. Alexander, and James Donaldson, eds. *The Ante-Nicene Fathers: Translations of the Writings of the Fathers Down to A.D. 325,* vol. 1. Buffalo, NY: Christian Literature Company, 1885, 194–200.

AFTERMATH

By the middle of the second century, the rift between Christianity and Judaism was complete. Both sides mistrusted each other, especially since Christians were trying to convert the Jewish population to Christianity. The dialogue above reveals some of that tension. While Trypho did not convert to Christianity, the text of the *Dialogue* became an important one for later Christians. It was used by many in their own defense of Christianity, including Irenaeus, Tertullian, and Hippolytus. Many of the arguments used by Justin were repeated by these authors. Eusebius of Caesarea, in his *Ecclesiastical History* (4.18.6–7), specifically mentions Justin's *Dialogue*. He states: "He composed also a dialogue against the Jews, which he held in the city of Ephesus with Trypho, a most distinguished man among the Hebrews of that day. In it he shows how the divine grace urged him on to the doctrine of the faith, and with what earnestness he had formerly pursued philosophical studies, and how ardent a search he had made for the truth. And he records of the Jews in the same work, that they were plotting against the teaching of Christ, asserting the same things against Trypho: 'Not only did you not repent of the wickedness which you had committed, but you selected at that time chosen men, and you sent them out from Jerusalem through all the land, to announce that the godless heresy of the Christians had made its appearance, and to accuse them of those things which all that are ignorant of us say against us, so that you become the causes not only of your own injustice, but also of all other men's.' "

ASK YOURSELF

1. It appears that Justin asked someone to write down the discussion as he was speaking with Trypho. How does this affect your view of the *Dialogue* itself? Can it be trusted?

2. Justin, as a Christian, was wearing the traditional clothing of a philosopher, even though he was a Christian. What does that tell you about Justin's form of Christianity?

3. Justin quoted the Old Testament a few times to Trypho. Why do you think Justin picked those particular passages? What point was he trying to make to Trypho? Ask yourself how Trypho would have felt with Justin, a Christian, making use of the Old Testament.

TOPICS TO CONSIDER

 Justin became involved in Christianity after learning about Greek philosophy. Consider the effect of Greek philosophy on the spread of Christianity. Do you think it played a big part in gaining converts? Does Greek philosophy play an important role in modern-day Christianity?

 Read the rest of the *Dialogue* with Trypho (link given below) and consider the other arguments that Justin gives to Trypho. The *Dialogue* ends with Trypho and his friends thanking Justin, and with Justin praying that Trypho would convert to Christianity. Consider the effects of this *Dialogue* on the Jewish population. Do you think that they would have converted after reading this work?

 The argument put forth by Justin for Christianity rested on Christians adopting the Old Testament for themselves. Consider what Christianity today would be like today if Christians did not use the Old Testament. Would it be very different, or would it not really affect the principles of Christianity?

Further Information

Barnard, L. W. *Justin Martyr.* Cambridge: Cambridge University Press, 1967.

Bokser, Ben Zion. "Justin Martyr and the Jews." *Jewish Quarterly Review,* n.s., 64, no. 2 (Oct., 1973): 97–122.

Bokser, Ben Zion. "Justin Martyr and the Jews: II." *Jewish Quarterly Review,* n.s., 64, no. 3 (Jan., 1974): 204–11.

Boyarin, Daniel. "Justin Martyr Invents Judaism." *Church History* 70, no. 3 (Sep., 2001): 427–61.

Higgins, A.J.B. "Jewish Messianic Belief in Justin Martyr's 'Dialogue with Trypho.' " *Novum Testamentum* 9, Fasc. 4 (Oct., 1967): 298–305.

Hirshman, M. "Polemic Literary Units in the Classical Midrashim and Justin Martyr's 'Dialogue with Trypho.'" *The Jewish Quarterly Review,* n.s. 83, no. 3/4 (Jan.–Apr., 1993): 369–84.

Martyr, Justin. *Dialogue with Trypho.* http://www.ccel.org/ccel/schaff/anf01.viii.iv.i.html.

Parvis, Sara, and Paul Foster, eds. *Justin Martyr and His Worlds.* Minneapolis, MN: Fortress Press, 2007.

Quasten, Johannes. *Patrology,* vol. 1. Allen, TX: RCL, 1986.

Rokeah, David. *Justin Martyr and the Jews,* Jewish and Christian Perspectives Series. Leiden, the Netherlands: Brill Academic Publishers, 2001.

Trakatellis, Demetrios. "Justin Martyr's Trypho." *Harvard Theological Review* 79, no. 1/3, Christians among Jews and Gentiles: Essays in Honor of Krister Stendahl on His Sixty-Fifth Birthday (Jan.–Jul., 1986): 287–97.

29. Irenaeus, *Against Heresies*

INTRODUCTION

Irenaeus (ca. 115–202) was a bishop in the city of Lugdunum, now Lyons, France. Though born in Asia Minor, Irenaeus made his way to Rome and ultimately settled in Lyons. Irenaeus was a prolific writer, and one of his most important texts was *Against Heresies*. It was one of the earlier Christian attempts to list and define what Irenaeus and others called heresy. In this particular instance, Irenaeus was writing against a large group of Christians called the Gnostics. The word *gnostic* comes from the Greek word *gnosis,* or "knowledge." The Gnostics believed they had access to secret knowledge of the message of Jesus. Irenaeus flatly refused to believe that Jesus gave anyone secret knowledge and thought that the entire Christian message could be found in the Hebrew Bible and in the genuine writings of the apostles. He also believed that there was only one belief for all Christians. Below is the preface to his book, as well as a section from book 1, chapter 10.

KEEP IN MIND WHILE YOU READ

1. Before Irenaeus was a bishop, but while he was living in Lyons, he was asked to go on a mission to talk to Eleutherus, the bishop of Rome. He was to urge the bishop to be tolerant of a group of Christians called the Montanists. When he returned to Lyons, he discovered that his bishop had been martyred and he had been chosen to be the next bishop.
2. Irenaeus had heard Bishop Polycarp of Smyrna when he was young. This probably influenced his desire to be a priest.
3. Irenaeus wrote on a number of different topics, but unfortunately many of these writings are no longer extant.

Irenaeus, Against Heresies, *preface*

1. Inasmuch as certain men have set the truth aside, and bring in lying words and vain genealogies, which, as the apostle says, "minister questions rather than godly edifying which is in faith" (1 Timothy 1:4), and by means of their craftily-constructed plausibilities draw away the minds of the inexperienced and take them captive, [I have felt constrained, my dear friend, to compose the following treatise in order to expose and counteract their machinations.] These men falsify the oracles of God, and prove themselves evil interpreters of the good word of revelation. They also overthrow the faith of many, by drawing them away, under a pretense of [superior] knowledge, from Him who rounded and adorned the universe; as if they had something more excellent and sublime to reveal, than that God who created the heaven and the earth, and all things that are therein. By means of specious and plausible words, they cunningly allure the simple-minded to inquire into their system; but they nevertheless clumsily destroy them, while they initiate them into their blasphemous and impious opinions respecting the **Demiurge;** and these simple ones are unable, even in such a matter, to distinguish falsehood from truth.

2. Error, indeed, is never set forth in its naked deformity, unless, being exposed, it should at once be detected. But it is craftily decked out in an attractive dress, so as, by its outward form, to make it appear to the inexperienced (ridiculous as the expression may seem) more true than the truth itself. **One far superior to me** has well said, in reference to this point, "A clever imitation in glass casts contempt, as it were, on that precious jewel the emerald (which is most highly esteemed by some), unless it come under the eye of one able to test and expose the counterfeit. Or, again, what inexperienced person can with ease detect the presence of brass when it has been mixed up with silver?" (source unknown). Lest, therefore, through my neglect, some should be carried off, even as sheep are by wolves, while they do not perceive the true character of these men,—because they outwardly are covered with sheep's clothing (against whom the Lord has enjoined us to be on our guard), and because their language resembles ours, while their sentiments are very different,—I have deemed it my duty, after reading some of the Commentaries, as they call them, of the disciples of **Valentinus,** and after making myself acquainted with their tenets through personal intercourse with some of them, to unfold to you, my friend, these portentous and profound mysteries, which do not fall within the range of every intellect, because all have not sufficiently purged their brains. I do this, in order that you, obtaining an acquaintance with these things, may in turn explain them to all those with whom you are connected, and exhort them to avoid such an abyss of madness and of blasphemy against Christ. I intend, then, to the best of my ability, with brevity and clearness to set forth the opinions of those who are now promulgating **heresy.** I refer especially to the disciples of **Ptolemæus,** whose school may be described as a bud from that of Valentinus. I shall also endeavor, according to my moderate ability, to furnish the means of overthrowing them, by showing how absurd and inconsistent with the truth are their statements. Not that I am practiced either in composition or eloquence; but my feeling of affection prompts me to make known to thee

---

Demiurge According to some Gnostic groups, the Demiurge was the creator of this world.

heresy For Irenaeus, a heresy was any belief that he thought differed from what the apostles taught.

One far superior to me It isn't clear who Irenaeus is referring to. Some have thought it may be Polycarp.

Ptolemæus A disciple of Valentinus.

Valentinus A Gnostic Christian who led a group called the Valentinians sometime during the middle of the second century.

---

and all thy companions those doctrines which have been kept in concealment until now, but which are at last, through the goodness of God, brought to light. "For there is nothing hidden which shall not be revealed, nor secret that shall not be made known" (Matthew 10:26).

3. You will not expect from me, who am resident among the Keltae, and am accustomed for the most part to use a barbarous dialect, any display of rhetoric, which I have never learned, or any excellence of composition, which I have never practiced, or any beauty and persuasiveness of style, to which I make no pretensions. But you will accept in a kindly spirit what I in a like spirit write to you simply, truthfully, and in my own homely way; while you yourself (as being more capable than I am) will expand those ideas of which I send you, as it were, only the seminal principles; and in the comprehensiveness of your understanding, you develop to their full extent the points on which I briefly touch, so as to set with power before your companions those things which I have uttered in weakness. In fine, as I (to gratify your long-cherished desire for information regarding the tenets of these persons) have spared no pains, not only to make these doctrines known to you, but also to furnish the means of showing their falsity; so you shall, according to the grace given to you by the Lord, prove an earnest and efficient minister to others, that men may no longer be drawn away by the plausible system of these heretics, which I now proceed to describe.

Irenaeus, Against Heresies *1.10.1–2*

1. The Church, though dispersed through the whole world, even to the ends of the earth, has received from the apostles and their disciples this faith: (She believes) in one God, the Father Almighty, Maker of heaven, and earth, and the sea, and all things that are in them; and in one Christ Jesus, the Son of God, who became incarnate for our salvation; and in the Holy Spirit, who proclaimed through the prophets the dispensations of God, and the advents, and the birth from a virgin, and the passion, and the resurrection from the dead, and the ascension into heaven in the flesh of the beloved Christ Jesus, our Lord, and His (future) manifestation from heaven in the glory of the Father "to gather all things in one," (Ephesians 1:10) and to raise up anew all flesh of the whole human race, in order that to Christ Jesus, our Lord, and God, and Savior, and King, according to the will of the invisible Father, "every knee should bow, of things in heaven, and things in earth, and things under the earth, and that every tongue should confess" (Philippians 2:10–11) to Him, and that He should execute just judgment towards all; that He may send "spiritual wickednesses," and the angels who transgressed and became apostates, together with the ungodly, the unrighteous, the wicked, and profane among men, into everlasting fire; but may, in the exercise of His grace, confer immortality on the righteous, the holy, and those who have kept His commandments, and have persevered in His love, some from the beginning (of their Christian course), and others from (the date of) their repentance, and may surround them with everlasting glory.

2. As I have already observed, the Church, having received this preaching and this faith, although scattered throughout the whole world, yet, as if occupying but one house, carefully preserves it. She also believes these points (of doctrine) just as if she had but one soul, and one and the same heart, and she proclaims them, teaches them, and hands them down, with perfect harmony, as if she possessed only one mouth. For, although the languages of the world are dissimilar, yet the import of the tradition is one and the same. For the Churches

which have been planted in Germany do not believe or hand down anything different, nor do those in Spain, nor those in Gaul, nor those in the East, nor those in Egypt, nor those in Libya, nor those which have been established in the central regions of the world. But as the sun, that creature of God, is one and the same throughout the whole world, so also the preaching of the truth shines everywhere, and enlightens all men that are willing to come to a knowledge of the truth. Nor will any one of the rulers in the Churches, however highly gifted he may be in point of eloquence, teach doctrines different from these (for no one is greater than the Master); nor, on the other hand, will he who is deficient in power of expression inflict injury on the tradition. For the faith being ever one and the same, neither does one who is able at great length to discourse regarding it, make any addition to it, nor does one, who can say but little diminish it . . .

Source: Roberts, Rev. Alexander, and James Donaldson, eds. *The Ante-Nicene Fathers: Translations of the Writings of the Fathers Down to* A.D. *325,* vol. 1. Buffalo, NY: Christian Literature Company, 1885, 315–31.

AFTERMATH

Irenaeus's *Against Heresies* was a very popular book in antiquity, primarily because of the detail he gives. There were many early Christians who made use of it, including Hippolytus of Rome. Hippolytus made his own list of heresies and modeled his on the writings of Irenaeus (*Refutation of All Heresies*). Eusebius, bishop of Caesarea, also had access to the writings of Irenaeus. In his *Ecclesiastical History,* Eusebius quotes Irenaeus many times, preserving pieces of writings that did not survive. The section from book 1, section 10 was also important because it stressed the unity of Christianity. This was a common theme in many early Christian writings.

ASK YOURSELF

1. *Against Heresies* is an extremely important text because it preserves the ideas of these so-called Gnostic groups. However, in many cases we do not have the writings of these Gnostic Christians. How do you think this affects our understanding of these Christian groups?
2. Where would the Christian Gnostics find their ideas? Did they find them in the New and Old Testaments, or did they have other sources for their information?
3. Twice Irenaeus downplays his learning and eloquence. This was a common practice among ancient (and some modern) writers. Why do you think he did this?
4. Do you believe Irenaeus is correct when he states that clergy in Germany would be teaching the exact same thing as the clergy in Egypt and elsewhere?

TOPICS TO CONSIDER

- ⮑ A few times Irenaeus makes use of the Old and New Testament to help his argument. Consider how this would help or hurt his argument against the Gnostics. Consider how the Gnostics would respond to Irenaeus.
- ⮑ Consider how mainstream Christian groups deal with heresy. Are those who are thought to be heretics attacked in a similar manner?

> As mentioned above, Irenaeus was sent on a mission to urge the Roman church to tolerate a group of Christians called the Montanists. Consider why Irenaeus would be so tolerant of this group but mercilessly attack the Gnostic Christians.

> The Catholic Church today is thought to practice what Irenaeus preached in terms of the solidarity of the clergy teaching the exact same things everywhere. Consider the mass of the Catholic Church from two different geographic areas—compare and contrast the various steps. Do you think the two areas would receive the same message?

Further Information

Grant, Robert M. "Irenaeus and Hellenistic Culture." *Harvard Theological Review* 42, no. 1 (Jan., 1949): 41–51.

Irenaeus's texts. http://www.ccel.org/ccel/schaff/anf01.ix.html.

Kaatz, Kevin W. *Early Controversies and the Growth of Christianity.* Santa Barbara, CA: Praeger, 2012.

Minns, Denis. *Irenaeus: An Introduction.* London: T & T Clark, 2010.

Osborn, Eric. *Irenaeus of Lyons.* Cambridge: Cambridge University Press, 2005.

Pagels, Elaine. "Irenaeus, the 'Canon of Truth,' and the 'Gospel of John': 'Making a Difference' through Hermeneutics and Ritual." *Vigiliae Christianae* 56, no. 4 (Nov., 2002): 339–71.

Quispel, Gilles. "The Original Doctrine of Valentinus the Gnostic." *Vigiliae Christianae* 50, no. 4 (1996): 327–52.

Quispel, Gilles. "Valentinus and the Gnostikoi." *Vigiliae Christianae* 50, no. 1 (1996): 1–4.

Thomassen, Einar. "Orthodoxy and Heresy in Second-Century Rome." *Harvard Theological Review* 97, no. 3 (Jul., 2004): 241–56.

30. TERTULLIAN, *AGAINST MARCION*

INTRODUCTION

Tertullian, a North African (ca. 160 CE to ca. 220 CE) wrote *Against Marcion* (ca. 70 CE to the late 150s CE). As will be seen, it was not the first time that he had written against Marcion since someone had stolen this first work and published it without his consent. The newer version is a very long work that was divided up into five books. Almost all of the early Christian texts were written in Greek, but Tertullian was one of the earliest to write Christian material in Latin. Although Tertullian touches on a number of different things that bothered him, he was particularly concerned about three things that Marcion believed. The first was that Marcion thought Christians should not be using the Old Testament. Marcion believed it belonged to another god (the God of the Hebrews) and, because of that, the message in the texts was not suitable for Christians. The second concern Tertullian had was that Marcion believed in two gods—one god from the Old Testament and another god from the New Testament. The third problem that bothered Tertullian was that Marcion did not accept all the writings from the New Testament. The books he accepted were Luke as the only Gospel, plus 10 letters of Paul (Galatians, 1 and 2 Corinthians, Romans, 1 and 2 Thessalonians, Laodiceans [which may have been Ephesians], Colossians, Philippians, and Philemon). Not only that, but Marcion changed these texts to what he thought were the original wordings. The following text is taken from Tertullian's *Against Marcion*.

KEEP IN MIND WHILE YOU READ

1. The area that Tertullian describes as being savage had been part of the Roman Empire since the middle of the first century BCE. It became a Roman province in 62 CE. However, it had received this reputation much earlier, starting in the fifth century BCE in the writings of Herodotus, who is considered to be the first historian.
2. Marcion had left Pontus and went to Rome to spread his ideas on Christianity. According to Tertullian and other writers, Marcion's father was a Christian bishop who had excommunicated Marcion from the church in Pontus. Although this cannot be proven, it may have had an impact on his reception in the Church at Rome.

3. Tertullian's attack on Marcion was a typical way to attack those who had different ideas. The character was usually denigrated first, and then the ideas.

Tertullian, Against Marcion *1:1–2*

Whatever in times past we have created in opposition to Marcion, is from the present moment no longer to be accounted of. It is a new work which we are undertaking in lieu of the old one. My original tract, as too hurriedly composed, I had subsequently superseded by a fuller treatise. This latter I lost, before it was completely published, by the fraud of a person who was then a brother, but became afterwards an apostate. He, as it happened, had transcribed a portion of it, full of mistakes, and then published it. The necessity thus arose for an amended work; and the occasion of the new edition induced me to make a considerable addition to the treatise. This present text, therefore, of my work—which is the third as superseding the second, but henceforward to be considered the first instead of the third—renders a preface necessary to this issue of the tract itself that no reader may be perplexed, if he should by chance fall in with the various forms of it which are scattered about. The Euxine Sea, as it is called, is self-contradictory in its nature, and deceptive in its name. As you would not account it hospitable from its situation, so is it severed from our more civilized waters by a certain stigma which attaches to its barbarous character. The fiercest nations inhabit it, if indeed it can be called habitation, when life is passed in wagons. They have no fixed abode; their life has no germ of civilization; they indulge their sexual desires without restraint, and for the most part naked. Moreover, when they gratify secret lust, they hang up their quivers on their car-yokes, to warn off the curious and rash observer. Thus without a blush do they prostitute their weapons of war. The dead bodies of their parents they cut up with their sheep, and devour at their feasts. They who have not died so as to become food for others, are thought to have died an accursed death. Their women are not by their sex softened to modesty. They uncover the breast, from which they suspend their battle-axes, and prefer warfare to marriage. In their climate, too, there is the same rude nature. The day-time is never clear, the sun never cheerful; the sky is uniformly cloudy; the whole year is wintry; the only wind that blows is the angry North. Waters melt only by fires; their rivers flow not by reason of the ice; their mountains are covered with heaps of snow.

All things are torpid, all stiff with cold. Nothing there has the glow of life, but that ferocity which has given to scenic plays their stories of the **sacrifices of the Taurians,** and **the loves of the Colchians,** and **the torments of the Caucasus.** Nothing, however, in Pontus is so barbarous and sad as the fact that Marcion was born there, fouler than any Scythian, **more roving than the wagon-life of the Sarmatian, more inhuman than the Massagete,** more audacious

---

the loves of the Colchians
   Mentioned in Euripedes's play *Medea.*

the torments of the Caucasus Taken from Euripides' play *Prometheus.*

more inhuman than the Massagete Herodotus, a fifth-century BCE Greek writer, describes a Massagete custom in which the elderly are sacrificed, along with the animals, and then are eaten (*Histories* 1.216).

more roving than the wagon-life of the Sarmatian The Sarmatians lived north of the Black Sea (north of Pontus). Strabo (63 BCE to 24 CE), a Greek who found himself living in the newly acquired Roman territory of Pontus, described the Sarmatians as being nomadic people who lived in wagons.

sacrifices of the Taurians In the play *Iphigenia of Taurus* by the Greek playwright Euripides the Taurians are described as performing human sacrifices.

than an **Amazon,** darker than the cloud, (of Pontus) colder than its winter, more brittle than its ice, more deceitful than the Ister, more craggy than Caucasus. Nay more, the true **Prometheus,** Almighty God, is mangled by Marcion's blasphemies. Marcion is more savage than even the beasts of that barbarous region. For what beaver was ever a greater emasculator than he who has abolished the nuptial bond? What Pontic mouse ever had such gnawing powers as he who has gnawed the Gospels to pieces? Yes, O Euxine, you have produced a monster more credible to philosophers than to Christians. For the **cynic Diogenes** used to go about, lantern in hand, at mid-day to find a man; whereas Marcion has quenched the light of his faith, and so lost the God whom he had found. His disciples will not deny that his first faith he held along with ourselves; a letter of his own proves this; so that for the future a heretic may from his case be designated as one who, forsaking that which was prior, afterwards chose out for himself that which was not in times past. For in as far as what was delivered in times past and from the beginning will be held as truth, in so far will that be accounted heresy which is brought in later. But another brief treatise will maintain this position against heretics, who ought to be refuted even without a consideration of their doctrines, on the ground that they are heretical by reason of the novelty of their opinions. Now, so far as any controversy is to be admitted, I will for the time (lest our compendious principle of novelty, being called in on all occasions to our aid, should be imputed to want of confidence) begin with setting forth our adversary's rule of belief, that it may escape no one what our main contention is to be.

Amazon According to Greek mythology, the Amazons were a tribe of women living in the Pontic region. Once a year they would leave their region and have sex with men who lived in a neighboring area so that they could have children. The girls would be kept, but the boys would be killed. They had no hesitation in going to war against men.

cynic Diogenes Diogenes (404 [?] BCE to 323 BCE) was a Greek philosopher.

Prometheus Prometheus, according to Greek myth, was a Titan who provided humanity with many aspects of civilization, including the use of fire, writing, and agriculture. Prometheus did this against the will of Zeus, and as a result, Zeus had him chained to the side of a mountain in the Caucasus, where an eagle would eat his liver. Because Prometheus was an immortal, his liver would regenerate and every day the eagle would come back.

Chapter 2

The heretic of Pontus introduces two Gods, like the twin Symplegades of his own shipwreck: One whom it was impossible to deny, i.e. our Creator; and one whom he will never be able to prove, i.e. his own god. The unhappy man gained the first idea of his conceit from the simple passage of our Lord's saying, which has reference to human beings and not divine ones, wherein He disposes of those examples of a good tree and a corrupt one; how that "the good tree does not bring forth corrupt fruit, neither the corrupt tree good fruit," (Matthew 7:18) which means, that an honest mind and good faith cannot produce evil deeds, any more than an evil disposition can produce good deeds. Now (like many other persons now-a-days, especially those who have an heretical proclivity), while morbidly brooding over the question of the origin of evil, his perception became blunted by the very irregularity of his researches; and when he found the Creator declaring, "I am He who creates evil," inasmuch as he had already concluded from other arguments, which are satisfactory to every perverted mind, that God is the author of evil, so he now applied to the Creator the figure of the corrupt tree bringing forth evil fruit, that is, moral evil, and then presumed that there ought to be another god, after the analogy of the good tree producing its good fruit. Accordingly, finding in Christ a different disposition, as it were—one of a simple and pure benevolence—differing from the Creator, he readily argued that in his Christ had been revealed a new and strange divinity; and then with a little leaven he leavened the whole lump of the faith, flavoring it with the acidity of his own heresy. He had, moreover, in one Cerdon, an abettor of this blasphemy,—a circumstance which made them the more readily think that they saw most clearly their two gods, blind though they were; for, in truth, they had not seen the one God with soundness of faith. To men of diseased vision, even one lamp looks like many. One of his gods, therefore, whom he was obliged to acknowledge, he destroyed by defaming his attributes in the matter of evil; the other, whom he worked so hard to devise, he constructed, laying his foundation in the principle of good. In what articles he arranged these natures, we show by our own refutations of them. . .

Source: Roberts, Rev. Alexander, and James Donaldson, eds. *The Ante-Nicene Fathers: Translations of the Writings of the Fathers Down to* A.D. *325,* vol. 4. New York: Charles Scribner's Sons, 1905, 271–73.

AFTERMATH

According to Tertullian and other early writers, Marcion was kicked out of the church in Rome for trying to spread his ideas. Despite this, Marcion managed to start his own church, and his message must have been popular because he organized a large number of them. The Marcionite church existed into the seventh century. Many writers throughout the second, third, and fourth centuries wrote against Marcion and his ideas. However, Marcion's alternative Christianity had some positive effects on later Christianity. Some scholars believe that because Marcion created a list of texts for his followers to use, other Christians decided to do the same, and this list became the New Testament.

ASK YOURSELF

1. How do you think Tertullian's description of Marcion affected those who read it? Would they be more or less likely to believe in Marcion's message, and why?
2. Why does Tertullian continually mention the place where Marcion is from? Do you think this is some type of literary technique, or were people from this area really like this?
3. Tertullian implies that Marcion held the same belief that Tertullian did but became an "apostate," or one who leaves the faith. If Marcion had not become an apostate (as Tertullian calls him), do you think that modern-day people would know about him?
4. How are biblical verses used in these two sections? Do you find Tertullian's arguments persuasive? How do you think Marcion and his followers would have reacted to the use of these verses?

TOPICS TO CONSIDER

- ⮞ Many of Tertullian's readers would have been familiar with the Amazons, Prometheus, and the cynic Diogenes. Consider how these individuals or groups would have made an impact on Tertullian's audience and how they make an impact on today's audience.

❧ As stated above, the region of Pontus was a Roman province. Consider whether Tertullian's descriptions of the Romans living in this area are true or not. Make a list and compare them to attributes of Romans living in other areas.

❧ Tertullian states that his first writing was lost, found, and published, and his second version had to be amended. Tertullian had to make a third version that superseded the rest, which he claims was the most correct. Consider how these multiple versions may have had an impact on the manuscript history of Tertullian's *Against Marcion*.

❧ Marcion has long been considered to be a heretic, but his ideas have had an important role in the history of Christianity. Consider how heretics are dealt with in the modern world. Do they contribute anything good to Christianity?

MARCION'S *ANTITHESIS*

Marcion's rejection by the Roman church leaders led him to create his own form of Christianity, now called Marcionism. The spread of his version of Christianity was noted by many early Christians. Justin Martyr (died around 165 CE) stated that Marcion's beliefs were discussed by "every nation" (*First Apology* 1:26) and that Marcion was alive and well at the time that Justin was writing. Many other early Christians wrote against Marcion. It appears that the most popular writing of Marcion was his *Antitheses,* in which he listed biblical verses from the Old Testament and compared them to the New Testament. He was trying to show that there was a vast difference between the messages found in these books, and with this, he believed that there were different gods—the true one found in the New Testament and an evil god found in the Old Testament. One example was his comparison between Genesis 3:9 and Luke 9:47. In Genesis 3:9, God is looking for Adam and Eve after they had hid from him, but in Luke 9:47, Jesus was aware of the inner thoughts of his disciples. This showed that the Hebrew God did not know everything and was therefore not a true God like Jesus was. The methods used in Marcion's *Antitheses* proved to be very popular for later writers who thought the Old Testament should not be read by Christians.

Further Information

Against Marcion. http://www.ccel.org/ccel/schaff/anf03.pdf.

Blackmann, E. C. *Marcion and His Influence.* Reprint. Eugene, OR: Wipf and Stock, 2004.

Dunn, Geoffrey R. *Tertullian,* The Early Church Fathers series. New York: Routledge, 2004.

Hoffmann, R. Joseph. *Marcion, on the Restitution of Christianity: An Essay on the Development of Radical Paulist Theology in the Second Century,* American Academy of Religion Academy Series. Atlanta: Scholars Press, 1984.

Osborn, Eric. *Tertullian, First Theologian of the West.* Cambridge: Cambridge University Press, 2003.

Quispel, Gilles. "Marcion and the Text of the New Testament." *Vigiliae Christianae* 52, no. 4 (Nov., 1998): 349–60.

Tyson, Joseph B. *Marcion and Luke-Acts: A Defining Struggle.* Columbia: University of South Carolina Press, 2006.

31. ORIGEN, *AGAINST CELSUS*

INTRODUCTION

Origen, born in 185 CE, was a Christian living in Alexandria, Egypt, until 234, when he moved to Caesarea in Palestine. He came from a Christian family, and his father was a martyr during the reign of the Roman emperor Septimius Severus (193–211 CE). Eusebius of Caesarea, in his *Church History,* states that Origen was a Christian and wanted to join his father in martyrdom. His mother, however, hid his clothes so he could not go outside. Origen went on to become an exceptional scholar who wrote many volumes on everything from Christian theology to works on textual criticism. One of his more famous works is *Contra Celsum,* or *Against Celsus,* written in 248 or 249 CE. His friend Ambrosius sent Origen a book titled *On True Doctrine,* written by Celsus, who had lived sometime during the latter part of the second century. Celsus was not a Christian and had decided to attack the new religion. Celsus's book was not widely read during his lifetime, but it must have been causing some problems for Christians since it was sent to Origen to refute it.

The structure of Origen's response would become a template to other Christians who defended their faith. He gives a short excerpt of *On True Doctrine* and then proceeds to argue against it. Celsus had many problems with Christianity, including its ties with Judaism and tricking the uneducated into becoming members, among others. The following excerpts discuss Origen's response to some of these complaints.

KEEP IN MIND WHILE YOU READ

1. Origen was well known and popular with other Christians during his lifetime, but after his death (and even for a while when he was alive) he was seen as unorthodox. In the fourth century it was dangerous for an official high in the church to defend the writings of Origen. Later, in the sixth century, Origen was officially condemned as a heretic. However, many now believe that the positions that are considered to be unorthodox were held by Origen's students and not Origen himself.

2. Unfortunately, *On True Doctrine* no longer exists, so we are dependent on Origen for knowledge of its contents.

3. Origen's attack on Celsus was a bit unusual for Origen. He was a prolific writer, and the thousands of books and letters he wrote primarily concerned Christian theology, as opposed to personal attacks.

4. Celsus's first charge against Christians was that they were part of a secret society. This was a very common charge against Christians. The Romans had made it illegal for groups of people to meet in secret, in case they were plotting to overthrow the government. The charge led to persecutions against the Christians, which is probably why Origen spends so much time refuting this charge.

5. Ambrosius was the patron of Origen. Ambrosius provided scribes and monetary support for Origen's work.

Origen, Against Celsus, *selections*

Book 1, Chapter 1: The first point which Celsus brings forward, in his desire to throw discredit upon Christianity, is, that the Christians entered into secret associations with each other contrary to law, saying, that "of associations some are public, and that these are in accordance with the laws; others, again, secret, and maintained in violation of the laws." And his wish is to bring into disrepute what are termed the "love-feasts" of the Christians, as if they had their origin in the common danger, and were more binding than any oaths. Since, then, he babbles about the public law, alleging that the associations of the Christians are in violation of it, we have to reply, that if a man were placed among Scythians, whose laws were unholy, and having no opportunity of escape, were compelled to live among them, such an one would with good reason, for the sake of the law of truth, which the Scythians would regard as wickedness, enter into associations contrary to their laws, with those like-minded with himself. So, if truth is to decide, the laws of the heathens, which relate to images, and an atheistical polytheism are "Scythian" laws, or more impious even than these, if there be any such. It is not irrational, then, to form associations in opposition to existing laws, if done for the sake of the truth. For as those persons would do well who should enter into a secret association in order to put to death a tyrant who had seized upon the liberties of a state, so Christians also, when tyrannized over by him who is called the devil, and by falsehood, form leagues contrary to the laws of the devil, against his power, and for the safety of those others whom they may succeed in persuading to revolt from a government which is, as it were, "Scythian," and despotic.

Book 1, Chapter 7: Moreover, since he frequently calls the Christian doctrine a secret system (of belief), we must confute him on this point also, since almost the entire world is better acquainted with what Christians preach than with the favorite opinions of philosophers. For who is ignorant of the statement that Jesus was born of a virgin, and that He was crucified, and that His resurrection is an article of faith among many, and that a general judgment is announced to come, in which the wicked are to be punished according to their deserts, and the righteous to be duly rewarded? And yet the mystery of the resurrection, not being understood, is made a subject of ridicule among unbelievers. In these circumstances, to speak of the Christian doctrine as a secret system, is altogether absurd. But that there should be certain doctrines, not made known to the multitude, which are (revealed) after the exoteric ones have been taught, is not a peculiarity of Christianity alone, but also of philosophic systems, in which certain truths are exoteric and others esoteric. Some of the hearers of Pythagoras were content with his sayings; while others were taught in secret those doctrines which were not deemed fit to be communicated to profane and insufficiently prepared ears. Moreover, all the mysteries that are celebrated everywhere throughout Greece and barbarous countries, although held in secret, have no discredit thrown upon them, so that it is in vain that he endeavors to make false statements about the secret doctrines of Christianity, seeing he does not correctly understand its nature.

Book 3, Chapter 55: But as Celsus delights to heap up lies against us, and, in addition to those which he has already uttered, has added others, let us examine these also, and see whether it be the Christians or Celsus who have reason to be ashamed of what is said. He asserts, "We see, indeed, in private houses workers in wool and leather, and fullers, and persons of the most uninstructed and rustic character, not venturing to utter a word in the presence of their elders and wiser masters; but when they get hold of the children privately, and certain women as ignorant as themselves, they pour forth wonderful statements, to the effect that they ought not to give heed to their father and to their teachers, but should obey them; that the former are foolish and stupid, and neither know nor can perform anything that is really good, being preoccupied with empty trifles; that they alone know how men ought to live, and that, if the children obey them, they will both be happy themselves, and will make their home happy also. And while thus speaking, if they see one of the instructors of youth approaching, or one of the more intelligent class, or even the father himself, the more timid among them become afraid, while the more forward incite the children to throw off the yoke, whispering that in the presence of father and teachers they neither will nor can explain to them any good thing, seeing they turn away with aversion from the silliness and stupidity of such persons as being altogether corrupt, and far advanced in wickedness, and such as would inflict punishment upon them; but that if they wish (to avail themselves of their aid) they must leave their father and their instructors, and go with the women and their playfellows to the women's apartments, or to the leather shop, or to the fuller's shop, that they may attain to perfection;—and by words like these they gain them over."

Book 3, Chapter 56: Observe now how by such statements he depreciates those among us who are teachers of the word, and who strive in every way to raise the soul to the Creator of all things, and who show that we ought to despise things "sensible," and "temporal," and "visible," and to do our utmost to reach communion with God, and the contemplation of things that are "intelligent," and "invisible," and a blessed life with God, and the friends of God; comparing them to "workers in wool in private houses, and to leather-cutters, and to fullers, and to the most rustic of mankind, who carefully incite young boys to wickedness, and women to forsake their fathers and teachers, and follow them." Now let Celsus point out from what wise parent, or from what teachers, we keep away children and women, and let him ascertain by comparison among those children and women who are adherents of our doctrine, whether any of the opinions which they formerly heard are better than ours, and in what manner we draw away children and women from noble and venerable studies, and incite them to worse things. But he will not be able to make good any such charge against us, seeing that, on the contrary, we turn away women from a dissolute life, and from being at variance with those with whom they live, from all mad desires after theatres and dancing, and from superstition; while we train to habits of self-restraint boys just reaching the age of puberty, and feeling a desire for sexual pleasures, pointing out to them not only the disgrace which attends those sins, but also the state to which the soul of the wicked is reduced through practices of that kind, and the judgments which it will suffer, and the punishments which will be inflicted.

Source: Roberts, Rev. Alexander, and James Donaldson, eds. *The Ante-Nicene Fathers: Translations of the Writings of the Fathers Down to* A.D. *325,* vol. 4. New York: Charles Scribner's Sons, 1905, 397, 399, 486.

AFTERMATH

Celsus was long dead by the time Origen had written against his *On True Doctrine.* However, soon after the publication of *Contra Celsum,* Celsus became known as an archenemy of the Christians. This was especially the case when *Contra Celsum* became more well known, and persecutions against the Christians once again were on the rise. Origen's work was used by many to counter the claims put forth by Celsus. *Contra Celsum* was Origen's last major work. Emperor Decius, who ruled from 249 to 251 CE, did not like Christians and began to persecute them, including Origen. He was tortured but was not executed. However, he died three years later from the after effects.

ASK YOURSELF

1. Christians would gather and celebrate the Lord's Supper, which commemorated the last dinner that Christ had before he was crucified. What parts of that ceremony would lead Celsus and other non-Christians to assume it was a "love-feast"?
2. Origen mentions that there were other groups that kept secrets from their members until they were ready. Why would many groups in antiquity do this? What is the appeal of keeping and telling these secrets?
3. Do modern-day Christian groups still keep secrets from those not involved in their specific group? If so, are there people who attack in the same way that Celsus did?

TOPICS TO CONSIDER

- Origen argues that Christians did not have a secret religion, yet at the same time he states that there were secrets held from those who were not ready to hear them. What were these secrets?
- Another common charge (which Celsus repeats) against the Christians was that their group was made up of the poor, the uneducated, and women. Consider if this charge was true. How does Origen treat this accusation?
- Origen copied parts of *On True Doctrine* in order to refute it. How does knowing that affect the way you think of *Contra Celsum*?
- Consider how other non-Christians would feel about Celsus's *On True Doctrine.* Did they have the same complaints as Celsus?

ACCUSATIONS AGAINST THE CHRISTIANS

There were many accusations aimed at the Christians, even before the time of Celsus in the late second century. One accusation stated that Christians were cannibals because of the taking of communion. Christ, in the New Testament, asked his disciples to take a cup of wine as his blood and to eat bread as his body. Ancient Christians (like some Christians today) believed that the bread and wine were literally the body and blood of Christ. Another accusation stated that Christians had wild sex parties in the dark. This rumor stemmed from the fact that Christians met in small groups, away from the public, and that non-Christians could only guess what they were doing. Christians had to meet away from the public eye because Christianity was illegal until the time of Emperor Constantine (early 300s). Another accusation related to these secret meetings was that Christians were plotting to overthrow the Roman government. Because of this the Romans passed laws that stated small groups of people (including Christians) could not meet. Another common charge was that the Christians were atheists because they refused to worship the Roman gods, goddesses, and the emperors.

Further Information

"Celsus the Platonist." *The Catholic Encyclopedia* website. http://www.newadvent.org/cathen/03490a.htm.

Chadwick, Henry. "Origen, Celcus, and the Resurrection of the Body." *Harvard Theological Review* 41, no. 2 (Apr., 1948): 83–102.

De Lubac, Henri. *History and Spirit: The Understanding of Scripture According to Origen.* San Francisco: Ignatius Press, 2007.

Feldman, Louis H. "Origen's 'Contra Celsum' and Josephus' 'Contra Apionem': The Issue of Jewish Origins." *Vigiliae Christianae* 44, no. 2 (Jun., 1990): 105–35.

Origen. *Against Celsus.* http://www.ccel.org/ccel/schaff/anf04.vi.ix.i.i.html.

Richardson, Cyril C. "The Condemnation of Origen." *Church History* 6, no. 1 (Mar., 1937): 50–64.

Trigg, Joseph W. *Origen.* New York: Routledge, 1998.

Van Winden, J.C.M. "Notes on Origen, Contra Celsum." *Vigiliae Christianae* 20, no. 4 (Dec., 1966): 201–13.

32. ALEXANDER OF ALEXANDRIA, *CATHOLIC EPISTLE*

INTRODUCTION

In the year 318 or 319 CE, Arius, a priest from Alexandria, Egypt, began to openly complain about the teachings of his bishop, Alexander. Alexander had been stating that God and the Son were coeternal, meaning that they both existed from the very beginning. However, Arius did not agree. He believed that God had been in existence first, and the Son (Jesus) was created at a later point. Arius thought that if Jesus was really the Son, then God had to come first. Arius, like many other Christians, backed up his ideas with the Bible. His favorite text to use was Proverbs 8:22–25: "The Lord created me at the beginning of his work, the first of his acts of long ago." To Arius, this proved that God had created the Son first, which implied that God was here before the Son. The debate over this issue spilled over into other parts of the Mediterranean when both sides (Arius and Alexander) began writing letters to their supporters. The issue was brought to the attention of Emperor Constantine, who called the first ecumenical church council to decide the issue (the Council of Nicea in 325 CE). The letter below was written by Bishop Alexander in 320 CE to the bishops he believed followed his beliefs. It is important because it gives the beliefs of both the Arians and those who thought differently from them.

KEEP IN MIND WHILE YOU READ

1. The emperor at the time was the Christian Constantine, who had been involved in this controversy from its beginning. Constantine was no stranger to controversies during his rule. Soon after becoming the emperor of the west in 306 CE, Constantine also had to deal with the Donatists.
2. By the time the letter below was composed, Arius had already written a letter to Eusebius, bishop of Nicomedia, and had gone to visit him. It was after this meeting that Eusebius of Nicomedia played an important role in spreading the ideas of Arius.
3. The church in Alexandria, Egypt, had had a long history before this. It was considered to be one of the most important churches in all of Christianity. This

probably explains why the bishops of this city had to spend so much effort trying to contain Arianism.

4. The basis of most arguments between various Christian groups was the interpretation of biblical passages. The following letter is very similar.

Alexander of Alexandria, Catholic Epistle

To our beloved and most reverend fellow-ministers of the Catholic Church in every place, Alexander sends greeting in the Lord:

apostatize To leave a set of beliefs that are thought to be the most accurate.

Berytus Modern-day Beirut.

diocese An area that encompasses the territory controlled by the church. It can sometimes have many bishops.

Eusebius, the present bishop of Nicomedia Eusebius played a very important role in spreading the ideas of Arius. After the death of Constantine he became the bishop of Constantinople, making him one of the most powerful bishops.

1. Since the body of the Catholic Church is one, and it is commanded in Holy Scripture that we should keep the bond of unanimity and peace, it follows that we should write and signify to one another the things which are done by each of us; that whether one member suffer or rejoice we may all either suffer or rejoice with one another. In our **diocese**, then, not so long ago, there have gone forth lawless men, and adversaries of Christ, teaching men to **apostatize;** which thing, with good right, one might suspect and call the precursor of Antichrist. I indeed wished to cover the matter up in silence, that so perhaps the evil might spend itself in the leaders of the heresy alone, and that it might not spread to other places and defile the ears of any of the more simple-minded. But since **Eusebius, the present bishop of Nicomedia,** imagining that with him rest all ecclesiastical matters, because, having left **Berytus** and cast his eyes upon the church of the Nicomedians, and no punishment has been inflicted upon him, he is set over these apostates, and has undertaken to write everywhere, commending them, if by any means he may draw aside some who are ignorant to this most disgraceful and anti-Christian heresy; it became necessary for me, as knowing what is written in the law, no longer to remain silent, but to announce to you all, that you may know both those who have become apostates, and also the wretched words of their heresy; and if Eusebius write, not to give heed to him. For he, desiring by their assistance to renew that ancient wickedness of his mind, with respect to which he has for a time been silent, pretends that he is writing in their behalf, but he proves by his deed that he is exerting himself to do this on his own account.

2. Now the apostates from the Church are these: Arius, Achilles, Aithales, Carpones, the other Arius, Sarmates, who were formerly priests; Euzoius, Lucius, Julius, Menas, Helladius, and Gaius, formerly deacons; and with them Secundus and Theonas, who were once called bishops. And the words invented by them, and spoken contrary to the mind of Scripture, are as follows:

3. "God was not always the Father; but there was a time when God was not the Father. The Word of God was not always, but was made from things that are not; for He who is God fashioned the non-existing from the non-existing; wherefore there was a time when He was not. For the Son is a thing created, and a thing made: nor is He like to the Father in substance; nor is He the true and natural Word of the Father; nor is He His true Wisdom;

but He is one of the things fashioned and made. And He is called, by a misapplication of the terms, the Word and Wisdom, since He is Himself made by the proper Word of God, and by that wisdom which is in God, in which, as God made all other things, so also did He make Him. Wherefore, He is by His very nature changeable and mutable, equally with other rational beings. The Word, too, is alien and separate from the substance of God. The father also is **ineffable** to the Son; for neither does the Word perfectly and accurately know the Father, neither can He perfectly see Him. For neither does the Son indeed know His own substance as it is. Since He for our sakes was made, that by Him as by an instrument God might create us; nor would He have existed had not God wished to make us. Someone asked of them whether the Son of God could change even as the devil changed; and they feared not to answer that He can; for since He was made and created, He is of mutable nature."

> **ineffable** Unable to be described because of his greatness.

4. Since those about Arius speak these things and shamelessly maintain them, we, coming together with the Bishops of Egypt and the Libya, nearly a hundred in number, have anathematized them, together with their followers. But those about Eusebius have received them, earnestly endeavoring to mix up falsehood with truth, impiety with piety. But they will not prevail; for the truth prevails, and there is no communion between light and darkness, no concord between Christ and Belial. For who ever heard such things? Or who, now hearing them, is not astonished, and does not stop his ears that the pollution of these words should not touch them? Who that hears John saying, "In the beginning was the Word," (John 1:1) does not condemn those who say there was a time when He was not? Who that hears these words of the Gospel, "the only-begotten Son;" (John 1:18) and, "by Him were all things made," (John 1:3) will not hate those who declare He is one of the things made? For how can He be one of the things made by Him? Or how shall He be the only-begotten who, as they say, is reckoned with all the rest, if indeed He is a thing made and created? And how can He be made of things which are not, when the Father says, "My heart belched forth a good Word" (Psalms 45:1) and, "From the womb, before the morning have I begotten Thee?" (Psalms 110:3). Or how is He unlike to the substance of the Father, who is the perfect image and brightness of the Father, and who says, "He who has seen Me has seen the Father?" (John 14:9). And how, if the Son is the Word or Wisdom and Reason of God, was there a time when He was not? It is all one as if they said, that there was a time when God was without reason and wisdom. How, also, can He be changeable and mutable, who says indeed by Himself: "I am in the Father, and the Father in Me," (John 14:10) and, "I and My Father are one;" (John 10:30) and by the prophet, "I am the Lord, I change not?" (Malachi 3:6). For even though one saying may refer to the Father Himself, yet it would now be more aptly spoken of the Word, because when He became man, He changed not; but, as says the apostle, "Jesus Christ, the same yesterday, today, and forever" (Hebrews 13:8). Who hath induced them to say, that for our sakes He was made; although Paul says, "for whom are all things, and by whom are all things?" (Hebrews 11:10).

5. Now concerning their blasphemous assertion who say that the Son does not perfectly know the Father, we need not wonder: for having once purposed in their mind to wage war against Christ, they impugn also these words of His, "As the Father knows Me, even so I know the Father" (John 10:15). Wherefore, if the Father only in part knows the Son, then it is evident that the Son does not perfectly know the Father. But if it be wicked thus to speak, and if the Father perfectly knows the Son, it is plain that, even as the Father knows His own Word, so also the Word knows His own Father, of whom He is the Word.

> **Hymenæus and Philetus suffered**
>
> Alexander is referring to 2 Timothy 2:16–18: "Avoid profane chatter, for it will lead people into more and more impiety, and their talk will spread like gangrene. Among them are Hymenæus and Philetus, who have swerved from the truth by claiming that the resurrection has already taken place. They are upsetting the faith of some."

6. By saying these things, and by unfolding the divine Scriptures, we have often refuted them. But they, chameleon-like, changing their sentiments, endeavor to claim for themselves that saying: "When the wicked comes, then comes contempt" (Proverbs 18:3). Before them, indeed, many heresies existed, which, having dared more than was right, have fallen into madness. But these by all their words have attempted to do away with the Godhead of Christ, have made those seem righteous, since they have come nearer to Antichrist. Wherefore they have been excommunicated and anathematized by the Church. And indeed, although we grieve at the destruction of these men, especially that after having once learned the doctrine of the Church, they have now gone back; yet we do not wonder at it; for this very thing **Hymenæus and Philetus suffered,** (1 Timothy 2:17) and before them Judas, who, though he followed the Savior, afterwards became a traitor and an apostate. Moreover, concerning these very men, warnings are not wanting to us, for the Lord foretold: "Take heed that you are not deceived: for many shall come in My Name, saying, I am Christ; and the time draws near: therefore do not go after them" (Luke 21:8). Paul, too, having learnt these things from the Savior, wrote, "In the latter times some shall depart from the faith, giving heed to seducing spirits, and doctrines of devils which turn away from the truth" (2 John 10).

6. Since, therefore, our Lord and Savior Jesus Christ has thus Himself exhorted us, and by His apostle has signified such things to us; we, who have heard their impiety with our own ears, have consistently anathematized such men, as I have already said, and have declared them to be aliens from the Catholic Church and faith, and we have made known the thing, beloved and most honored fellow-ministers, to your piety, that you should not receive any of them, should they venture rashly to come unto you, and that you should not trust Eusebius or anyone else who writes concerning them. For it becomes us as Christians to turn with aversion from all who speak or think against Christ, as the adversaries of God and the destroyers of souls, and "not even to wish them Godspeed, lest at any time we become partakers of their evil deeds," (2 John 10) as the blessed John enjoins. Salute the brethren who are with you. Those who are with me salute you.

Signators:

(The text ends with many people signing the letter)

Source: Roberts, Rev. Alexander, and James Donaldson, eds. *Ante-Nicene Christian Library: Translations of the Writings of the Fathers Down to A.D. 325,* vol. 14. London: T & T Clark, 1880, 348–52.

AFTERMATH

Both Eusebius of Nicomedia and Arius sent at least one other letter to Alexander after this. Eusebius of Nicomedia asked Alexander to take Arius back into communion. Alexander refused, and there followed a number of local church councils that sided either with Alexander or with Arius. The situation continued to escalate, and Emperor Constantine decided to get personally involved. He wrote to both men and pleaded with them to settle their differences since they were giving Christians a bad name. This did not work, and in 325 CE Constantine convened the Council of Nicea to settle the issue.

ASK YOURSELF

1. What is the danger (according to Alexander) with Eusebius of Nicomedia siding with Arius?
2. To many (especially the emperor), the differences between Arius and Alexander were not serious enough to be called a heresy. Examine the differences and consider whether they warranted the intervention of the emperor and a church council. Consider your own religious beliefs—are they similar to those of Arius?
3. Emperor Constantine had no difficulty getting involved with the affairs of the church, and this intrusion sometimes led to arguments between the later emperors and the leaders of the church. How does this differ from the actions of political figures today?
4. There were many recipients of this letter. What factors would be involved with accepting either the claims of Alexander or those of Arius? Do you think Alexander would have sent this letter to the supporters of Arius?

TOPICS TO CONSIDER

- Recreate the beliefs of Arius just from the letter of Alexander. Consider whether Alexander is a good source for the history of Arianism.
- Create a list of all the biblical quotations that Alexander uses, both for the Arians and for the Catholics. Compare and contrast the list. Consider how the Catholics could use the biblical quotes attributed to Arius, and vice versa.
- The history of Christianity is full of arguments and schisms. Consider what Christianity would have been like if the Arians had won their arguments.
- In its early years the geographic spread of Arianism and the reaction to it only reached the eastern side of the Roman Empire. Consider why it did not spread to the western side until a few decades after the Council of Nicea in 325.

Further Information

"Alexander of Alexandria." *Catholic Encyclopedia.* http://www.newadvent.org/cathen/01296a.htm.

Barnard, L. W. "The Antecedents of Arius." *Vigiliae Christianae* 24, no. 3 (Sep., 1970): 172–88.

Haas, Christopher. "The Arians of Alexandria." *Vigiliae Christianae* 47, no. 3 (Sep., 1993): 234–45.

Hanson, R. P. C. *The Search for the Christian Doctrine of God: The Arian Controversy, 318–381.* Grand Rapids, MI: Baker Academic, 1988.

Haugaard, William P. "Arius: Twice a Heretic? Arius and the Human Soul of Jesus Christ." *Church History* 29, no. 3 (Sep., 1960): 251–63.

Rubenstein, Richard E. *When Jesus Became God: The Struggle to Define Christianity during the Last Days of Rome.* Orlando, FL: Harcourt, 1999.

33. ATHANASIUS, *DISCOURSE ONE AGAINST THE ARIANS*

INTRODUCTION

One of the more important people in the Arian controversy was Athanasius, who became the bishop of Alexandria, Egypt, in 327 and remained in his office until 373 CE. Athanasius was also present at the Council of Nicea in 325 when he was a deacon and where he acted as the secretary to Bishop Alexander of Alexandria. Athanasius's account of the history of Arianism is of extreme importance because he preserved many primary texts from this controversy as well as being an eyewitness. Athanasius, once he became the bishop of Alexandria, fought constantly to destroy the Arian beliefs, and his eagerness for argumentation and for the defense of the Nicene Creed led to him being exiled from Alexandria a total of four times, plus one period where he had to go into hiding. Many of these exiles were due to the fact that Emperor Constantius II (a son of Constantine) favored the Arian form of Christianity and clashed often with Athanasius. There are four *Discourses,* although there is debate on whether the fourth was written by Athanasius, and recently it has been questioned whether he wrote the third (but this has not found acceptance). The genuine *Discourses* were written sometime between 339 and 361, but the most probable date is around 340 when Athanasius was in Rome, where he had fled into exile for the second time (Barnes 53–55).

KEEP IN MIND WHILE YOU READ

1. By this time Arius was dead. His friend and supporter Eusebius (formerly bishop of Nicomedia) was now the bishop of Constantinople, which was the second most important city in the Roman Empire (behind Rome). This put Eusebius in a very powerful position.
2. Athanasius had been a deacon in Alexandria and had traveled to the Council of Nicea with his bishop, Alexander, in 325. Athanasius personally knew Arius and Eusebius, now bishop of Constantinople.
3. Athanasius had been exiled by Emperor Constantius during this period, but he was also exiled by Constantius II's father, Emperor Constantine. During the time of Constantine he fled to Gaul (now France) and spent 18 months there.

4. Emperor Constantine died in 337, and the royal power was split between his three sons, Constantius II (337–350), Constantine II (337–340), and Constans I (337–350). Each had a separate sphere of control. Constans I supported Athanasius and controlled the western side of the empire (including Italy, Greece, and Macedonia). Constantius II was partial to Arianism and controlled the east. It is not clear which side Constantine II supported. He controlled Britain, Gaul (modern-day France and Germany), and Spain.

Athanasius, Discourse One against the Arians *1:1–4*

1. Of all other heresies which have departed from the truth it is acknowledged that they have but devised a madness, and their irreligiousness has long since become notorious to all men. For that their authors went out from us, it plainly follows, as the blessed John has written, that they never thought nor now think with us. Wherefore, as the Savior says, in that they do not gather with us, they scatter with the devil, and keep an eye on those who slumber, that, by this second sowing of their own mortal poison, they may have companions in death. But, whereas one heresy, and that the last, which has now risen as harbinger of Antichrist, the Arian, as it is called, considering that other heresies, her elder sisters, have been openly proscribed, in her craft and cunning, affects to array herself in Scripture language, like her father the devil, and is forcing her way back into the Church's paradise,—that with the pretense of Christianity, her smooth sophistry (for reason she has none) may deceive men into wrong thoughts of Christ,—since she has already seduced certain of the foolish, not only to corrupt their ears, but even to take and eat with Eve, till in their ignorance which ensues they think bitter sweet, and admire this loathsome heresy, on this account I have thought it necessary, **at your request,** to rip the "folds of its breast-plate" and to show the ill savor of its folly. So while those who are far from it may continue to shun it, those whom it has deceived may repent; and, opening the eyes of their heart, may understand that darkness is not light, nor falsehood truth, nor Arianism good; that those who call these men Christians are in great and grievous error, as neither having studied Scripture, nor understanding Christianity at all, and the faith which it contains.

2. For what have they discovered in this heresy like to the religious Faith, that they vainly talk as if its supporters said no evil? This in truth is to call even **Caiaphas** a Christian, and to reckon the traitor Judas still among the Apostles, and to say that they who asked Barabbas instead of the Savior did no evil, and to recommend **Hymenæus** and Alexander as right-minded men, and as if the Apostle slandered them. But neither can a Christian bear to hear this, nor can he consider the man who dared to say it sane in his understanding. For with them for Christ is Arius, as with the Manichees **Manichæus**; and for Moses and the other saints they

at your request It isn't clear to whom this might be referring. If Athanasius wrote this around 340 CE during his exile at Rome, it could be that he was writing the *Discourses* for the bishop of that city, Julius I. It has also been suggested that the *Discourses* were requested by some of Athanasius's monastic friends (Kannengiesser 139).

Caiaphas The high priest who conspired to kill Jesus (Matthew 26:3). Caiaphas also questioned Jesus when he was captured.

Hymenaeus Hymenaeus is mentioned in 1 Timothy 1:20, who, along with Alexander, was kicked out of their Christian group by Paul.

Manichaeus Manichaeus (or Mani) was the founder of Manichaeism, a Christian group that spread quickly through the Roman Empire.

have made the discovery of one Sotades, a man whom even Gentiles laugh at, and of the daughter of Herodias. For of the one has Arius imitated the dissolute and effeminate tone, in writing **Thalia** on his model; and the other he has rivaled in her dance, reeling and frolicking in his blasphemies against the Savior; till the victims of his heresy lose their wits and go foolish, and change the Name of the Lord of glory into the likeness of the image of corruptible man, and for Christians come to be called Arians, bearing this badge of their irreligion. For let them not excuse themselves; nor retort their disgrace on those who are not as they, calling Christians after the names of their teachers, that they themselves may appear to have that Name in the same way. Nor let them make a jest of it, when they feel shame at their disgraceful appellation; rather, if they be ashamed, let them hide their faces, or let them recoil from their own irreligion. For never at any time did Christian people take their title from the Bishops among them, but from the Lord, on whom we rest our faith. Thus, though the blessed Apostles have become our teachers, and have ministered the Savior's Gospel, yet not from them have we our title, but from Christ we are and are named Christians. But for those who derive the faith which they profess from others, good reason is it they should bear their name, whose property they have become.

3. Yes surely, while all of us are called Christians after Christ, Marcion broached a heresy a long time since and was cast out; and those who continued with him who ejected him remained Christians; but those who followed Marcion were called Christians no more, but henceforth Marcionites. Thus Valentinus also, and Basilides, and Manichæus, and **Simon Magus,** have imparted their own name to their followers; and some are accosted as Valentinians, or as Basilidians, or as Manichees, or as Simonians; and other, Cataphrygians from Phrygia, and from Novatus Novatians. So too Meletius, when ejected by Peter the Bishop and Martyr, called his party no longer Christians, but **Meletians,** and so in consequence when Alexander of blessed memory had cast out Arius, those who remained with Alexander, remained Christians; but those who went out with Arius, left the Savior's name to us who were with Alexander, and as to them they were hence-forward denominated Arians. Behold then, after Alexander's death too, those who communicate with his successor Athanasius, and those with whom the said Athanasius communicates, are instances of the same rule; none of them bear his name, nor is he named from them, but all in like manner, and as is usual, are called Christians. For though we have a succession of teachers and become their disciples, yet, because we are taught by them the things of Christ, we both are, and are called, Christians all the same. But those who follow the heretics, though they have innumerable successors in their heresy, yet anyhow bear the name of him who devised it. Thus, though Arius is dead, and many of his party have succeeded him, yet those who think with him, as being known from Arius, are called Arians. And, what is a remarkable evidence of this, those of the Greeks who even at this time come into the Church, on giving up the superstition of idols, take the name, not of their catechists, but of the Savior, and begin to be called Christians instead of

Meletians The founder of this group was Melitius. Melitius had an argument with Peter, the bishop of Alexandria over allowing some priests and bishops to regain their offices after they had lapsed during the persecution under Emperor Diocletian. Melitius believed that those who had lapsed should not be allowed back into the church. He broke away from Peter and started his own movement.

Simon Magus Simon the Great is mentioned in Acts 8:9–24. He is described as being a magician. He converted to Christianity, and when he saw the apostles laying hands on people and bringing the Holy Spirit, Simon offered the apostles money to learn how to do this himself. He was thrown out of the group. This is where the word *simony* comes from.

Thalia A writing by Arius, also known as The Banquet. Unfortunately, the original text has been lost, but some of it is preserved in the writings of Athanasius.

Greeks: while those of them who go off to the heretics, and again all who from the Church change to this heresy, abandon Christ's name, and henceforth are called Arians, as no longer holding Christ's faith, but having inherited Arius's madness.

4. How then can they be Christians, who for Christians are Ario-maniacs? Or how are they of the Catholic Church, who have shaken off the Apostolical faith, and become authors of fresh evils, who, after abandoning the oracles of divine Scripture, call Arius's Thalia a new wisdom? And with reason too, for they are announcing a new heresy. And hence a man may marvel, that, whereas many have written many treatises and abundant homilies upon the Old Testament and the New, yet in none of them is a Thalia found; nay nor among the more respectable of the Gentiles, but among those only who sing such strains over their cups, amid cheers and jokes, when men are merry, that the rest may laugh; till this marvelous Arius, taking no grave pattern, and ignorant even of what is respectable, while he stole largely from other heresies, would be original in the ludicrous, with none but Sotades for his rival. For what suited him more, when he would dance forth against the Savior, than to throw his wretched words of irreligion into dissolute and loose meters? That, while a man, as Wisdom says, "is known from the utterance of his word," so from those numbers should be seen the writer's effeminate soul and corruption of thought. In truth, that crafty one did not escape detection; but, for all his many writings to and fro, like the serpent, he did but fall into the error of the Pharisees. They, that they might transgress the Law, pretended to be anxious for the words of the Law, and that they might deny the expected and then present Lord, were hypocritical with God's name, and were convicted of blaspheming when they said, Why do you, being a man, make yourself God,' and say, "I and the Father are one?" And so too, this counterfeit and Sotadean Arius, feigns to speak of God, introducing Scripture language, but is on all sides recognized as godless Arius, denying the Son, and reckoning Him among the creatures.

Source: Wace, Henry, and Philip Schaff, eds. *A Select Library of Nicene and Post-Nicene Fathers of the Christian Church, Vol. I*. Oxford: Parker and Company, 1890, 306–08.

AFTERMATH

Athanasius had written the *Discourses* primarily as an attack against the spread of Arianism. Arius had recently died, and it was the hope of many that this would put an end to the Arian movement, but this was not the case. Arianism continued to be a large movement, primarily in the eastern side of the Roman Empire, and for the entire time that Athanasius was bishop of Alexandria, the Arians would be a source of conflict for him. Many Christians who followed the form of Christianity espoused by Athanasius read this work (and his other anti-Arian writings) and it helped them to combat Arianism. Athanasius was a prolific writer and he continued to attack Arianism until his death in 373.

ASK YOURSELF

1. Athanasius probably wrote this first *Discourse* while he was in exile at Rome. The Bishop of Rome at that time was Julius and he had wholeheartedly accepted Athanasius, as well as Emperor Constans I. However, Constantius II usually did not support him. How do you think this affected what Athanasius had written?
2. How do you think Athanasius' exiles affected his writings and his life in general?

3. Athanasius spent many years in exile outside of his native Alexandria. How do you think this affected his parishioners, both when he was in exile and when he was back in his see?
4. What role did the Bible play in arguing against the ideas of Arius?
5. One argument that Athanasius makes is that heretical groups are named after their founders. However, these groups usually did not name themselves, but were named by other Christian groups who were arguing against them. Knowing this, do you think this hurts the arguments of Athanasius?

TOPICS TO CONSIDER

☙ Arius believed that Christ was the Son of God and that Christ was divine, but he believed that the Son was created second. His reasoning was that if God was the Father, then the Son must come after. If someone held these views today, would they be attacked in the same way Athanasius attacked Arius?

☙ During this period, the Arians and the Nicenes (the Catholics) fought for supremacy, especially with gaining the ear of the emperors. Consider the importance of having the support of the emperor for this religion. Would it hurt or help? Also consider whether the man or woman on the street would care what the emperors believed in.

☙ There are many different versions of Christianity today. Consider how these different groups deal with each other. Consider who in modern Christianity is doing the same things that Athanasius did to religious groups that differed with him.

Further Information

Athanasius, *The Discourses* (including the fourth, which is generally thought not to have been written by Athanasius). http://www.ccel.org/ccel/schaff/npnf204.xxi.ii.i.i.html.

Barnard, L. W. "The Antecedents of Arius." *Vigiliae Christianae* 24, no. 3 (Sep., 1970): 172–88.

Barnard, L. W. "Athanasius and the Meletian Schism in Egypt." *The Journal of Egyptian Archaeology* 59 (Aug., 1973): 181–89.

Barnes, Timothy. *Athanasius and Constantius: Theology and Politics in the Constantinian Empire*. Cambridge, MA: Harvard University Press, 1993.

Brakke, David. *Athanasius and Asceticism*. Baltimore: Johns Hopkins University Press, 1995.

Ernest, James D. "Athanasius of Alexandria: The Scope of Scripture in Polemical and Pastoral Context." *Vigiliae Christianae* 47, no. 4 (Dec., 1993): 341–62.

Kannengiesser, Charles. "Athanasius." In *Encyclopedia of Early Christianity*, pp. 137–40, 2nd ed., edited by Everett Ferguson. New York: Garland, 1998.

Pettersen, Alvyn. *Athanasius*. Harrisburg, PA: Morehouse, 1995.

34. A Manichaean Psalm

INTRODUCTION

The Manichaeans were a Christian group that had formed around the ideas of Mani (216–276 CE), a prophet from the Persian Empire. According to Manichaean texts, King Shapur, the great Sassanian king, was good friends with Mani, and he allowed Mani to travel throughout his kingdom. However, after the death of Shapur, Mani and his followers began to be persecuted. At this time a large number of Manichaeans began to leave Persia and to go east to Central Asia and ultimately to China, or to go west into the Roman Empire. The Manichaeans were skilled at adapting their religious beliefs and texts to the local regions. Manichaean Christianity was slightly different from other forms of Christianity, especially when it came to the origin of evil. Many Christians, at least from the time of Tertullian (around 200 CE), believed that people were given free will, which they could then use to do either good or evil. This made sure that God was not responsible for evil actions. However, the Manichaeans believed that there was an evil deity. Although there is considerable debate on this point, it appears that the Manichaeans believed that the evil deity was responsible for making people do evil.

The following text is from the *Manichaean Psalm Book,* part 2, the largest collection of psalms in antiquity. It was written in Egypt sometime in the 300s CE. This psalm describes Manichaean cosmology (or how the universe was put together) in great detail and the Three Times—the Beginning, Middle, and End. Evil existed in the Beginning time, and in the Middle time it came to the world through a war between the Kingdom of Light and the Kingdom of Darkness. The text then explains how, during the End time, evil will be vanquished once and for all.

KEEP IN MIND WHILE YOU READ

1. The *Manichaean Psalm Book* was written in Coptic, which is an Egyptian language using mostly Greek letters. However, there is the occasional whole Greek word found in the Coptic manuscript. For example, the words *world, error,* and *natures* found in the text are Greek words. Many Christian texts (including those from Nag Hammadi) were written in Coptic.

2. The Manichaeans had arrived in Egypt very early on, probably in the late 200s CE. Certainly by the middle of the 300s Manichaeans were found all over the Roman Empire.

3. The Spirit of the Paraclete is Mani, the founder of the religion. In some texts Mani is described as being the Holy Spirit. Mani was seen as the last prophet of mankind.

4. Jesus played an important role in Manichaeism, as can be seen from the text. It was Jesus who sent Mani to rescue humanity.

5. There are a few places where the text was damaged. This is indicated by ". . ." There are also a few places where the meaning of the word is unclear. This has been indicated by a question mark.

Manichaean Psalm Book, *Part 2, pp. 9–11*

Let us worship the Spirit of the Paraclete. Let us bless our Lord Jesus who sent us the Spirit of Truth. He came and separated us from the Error of the world. He brought a mirror to us—we looked and saw all things in it. When the Holy Spirit came he revealed for us the truth and taught us the two natures: the Light and the Darkness which are separate from each other from the beginning. On the one hand the Kingdom of Light consists of five Greatnesses: The Father and his Twelve Aeons and the Aeons of the Aeons; the Living Air, the Land of Light, The great Sprit breathing in them, nourishing them with his light. The Kingdom of Darkness consists of five storehouses, which are smoke, fire, wind, water, and darkness; their counsel creeping in them, moving them and . . . them to make war with one another.

Now as they were making war with one another they dared to make an attempt upon the Land of Light, thinking they would be able to conquer it. But they did not know that what they were planning will bring down (a disaster) on their own heads. But there was a multitude of angels in the Land of Light, who had the power to go forth and subdue the enemy of the Father, whom was pleased that by his word he would send, he should subdue the rebels who desired to exalt themselves over that which was more exalted than they. The Father, like a shepherd who will see a lion coming to destroy his sheep, uses trickery and takes a lamb and sets it as a snare so that he might catch the lion by it. By this method he saves his sheep. After doing these things he heals the lamb which has been wounded by the lion.

This is the way of the Father, who sent his strong son. And the strong son produced from himself his Virgin (or maiden), equipped with five powers so that she might fight against the five abysses of the Darkness. When the Watcher stood firm in the boundaries of the light, he showed them his Virgin, who is his soul. The powers of Darkness stirred in their abysses, desiring to exalt themselves over her. They opened their mouths, desiring to swallow her. The Watcher held firm her power. He spread her upon them like nets over fish. He made her rain down upon the powers of Darkness like purified clouds of water. She thrust herself within them like piercing lightning. She crept into their inner parts, bounding all of them but they didn't know this. When the First Man finished his war, the Father sent his second son. He came and helped his brother (the Virgin, who was his soul) out of the abyss. He constructed the entire world out of the mix, which consisted of the Light and Darkness. He scattered all the powers of the abyss to the ten heavens and the eight earths. He shut them up in this world once. He made it a prison for all the powers of Darkness. It is also a place of purification of the soul, which was swallowed by them.

He established the sun and the moon and he set them in the highest part to purify the soul. Every day they take up the purified part to the height, but they erase the dregs (the evil parts). . . . (text is corrupted for a few words) . . . (they?) mixed (joined?) it, and conveyed it above and below. This entire world stands firm for a season. There is a great building being built outside of this world. As soon as the builder will complete it, the entire world will be destroyed and will be set on fire so that the fire will smelt it down. All the living, the remnant of the light which is everywhere, will be gathered to him and he will make a painting and an image of it. And the counsel of death, all of the Darkness, will be gathered and he will make a painting of it . . . and the ruler (of Darkness). The Living spirit will come suddenly . . . he will help the Light. However, he will shut up the Counsel of Death and the Darkness into a storehouse which was constructed for it so that it will be bound in it forever. There is no other way to bind the enemy except for this way and it will not be received by the light because it is a stranger to it, nor will it be allowed to remain in the Land of Darkness to wage a war greater than the first. A new aeon will be built in the place of this world, which will be destroyed, but the powers of the Light will rule because they have completed the whole will of the Father—they subdued the enemy, they . . . upon it forever.

This is the knowledge of Mani. Let us worship him and bless him. Blessed is everyone who will believe in him for he is the one who will live will all the righteous. Glory and victory to our lord Mani, the Spirit of the Truth, who comes from our Father. He has revealed to us the Beginning, the Middle and the End. Victory to the soul of the Blessed Mary, Theona, and Pshaijmnoute.

Source: *Manichaean Psalm Book,* part 2, p. 9–11. Translated by Kevin Kaatz, 2012.

AFTERMATH

The Manichaeans were first persecuted by Emperor Diocletian in 296 CE. The emperor was mostly concerned that the Manichaeans were seen as Persian infiltrators. However, like most persecutions, this only caused the Manichaeans to spread. By the end of the 300s many non-Manichaean Christian writers were attacking them, especially Augustine, Bishop of the North African city of Hippo. The fact that many Christians wrote against the Manichaeans shows that their ideas were very popular with some people.

The ideas found not only in this Psalm but in other Manichaean writings were used against them, including their ideas about the origin of evil. By the 400s the Manichaeans had been largely driven from the Roman Empire (what was left of it in the west), but they continued to make inroads into Central Asia and ultimately into China, where they lasted until sometime in the 1600s.

ASK YOURSELF

1. What parts of this document were appealing to those who were thinking about joining the Manichaeans, especially if they were Christian? What parts do you think were not appealing?
2. During the fourth century many Romans still worshipped the Roman gods. What are some of the parallels of the Roman religion to the Manichaean Christian

religion? Do you think those who followed the Roman religion would be attracted to this new belief system?

3. What role does Mani play in this document?

4. How does the Land of Light keep itself pure from the stain of the Land of Darkness?

5. It isn't clear who the people are at the end of the psalm. Their names appear many times in the rest of the *Psalm Book.* Who do you think these people might be?

TOPICS TO CONSIDER

- ☞ Early Christians debated the idea of free will. Consider how Christians today deal with this topic. Consider whether the Manichaean ideas have any impact on Christianity today.

- ☞ Compare the Catholic Christian idea of free will with that of the Manichaeans. Consider whether or not either side had valid points. Could there be other explanations for where evil comes from?

- ☞ The Manichaean Christians were heavily persecuted for the entire time they existed in the Roman Empire. Consider the reasons why the Manichaeans were such a threat to the Catholics.

SOURCES FOR MANICHAEISM

The *Manichaean Psalm Book* is not the only primary source we have from the Manichaeans. There exists a very large book called the *Kephalaia,* or the Main Teaching. Like the *Psalm Book,* it is written in Coptic (an Egyptian language). *The Kephalaia* contains a large amount of information about the Manichaeans and the Christian religion that they followed. The very first chapter contains the story of the Manichaean cosmogony and is very similar to that found in the Manichaean Psalm above. The second chapter states that Mani, the founder of Manichaeism, was the last of the apostles to mankind, following Adam, Enoch, Buddha, Zarathustra (or Zoroaster, a Persian prophet), and Paul. In 1969 a new manuscript was discovered that has since been titled the *Cologne Mani Codex.* This is a very tiny manuscript (about 1.5 inches by nearly 2 inches) and contains the story of Mani as a child (among many other things). It has been suggested that the size of the manuscript allowed Manichaeans to carry it easily. The first part describes the revelations that were revealed to Mani, as well as the persecution he received when he tried to spread his new faith.

Further Information

Allberry, C.R.C., ed., with a contribution by H. Ibscher. *A Manichaean Psalm-Book: Part II,* Manichaean Manuscripts in the Chester Beatty Collection, 2. Stuttgart, Germany: W. Kohlhammer, 1938.

Brown, Peter. *Augustine of Hippo: A Biography.* New ed. Berkeley: University of California Press, 2000.

Evans, G. R. *Augustine on Evil.* Cambridge: Cambridge University Press, 1993.

Gardner, Iain, and Klass A. Worp. "Leaves from a Manichaean Codex (Pl.s VIII–X)." *Zeitschrift für Papyrologie und Epigraphik* 117 (1997): 139–55.

International Association of Manichaean Studies. http://www.manichaeism.de/.

Lieu, S.N.C. *Manichaeism in the Later Roman Empire and Medieval China: A Historical Survey.* Rev.. 2nd ed. Tübingen, Germany: Mohr Siebeck, 1992.

35. Mani, *Foundation Letter*

INTRODUCTION

Mani (216–276 CE) was the founder of a religion that spread outward from the Atlantic to the Pacific Oceans. He grew up in Mesopotamia (now modern-day Iraq) in a Jewish Christian sect called the Elchasaites. Mani began receiving visions when he was young. Later he decided to break away from the Elchasaites and started his own religion. As will be seen in his letter, Mani called himself an Apostle of Jesus Christ. Manichaeism (the name given to his religion) was a Christian religion. The religion was highly adaptable, so in the Roman west it was Christian, while in China it was more Buddhist. The Manichaeans were a highly persecuted group wherever they were found.

Sometime toward the middle/end of the fourth century, Augustine became a Manichaean. Later, Augustine would leave the Manichaeans and become their greatest enemy, especially after he became the Catholic bishop of Hippo, a Roman city in North Africa. Augustine wrote many books against his former friends, including *Against the Letter Which They Call Foundation* (in 396 CE). This *Foundation Letter* is a letter written by Mani that is preserved mostly in Augustine's writings. We don't have the original, nor do we know the entire contents. Like many early Christian writers, Augustine took parts of the original letter from Mani and created a commentary to go with it. The following sections of Mani's letter are taken from Augustine's *Against the Letter Which They Call Foundation*. The numbers in parentheses are the chapter numbers in Augustine's work.

KEEP IN MIND WHILE YOU READ

1. Mani was writing this letter to one of his disciples named Patticius. Patticius must have asked about the creation of Adam and Eve, and this *Foundation Letter* is Mani's response.
2. It is not known when Mani wrote this letter, but later in Manichaean history it became a very important text for Manichaeans to use, primarily because of its detail on the Land of Light and the Land of Darkness. Notice that Augustine states that the letter was read to him aloud when he was a Manichaean.
3. The excerpt below is only part of the *Foundation Letter*. The end has been lost.

4. Mani sent his disciples out to different areas, which probably included the Roman Empire. The Manichaeans were certainly in Egypt by the last decade of the third century since the Roman emperor Diocletian issued an edict of persecution against them.

5. The Manichaean religion died out in the west sometime in the 600s. It survived, however, until the early 1600s CE in China, where at least one Manichaean temple remained.

Mani, Foundation Letter

(5) Therefore let us see what **Manichaeus** teaches me and in particular, let us examine that book which you Manichaeans call the *Letter of the Foundation* where practically everything that you (plur.) believe is contained. For at that time, when this was read aloud to us wretched people, we were referred to by you as enlightened ones. At any rate it begins as follows: "I, Manichaeus, an apostle of Jesus Christ, by the Providence of God the Father. These are the beneficial words from the immortal and living fount, (11) words which whoever in the first place hears and believes them, then observes what they convey, will never be subject to death, but will enjoy the eternal and glorious life. For undoubtedly he must be judged blessed who will be instructed by this divine knowledge, through which he is made free and will remain in everlasting life. May the Peace of the invisible God and the knowledge of truth be with my holy and most dear brothers, who believe and at the same time observe the heavenly commands, and also may your **right hand of light** protect and snatch you away from every evil invasion and from the snares of the world. (12) Therefore about that matter which you indicated to me, most beloved brother Patticius, saying that you desire to be acquainted with how Adam and Eve were born, whether they came into being by a word or were born from a body, it will be replied to you as is appropriate. For about those things it was introduced and mentioned in various scriptures and revelations in a dissimilar way by a great number of people. Hence, the truth of this matter as it finds itself is unknown to virtually the entire race and by all who up to this day disputed this at length for a long time. For if by these means they had come to know clearly about the generation of Adam and Eve, they would have never been subjected to corruption and death. Therefore it is necessary that there are many things that must be kept in mind beforehand so that one can arrive at this mystery without any ambiguity. Therefore, if it pleases you hear first what happened before the construction of the world and by which manner the conflict was set into motion, so that you are able to distinguish the nature of the **Light and of the Darkness.**

(13) For these two substances were divided from each other in the beginning and indeed God the Father was occupying the dominion of Light, He who is perpetual in His holy origin, magnificent in His virtue, true in His very nature, always exulting in His eternal being, keeping within Himself wisdom and attributes

Light and of the Darkness Two areas in the Manichaean cosmology that are totally separated in the beginning of time. In the second period the two become mixed. In the third and last time period, the two are once again separated, and the Darkness is totally enclosed so that it can never escape.

Manichaeus A Latin version of Mani's name, which originally came from the Syriac, in which Mani was called the Living Mani. The version *Manichaeus* is found in numerous documents.

right hand of light In Manichaean mythology, the Right Hand is a deity. In their creation story, the Right Hand is extended downward in order to rescue the good parts of the soul. In Manichaean religious practice, the grasping of right hands became important.

of life, through which also He unites the twelve members of His own light, that is to say the overflowing riches of His own kingdom. Also in each of His own members are hidden thousands of innumerable and immense treasures. Truly this Father, outstanding in His own praise, incomprehensible in His own greatness, has joined to Himself blessed and glorious worlds, which can be measured neither in number nor duration, in which this holy and illustrious Father and Creator lives, having created nothing in His own glorious kingdoms either in need or having any weakness. Also in this way His most splendid kingdoms are established above the clear and blessed earth so that they can never be moved or upset by anything. (15) Now near one part and side of that bright and holy land was the land of darkness, deep and immense in magnitude, in which fiery bodies lived, this is to say, destructive races. Here is the infinite darkness flowing immeasurably from the same nature, with its own special offspring. Beyond this were filthy and turbid waters with their own inhabitants; inside of these were horrible and violent winds with their own prince and fathers. In addition there was a fiery and destructive region also with its own leaders and peoples. In equal fashion inside of this a race full of murkiness and smoke, in which the savage leader and commander of all of them stayed, having surrounded himself with countless leaders of whom he was the mind and origin of all. These were the five natures of the destructive land.

Source: Mani. *Foundation Letter*, 396 CE. Translated by Kevin Kaatz, 2012.

AFTERMATH

The *Against the Letter Which They Call Foundation* was Augustine's first attempt to directly attack a text written by Mani. During this period the Manichaeans were very active both in North Africa and in Italy. Augustine, now a Catholic bishop, felt that he had to convince people he was no longer a Manichaean. Soon after this book was published Augustine wrote another book titled *Against Faustus*. Faustus was a high-ranking Manichaean, and in his *Against Faustus,* Augustine used the *Foundation Letter* against him. Soon after this Augustine had a public debate in Hippo with a Manichaean named Felix. Again, Augustine used the *Foundation Letter* against him, so this letter of Mani became a useful weapon that Augustine could use against the Manichaeans. Augustine's rebuttal to Manichaeism at every turn had a profound effect on the Manichaeans in North Africa since it was soon after that they started to disappear from this area.

ASK YOURSELF

1. As stated above, Augustine was a Manichaean (for at least 10 years) before he converted to Catholicism. How would his past as a Manichaean affect his ability to discuss the Manichaean faith?
2. Mani's religion was Christian, but there were obvious differences between his version of Christianity and that of Catholicism. We know that there were converts and that his religion seemed fairly popular. If you are Christian, what parts of this letter sound like Christianity? If you are not Christian, what parts of this letter would make you consider converting to Manichaeism?
3. As stated above, the Manichaeans were heavily persecuted. Is there anything in Mani's letter that would force the Roman government or those in the Catholic hierarchy to persecute the Manichaeans?

TOPICS TO CONSIDER

- ⮞ Consider the effect Mani's self-title of Apostle of Jesus Christ would have had on his audience. Consider that Paul, the author of several parts of the New Testament, also called himself an apostle.
- ⮞ Manichaean history is full of persecutions. Mani himself was persecuted when he broke away from the Elchasaites. The Manichaeans were persecuted in the Persian Empire under Bahram I (ruled 273–276 CE). They were persecuted in the Roman Empire under Emperor Diocletian, followed by numerous persecutions directed by the Catholic Church. Consider the effect of persecution on Manichaeism. Consider how persecution affects modern-day religions.
- ⮞ Mani's letter, although it was directed to Patticius, was later used by many Manichaeans, in much the same way that Paul's letters were used. Consider how the personal letters of religious founders can be used to spread their own versions of religion.

Further Information

Baker-Brian, Nicholas J. *Manichaeism: An Ancient Faith Rediscovered.* New York: T & T Clark, 2011.

Beduhn, Jason, and Paul Mirecki, eds. *Frontiers of Faith: The Christian-Manichaean Encounter in the Acts of Archelaus.* Leiden, the Netherlands: Brill: 2007.

Gardner, Iain, and Sam N. C. Lieu, eds. *Manichaean Tests from the Roman Empire.* Cambridge: Cambridge University Press, 2004.

Wermelinger, Otto, Gregor Wurst, and Johannes Van Oort, eds. *Augustine and Manichaeism in the Latin West: Proceedings of the Fribourg-Utrecht Symposium of the International Association of Manichaean Studies.* Leiden, the Netherlands: Brill, 2001.

PERSECUTION

36. *The Martyrdom of Polycarp*

INTRODUCTION

Christians were persecuted in larger numbers starting soon after the death of Jesus. Many became martyrs, or people who died for their faith. Polycarp, the bishop of Smyrna, was one of them. Not much is known about the life of Polycarp. Irenaeus (ca. 115 to ca. 202) thought that Polycarp was made bishop of Smyrna by the original apostles of Jesus. There also exists a letter from Ignatius, the bishop of Antioch, who had written to Polycarp on the way to his own martyrdom. When he was a bishop, Polycarp wrote some letters to churches outside of Smyrna, but unfortunately only his *Letter to the Philippians* survive. Polycarp's martyrdom is the earliest account we have of an official persecution of Christians. The following excerpt was written by someone in the church of Smyrna, the church of Polycarp, a year after his death (between 156 and 177 CE).

KEEP IN MIND WHILE YOU READ

1. The Jewish population is mentioned a few times in the text. By the middle of the second century, the Christians and Jews had become totally separated. The early Christians had blamed the Jewish population for the death of Christ.
2. Even in the middle of the second century the role of the bishop was not totally defined. Polycarp was asked to write his *Letter to the Philippians* by the citizens of Philadelphia, who had their own bishop.
3. The author of the text sent the account of the martyrdom of Polycarp to the Christian community at Philomelium, in the Roman province of Phrygia (central Turkey), and to all the other Christian communities. It was common by this time for Christians in different communities to communicate with each other about various issues.

The Martyrdom of Polycarp, *excerpts*

The Church of God which sojourns at Smyrna, to the Church of God sojourning in Philomelium, and to all the congregations of the Holy and Catholic Church in every place: Mercy, peace, and love from God the Father, and our Lord Jesus Christ, be multiplied.

Chapter 1: We have written to you, brethren, as to what relates to the martyrs, and especially to the blessed Polycarp, who put an end to the persecution, having, as it were, set a seal upon it by his martyrdom. For almost all the events that happened previously (to this one), took place that the Lord might show us from above a martyrdom becoming the Gospel. For he waited to be delivered up, even as the Lord had done, that we also might become his followers, while we look not merely at what concerns ourselves but have regard also to our neighbors. For it is the part of a true and well-founded love, not only to wish one's self to be saved, but also all the brethren.

Chapter 9: Now, as Polycarp was entering into the stadium, there came to him a voice from heaven, saying, "Be strong, and show yourself a man, O Polycarp!" No one saw who it was that spoke to him; but those of our brethren who were present heard the voice. And as he was brought forward, the tumult became great when they heard that Polycarp was taken. And when he came near, the **proconsul** asked him whether he was Polycarp. On his confessing that he was, (the proconsul) sought to persuade him to deny Christ, saying, "Have respect for your old age," and other similar things, according to their custom, (such as), "Swear by the fortune of **Caesar**; repent, and say, Away with the **Atheists**." But Polycarp, gazing with a stern countenance on all the multitude of the wicked heathen then in the stadium, and waving his hand towards them, while with groans he looked up to heaven, said, "Away with the Atheists." Then, the proconsul urging him, and saying, "Swear, and I will set you free: reproach Christ." Polycarp declared, "Eighty and six years have I served Him, and He never did me any injury: how then can I blaspheme my King and my Savior?"

Chapter 10: And when the proconsul yet again pressed him, and said, "Swear by the fortune of Caesar," he answered, "Since you are vainly urgent that, as you say, I should swear by the fortune of Caesar, and pretend not to know who and what I am, hear me declare with boldness, I am a Christian. And if you wish to learn what the doctrines of Christianity are, appoint me a day, and you shall hear them." The proconsul replied, "Persuade the people." But Polycarp said, "To you I have thought it right to offer an account (of my faith), for we are taught to give all due honor (which entails no injury upon ourselves) to the powers and authorities which are ordained of God. But as for these, I do not deem them worthy of receiving any account from me."

Chapter 11: The proconsul then said to him, "I have wild beasts at hand; I will cast you to these unless you repent." But he answered, "Call them then, for we are not accustomed to repent of what is good in order to adopt that which is evil; and it is well for me to be changed from what is evil to what is righteous." But again the proconsul said to him,

Atheists The title given to Christians by those who were not. Since the Christians rejected the Roman pantheon, it was thought that they were atheists. To the Christians (as noted by Polycarp), those who followed the Roman religion were atheists because they did not believe in the Christian god.

Caesar The emperor. Because the exact date of Polycarp's death is not known, the emperor could have been Antonius Pius or Marcus Aurelius.

proconsul A governor of a Roman province.

"I will cause you to be consumed by fire, seeing you despise the wild beasts, if you will not repent." But Polycarp said, "You threaten me with fire which burns for an hour, and after a little is extinguished, but are ignorant of the fire of the coming judgment and of eternal punishment, reserved for the ungodly. But why do you hesitate? Bring forth what you will."

Chapter 12: While he spoke these and many other like things, he was filled with confidence and joy, and his countenance was full of grace, so that not merely did it not fall as if troubled by the things said to him, but, on the contrary, the proconsul was astonished, and sent his herald to proclaim in the midst of the stadium three times, "Polycarp has confessed that he is a Christian." This proclamation having been made by the herald, the whole multitude both of the heathen and Jews, who lived at Smyrna, cried out with uncontrollable fury, and in a loud voice, "This is the teacher of Asia, the father of the Christians, and the overthrower of our gods, he who has been teaching many not to sacrifice, or to worship the gods." Speaking thus, they cried out, and sought Philip the Asiarch to let loose a lion upon Polycarp. But Philip answered that it was not lawful for him to do so, seeing the shows of wild beasts were already finished. Then it seemed good to them to cry out with one voice, that Polycarp should be burnt alive. For thus it behooved the vision which was revealed to him in regard to his pillow to be fulfilled, when, seeing it on fire as he was praying, he turned about and said prophetically to the faithful that were with him, "I must be burnt alive."

Chapter 13: This, then, was carried into effect with greater speed than it was spoken, the multitudes immediately gathering together wood and sticks out of the shops and baths; the Jews especially, according to custom, eagerly assisting them in it. And when the funeral pile was ready, Polycarp, laying aside all his garments, and taking off his girdle, sought also to take off his sandals,—a thing he was not accustomed to do, inasmuch as every one of the faithful was always eager who should first touch his skin. For, on account of his holy life, he was, even before his martyrdom, adorned with every kind of good. Immediately then they surrounded him with those substances which had been prepared for the funeral pile. But when they were about also to fix him with nails, he said, "Leave me as I am; for He that gives me strength to endure the fire, will also enable me, without your securing me by nails, to remain without moving in the pile."

Chapter 14: They did not nail him then, but simply bound him. And he, placing his hands behind him, and being bound like a distinguished ram (taken) out of a great flock for sacrifice, and prepared to be an acceptable burnt-offering unto God, looked up to heaven, and said, "O Lord God Almighty, the Father of your beloved and blessed Son Jesus Christ, by whom we have received the knowledge of You, the God of angels and powers, and of every creature, and of the whole race of the righteous who live before you, I give You thanks that You have counted me worthy of this day and this hour, that I should have a part in the number of Your martyrs, in the cup of your Christ, to the resurrection of eternal life, both of soul and body, through the incorruption (imparted) by the Holy Ghost. Among whom may I be accepted this day before You as a fat and acceptable sacrifice, according as You, the ever-truthful God, have foreordained, have revealed beforehand to me, and now have fulfilled. Wherefore also I praise You for all things, I bless You, I glorify You, along with the everlasting and heavenly Jesus Christ, Your beloved Son, with whom, to You, and the Holy Ghost, be glory both now and to all coming ages. Amen."

Chapter 15: When he had pronounced this amen, and so finished his prayer, those who were appointed for the purpose kindled the fire. And as the flame blazed forth in great fury, we, to whom it was given to witness it, beheld a great miracle, and have been preserved that we might report to others what then took place. For the fire, shaping itself into the form of an arch, like the sail of a ship when filled with the wind, encompassed as by a circle the body of the martyr. And he appeared within not like flesh which is burnt, but as bread that is baked, or as gold and silver glowing in a furnace. Moreover, we perceived such a sweet odor (coming from the pile), as if frankincense or some such precious spices had been smoking there.

Chapter 16: At length, when those wicked men perceived that his body could not be consumed by the fire, they commanded an executioner to go near and pierce him through with a dagger. And on his doing this, there came forth a dove and a great quantity of blood, so that the fire was extinguished; and all the people wondered that there should be such a difference between the unbelievers and the elect, of whom this most admirable Polycarp was one, having in our own times been an apostolic and prophetic teacher, and bishop of the Catholic Church which is in Smyrna. For every word that went out of his mouth either has been or shall yet be accomplished.

Chapter 17: But when the adversary of the race of the righteous, the envious, malicious, and wicked one, perceived the impressive nature of his martyrdom, and (considered) the blameless life he had led from the beginning, and how he was now crowned with the wreath of immortality, having beyond dispute received his reward, he did his utmost that not the least memorial of him should be taken away by us, although many desired to do this, and to become possessors of his holy flesh. For this end he suggested it to Nicetes, the father of Herod and brother of Alce, to go and entreat the governor not to give up his body to be buried, "lest," said he, "forsaking Him that was crucified, they begin to worship this one." This he said at the suggestion and urgent persuasion of the Jews, who also watched us, as we sought to take him out of the fire, being ignorant of this, that it is neither possible for us ever to forsake Christ, who suffered for the salvation of such as shall be saved throughout the whole world (the blameless one for sinners), nor to worship any other. For Him indeed, as being the Son of God, we adore; but the martyrs, as disciples and followers of the Lord, we worthily love on account of their extraordinary affection towards their own King and Master, of whom may we also be made companions and fellow-disciples!

Chapter 18: The centurion then, seeing the strife excited by the Jews, placed the body in the midst of the fire, and consumed it. Accordingly, afterwards we took up his bones, as being more precious than the most exquisite jewels, and more purified than gold, and deposited them in a fitting place, whither, being gathered together, as opportunity is allowed us, with joy and rejoicing, the Lord shall grant us to celebrate the anniversary of his martyrdom, both in memory of those who have already finished their course, and for the exercising and preparation of those yet to walk in their steps.

Chapter 19: This, then, is the account of the blessed Polycarp, who, being the twelfth that was martyred in Smyrna (reckoning those also of Philadelphia), yet occupies a place of his own in the memory of all men, insomuch that he is everywhere spoken of by the heathen themselves. He was not merely an illustrious teacher, but also a pre-eminent martyr, whose martyrdom all desire to imitate, as having been altogether consistent with the Gospel of Christ. For, having through patience overcome the unjust governor, and thus acquired the crown of immortality, he now, with the apostles and all the righteous (in heaven), happily glorifies God, even the Father, and blesses our Lord Jesus Christ, the Savior of our souls, the Governor of our bodies, and the Shepherd of the Catholic Church throughout the world.

Chapter 20: Since, then, you requested that we would at large make you acquainted with what really took place, we have for the present sent you this summary account through our brother Marcus. When, therefore, you have yourselves read this Epistle, be pleased to send it to the brethren at a greater distance, that they also may glorify the Lord, who makes such choice of His own servants. To Him who is able to bring us all by His grace and goodness into his everlasting kingdom, through His only-begotten Son Jesus Christ, to Him be glory, and honor, and power, and majesty, forever. Amen. Salute all the saints. They that are with us salute you, and Evarestus, who wrote this Epistle, with all his house.

Chapter 21: Now, the blessed Polycarp suffered martyrdom on the second day of the month Xanthicus just begun, the seventh day before the Kalends of May, on the great Sabbath, at the eighth hour. He was taken by Herod, Philip the Trallian being high priest, Statius Quadratus being proconsul, but Jesus Christ being King forever, to whom be glory, honor, majesty, and an everlasting throne, from generation to generation. Amen.

Chapter 22: We wish you, brethren, all happiness, while you walk according to the doctrine of the Gospel of Jesus Christ; with whom be glory to God the Father and the Holy Spirit, for the salvation of His holy elect, after whose example the blessed Polycarp suffered, following in whose steps may we too be found in the kingdom of Jesus Christ! These things Caius transcribed from the copy of Irenaeus (who was a disciple of Polycarp), having himself been intimate with Irenaeus. And I Socrates transcribed them at Corinth from the copy of Caius. Grace be with you all. And I again, Pionius, wrote them from the previously written copy, having carefully searched into them, and the blessed Polycarp having manifested them to me through a revelation, even as I shall show in what follows. I have collected these things, when they had almost faded away through the lapse of time, that the Lord Jesus Christ may also gather me along with His elect into His heavenly kingdom, to whom, with the Father and the Holy Spirit, be glory for ever and ever. Amen.

Source: Roberts, Rev. Alexander, and James Donaldson, eds. *The Ante-Nicene Fathers: Translations of the Writings of the Fathers Down to A.D. 325*, vol. 1. Buffalo, NY: Christian Literature Company, 1885, 83–96.

THE AFTERMATH

The account of the death of Polycarp had repercussions for early Christians. The examples of Polycarp's bravery in standing up to the proconsul and the miracles that occurred often get retold in later martyrdoms of other Christians. In addition, it discusses for the first time Christians celebrating the anniversary of someone who was killed for the faith. The anniversary celebration became common practice for early Christians in remembering other martyrs. Finally, the relics, or the bones of Polycarp, were revered by the Christians at Smyrna. The practice of collecting material (either body parts, bits of clothing, or anything the martyr may have owned or touched) became extremely popular and even today, many churches have relics on display.

ASK YOURSELF

1. Why would the Christian community at Philomelium request the story of Polycarp's martyrdom? How do modern Christian communities interact with one another?
2. How would Christian groups today react to a martyr? Would they act as the early Christians?

3. What aspect of Christianity did the Roman Empire dislike? Do you think the Christians could have been good Roman citizens while still being Christian? How do modern Christians view their relationship with their home countries?

4. Why do you think it was important to keep the list of transcribers, found at the end of the letter?

TOPICS TO CONSIDER

- There are many instances where the author makes use of the Bible, either directly or indirectly. Consider the reasons why the author would use these particular biblical verses and scenes.

- The numbers of martyrs dropped considerably when Christianity became legal in the Roman Empire (313 CE). Consider how Christians from the fourth century onward would have made use of these martyrdoms.

- While most modern Christians can practice their faith in peace, there are still a few places that actively persecute Christians. Consider how their persecutions compare to what was happening in the early Christian communities.

Further Information

Berding, Kenneth. *Polycarp and Paul: An Analysis of Their Literary and Theological Relationship in Light of Polycarp's Use of Biblical and Extra-Biblical Literature.* Leiden, the Netherlands: Brill Academic Publishers, 2002.

Early Church website: http://www.earlychurch.org.uk/polycarp.php.

Hareog, Paul. *Polycarp and the New Testament: The Occasion, Rhetoric, Theme, and Unity of the Epistle to the Philippians and Its Allusions to New Testament Literature.* Tübingen, Germany: Mohr Siebeck, 2001.

The Martyrdom of Polycarp. http://www.ccel.org/ccel/schaff/anf01.txt.

Mursurillo, Herbert, trans. *Acts of the Christian Martyrs,* vol. 2. Oxford: Clarendon Press, 1972.

Thompson, Leonard L. "The Martyrdom of Polycarp: Death in the Roman Games." *Journal of Religion* vol. 82, no. 1 (Jan., 2002): 27–52.

37. Martyrdom

INTRODUCTION

Cyprian was the bishop of Carthage, North Africa, starting in 248 CE. The bishoprics of Carthage and Alexandria, Egypt, were the most important dioceses in Africa. In 249, the new emperor Decius declared that everyone in the empire needed to burn incense and offer a sacrifice to his image. When Christians refused, Decius first attacked the bishops, including Cyprian. Cyprian went into exile in 250 CE, and during this time some Christians confessed and became martyrs, some confessed (called confessors) and were imprisoned, while others decided to sacrifice. While in prison, the confessors started to write letters for people who had originally sacrificed but were now trying to get back into the church (called the lapsed). Cyprian had to deal with all of these issues, primarily through letters. Unfortunately for Cyprian, Emperor Valerian (253–260) also persecuted the Christians. In 258, Cyprian was imprisoned and executed by beheading. The text below is Epistle 8 in Cyprian's collection. He probably wrote this epistle during his period of exile.

KEEP IN MIND WHILE YOU READ

1. This letter was originally labeled the 8th Letter of Cyprian, but in modern editions it is the 10th.
2. When Cyprian went into exile during the Decian persecution, many saw this as a cowardly act. Complaints were made in Rome, but he defended himself by stating that even though he had fled, he was in active correspondence with his flock.
3. Carthage had a long history of producing martyrs. As we have seen, Perpetua and Felicitas were martyred in the city at the beginning of the third century.
4. The confessors, if they died after their interrogation, were believed to go straight to heaven and sit next to Christ; at the end of time, they would help Christ judge (Patout Burns 21). This made the confessor/martyr a very important person in the Christian community.
5. Cyprian was not born a Christian. He was a member of an aristocratic family and taught rhetoric. He converted to Christianity just a few years before he was elected bishop. and because of this some complained that he was not properly prepared to be the bishop of a major city.

Cyprian, Epistle 8

Cyprian, to the martyrs and confessors in Christ our Lord and in God the Father, everlasting salvation: I gladly rejoice and am thankful, most brave and blessed brethren, at hearing of your faith and virtue, wherein the Church, our Mother, glories. Lately, indeed, she gloried, when, in consequence of an enduring confession, that punishment was undergone which drove the confessors of Christ into exile; yet the present confession is so much the more illustrious and greater in honor as it is braver in suffering. The combat has increased, and the glory of the combatants has increased also. Nor were you kept back from the struggle by fear of tortures, but by the very tortures themselves you were more and more stimulated to the conflict; bravely and firmly you have returned with ready devotion, to contend in the most extreme contest. Of you I find that some are already crowned, while some are even now within reach of the crown of victory; but all whom the danger has shut up in a glorious company are animated to carry on the struggle with an equal and common warmth of virtue, as it behooves the soldiers of Christ in the divine camp: that no allurements may deceive the incorruptible steadfastness of your faith, no threats terrify you, no sufferings or tortures overcome you, because "greater is He that is in us, than he that is in the world" (1 John 4:4), nor is the earthly punishment able to do more towards casting down, than is the divine protection towards lifting up. This truth is proved by the glorious struggle of the brethren, who, having become leaders to the rest in overcoming their tortures, afforded an example of virtue and faith, contending in the strife, until the strife yielded, being overcome. With what praises can I commend you, most courageous brethren? With what vocal proclamation can I extol the strength of your heart and the perseverance of your faith? You have borne the sharpest examination by torture, even unto the glorious consummation, and have not yielded to sufferings, but rather the sufferings have given way to you. The end of torments, which the tortures themselves did not give, the crown has given. The examination by torture waxing severer, continued for a long time to this result, not to overthrow the steadfast faith, but to send the men of God more quickly to the Lord. The multitude of those who were present saw with admiration the heavenly contest,—the contest of God, the spiritual contest, the battle of Christ,—saw that His servants stood with free voice, with unyielding mind, with divine virtue—bare, indeed, of weapons of this world, but believing and armed with the weapons of faith. The tortured stood more bravely than the torturers; and the limbs, beaten and torn as they were, overcame the hooks that bent and tore them. The scourge, often repeated with all its rage, could not conquer invincible faith, even although the membrane which enclosed the entrails was broken, and it was no longer the limbs but the wounds of the servants of God that were tortured. Blood was flowing which might quench the blaze of persecution, which might subdue the flames of Gehenna with its glorious gore. Oh, what a spectacle was that to the Lord,—how sublime, how great, how acceptable to the eyes of God in the allegiance and devotion of His soldiers! As it is written in the Psalms, when the Holy Spirit at once speaks to us and warns us: "Precious in the sight of the Lord is the death of His saints" (Psalms 116:15). Precious is the death which has bought immortality at the cost of its blood, which has received the crown from the consummation of its virtues. How did Christ rejoice therein! How willingly did He both fight and conquer in such servants of His, as the protector of their faith, and giving to believers as much as he who takes believes that he receives! He was present at His own contest; He lifted up, strengthened, animated the champions and assertors of His name. And He who once conquered death on our behalf, always conquers it in us. "When they," says He, "deliver you up, take no thought what you will say: for it shall be given you in that hour what you shall speak. For it is not you that speaks, but the Spirit of your Father which speaks in you" (Matthew 10:19–20). The present struggle has afforded a proof of this saying. A voice filled with the Holy Spirit broke forth from the martyr's mouth when the most blessed Mappalicus said to the proconsul in the midst of his torments, "You shall see a contest tomorrow." And that which he said with the testimony of virtue and faith, the Lord fulfilled. A heavenly contest was exhibited, and the servant of God was crowned in the struggle of the promised fight. This is the contest which the prophet Isaiah of old predicted, saying, "It shall be no light contest for you with men, since God appoints the struggle" (Isaiah 7:13). And in order to show what this struggle would be, he added the words, "Behold, a virgin shall conceive and bear a son, and ye shall call His name Emmanuel" (Isaiah 7:14). This is the struggle of our faith in which we engage, in which we conquer, in which we are crowned. This is the struggle which the blessed Apostle Paul has shown to us, in which it behooves us to run and to attain the crown of glory. "Do you not know," says he, "that they which run in a race, run all indeed, but one receives the prize? So run that you may obtain. Now they do it that they may receive a corruptible crown, but we, an incorruptible one" (1 Corinthians 9:24–25). Moreover, setting forth his own struggle, and declaring that he himself should soon be a sacrifice for the Lord's sake, he says, "I am now ready to be offered, and the time of my assumption is at hand. I have fought a good fight, I have finished my course, I have kept the faith: henceforth there is laid up for me a crown of righteousness, which the Lord, the righteous judge, shall give me at that day; and not to me only, but unto all them also that love His appearing" (2 Timothy 4:6–8). This fight, therefore, predicted of old by the prophets, begun by the Lord, waged by the apostles, Mappalicus promised again to the proconsul in his own name and that of his colleagues. Nor did the faithful voice deceive in his promise; he exhibited the fight to which he had pledged himself, and he received the reward which he deserved. I not only beseech but exhort the rest of you, that you all should follow that martyr now most blessed, and the other partners of that engagement,—soldiers and comrades, steadfast in faith, patient in suffering, victors in tortures,—that those who are united at once by the bond of confession, and the entertainment of a dungeon, may also be united in the consummation of their virtue and a celestial crown; that you by your joy may dry the tears of our Mother, the Church, who mourns over the wreck and death of very many; and that you may confirm, by the provocation of your example, the steadfastness of others who stand also. If the battle shall call you out, if the day of your contest shall come engage bravely, fight with constancy, as knowing that you are fighting under the eyes of a present Lord, that you are attaining by the confession of His name to His own glory; who is not such a one as that He only looks on His servants, but He Himself also wrestles in us, Himself is engaged,—Himself also in the struggles of our conflict not only crowns, but is crowned. But if before the day of your contest, of the mercy of God, peace shall supervene, let there still remain to you the sound will and the glorious conscience. Nor let any one of you be saddened as if he were inferior to those who before you have suffered tortures, have overcome the world and trodden it under foot, and so have come to the Lord by a glorious road. For the Lord is the "searcher out of the reins and the hearts" (Revelation 2:23). He looks through secret things, and beholds that which is concealed. In order to merit the crown from Him, His own testimony alone is sufficient, who will judge us. Therefore, beloved brethren, either case is equally lofty and illustrious,—the former more secure, to wit, to hasten to the Lord with the consummation of our victory,—the latter more joyous; a leave of absence, after glory, being received to flourish in the praises of the Church. O blessed Church of ours, which the honor of the divine condescension illuminates, which in our own times the glorious blood of martyrs renders illustrious! She was white before in the works of the brethren; now she has become purple in the blood of the martyrs. Among her flowers are wanting neither roses nor lilies. Now let each one strive for the largest dignity of either honor. Let them receive crowns, either white, as of labors, or of purple, as of suffering. In the heavenly camp both peace and strife have their own flowers, with which the soldier of Christ may be crowned for glory. I bid you, most brave and beloved brethren, always heartily farewell in the Lord; and have me in remembrance. Farewell.

Source: Roberts, Rev. Alexander, and James Donaldson, eds. *The Ante-Nicene Fathers: Translations of the Writings of the Fathers Down to* A.D. *325*, vol. 5. Buffalo, NY: Christian Literature Company, 1886, 287–89.

AFTERMATH

Cyprian clearly had a lot of respect for those who were persecuted for their faith. He supported their choice to confess and in fact encouraged them to persevere. This persecution lasted until the beginning of 251. While the letters written by the confessors were a source of difficulty for his power as bishop, Cyprian was very clear on how the lapsed should be treated. He spent the next seven years stating that the lapsed had to perform some type of penance for abandoning Christianity during the persecution. He also spent a great deal of time stressing the unity of the church. As stated above, Cyprian himself was martyred during the Valerian persecution. Pontius, Cyprian's biographer, gives some details about his life (see web link below).

ASK YOURSELF

1. It is likely that the confessors knew that Cyprian had fled Carthage instead of staying to be tortured and executed. Do you think that this would have affected the reception of this letter? Do you think it mattered to them that the bishop fled while his flock suffered?
2. Imagine that there was a Christian persecution started by the government and that you had confessed to the authorities and were now awaiting execution. Do you think you would feel the same way as the confessors during the time of Cyprian?
3. Cyprian calls the persecution "a heavenly contest." He also uses explicit language to describe the torture that these people either underwent or were about to. Does this explicit language help his message?

TOPICS TO CONSIDER

- List all of the biblical passages that Cyprian uses. Consider how the use of the Bible would have helped the confessors await their persecution.
- The lapsed, or those who originally sacrificed and now wanted back into the church once the persecutions had stopped, were a large problem for Cyprian. Read his *On the Lapsed* (website given below) and consider how Cyprian's arguments differ from the letter given above.

    ☙ Consider how this letter would have affected those who sacrificed and cursed Christ. Consider the effect this would have had on the community, especially those who wanted back in and those who decided not to rejoin Christianity.

THE REAL PURPOSE OF THE MARTYRDOMS

People from all periods are fascinated by the tales of those who were persecuted for their faith. The stories of gladiators, tortures, and wild animals draw the reader in. However, for the early Christians, these martyrdoms served another purpose—that of instruction. Those who read or heard the stories were to understand how a Christian should act in the face of persecution, which remained a threat until the time of Emperor Constantine in the early fourth century. The act of dying as a martyr was seen as a very special death, and certainly not one to be afraid of. As the first chapter of the Martyrdom of Polycarp states, the martyrs were examples of Christ, considered to be the first martyr. Many of these martyrdoms also contain stories of miracles that took place during the persecution of the martyr. For example, Polycarp could not be burned by the fire, and when a soldier pierced his side, a dove flew out along with a large amount of blood that put out the fire. The bodies of the martyrs were also very important relics, and many churches today are built around the bodies of these ancient martyrs.

Further Information

Bakker, H., P. Van Geest, and H. Van Loon, eds. *Cyprian of Carthage: Studies in His Life, Language and Thought*. Louvain, Belgium: Peeters, 2010.

Brent, Allen. *Cyprian and Roman Carthage*. Cambridge: Cambridge University Press, 2010.

Cyprian. *On the Lapsed*. http://www.ccel.org/ccel/schaff/anf05.iv.v.iii.html.

Cyprian's works. http://www.ccel.org/ccel/schaff/anf05.iv.ii.html.

Knipfing, John R. "The Libelli of the Decian Persecution." *Harvard Theological Review* 16, no. 4 (Oct., 1923): 345–90.

Patout Burns, J., Jr. *Cyprian the Bishop*. New York: Routledge, 2002.

Pontius. *Life and Passion of Cyprian, Bishop and Martyr*. http://www.ccel.org/ccel/schaff/anf05.iv.iii.html.

Rives, J. B. "The Decree of Decius and the Religion of Empire." *Journal of Roman Studies* 89 (1999): 135–54.

38. Lactantius, *On the Deaths of the Persecutors*

INTRODUCTION

There were many times in early Christianity when persecution was a way of life for some Christians. The official persecution, by the Roman government, started as early as 40s CE. The first major persecution happened under the reign of Nero (54–68 CE), soon after a fire gutted a large section of Rome. Nero blamed the fire on the Christians. Their torture was horrific. While there were other sporadic persecutions, the worst came under the reign of Diocletian (284–305 CE). Lactantius, in his *On the Deaths of the Persecutors* (written sometime between 314–315), describes in vivid detail the punishments the Roman emperors received because of their persecution. Lactantius was convinced that the Christian god was punishing these men. I have included the introduction, and the sections on emperor's Nero, Valerian (253–260 CE), and Diocletian.

KEEP IN MIND WHILE YOU READ

1. Lactantius was appointed as a teacher of Rhetoric in the city of Nicomedia by Emperor Diocletian. Lactantius was forced out when Diocletian began his persecution of Christians.
2. While Emperor Diocletian certainly persecuted Christians, it appears that his Caesar, Galerius, was responsible for convincing Diocletian to increase the persecution to physical torture and destruction of church property.
3. Lactantius was not a Christian when he was growing up. It isn't known when he converted to Christianity.
4. By the time Lactantius had written this text (314–315), Constantine had been emperor for eight years. Emperors Constantine and Licinius (emperor of the east from 308–324) had issued their Edict of Milan in 313 CE, which officially made Christianity a legal religion in the Roman Empire.
5. Donatus, to whom this work was dedicated, was tortured many times for being a Christian. He was finally freed when Galerius issued his amnesty (Barnes 1973, 30).

Lactantius, On the Deaths
of the Persecutors, *excerpts*

Chap. 1. The Lord has heard those supplications which you, my best beloved Donatus, pour forth in His presence all the day long, and the supplications of the rest of our brethren, who by a glorious confession have obtained an everlasting crown, the reward of their faith. Behold, all the adversaries are destroyed, and tranquility having been re-established throughout the Roman Empire, the late oppressed Church arises again, and the temple of God, overthrown by the hands of the wicked, is built with more glory than before. For God has raised up princes to rescind the impious and sanguinary edicts of the tyrants and provide for the welfare of mankind; so that now the cloud of past times is dispelled, and peace and serenity gladden all hearts. And after the furious whirlwind and black tempest, the heavens are now become calm, and the wished-for light has shone forth; and now God, the hearer of prayer, by His divine aid has lifted His prostrate and afflicted servants from the ground, has brought to an end the united devices of the wicked, and wiped off the tears from the faces of those who mourned. Those who insulted over the Divinity, lie low; they who cast down the holy temple, are fallen with more tremendous ruin; and the tormentors of just men have poured out their guilty souls amidst plagues inflicted by Heaven, and amidst deserved tortures. For God delayed to punish them, that, by great and marvelous examples, He might teach posterity that He alone is God, and that with fit vengeance He executes judgment on the proud, the impious, and the persecutors. Of the end of those men I have thought good to publish a narrative, that all who are afar off and all who shall arise hereafter, may learn how the Almighty manifested His power and sovereign greatness in rooting out and utterly destroying the enemies of His name. And this will become evident, when I relate who were the persecutors of the Church from the time of its first constitution, and what were the punishments by which the divine Judge, in His severity, took vengeance on them.

Chap. 2. In the latter days of the Emperor Tiberius, in the consulship of Ruberius Geminus and Fufius Geminus, and on the tenth of the kalends of April, as I find it written, Jesus Christ was crucified by the Jews. After He had risen again on the third day, He gathered together His apostles, whom fear, at the time of His being laid hold on, had put to flight; and while He sojourned with them forty days, He opened their hearts, interpreted to them the Scripture, which hitherto had been wrapped up in obscurity, ordained and fitted them for the preaching of His word and doctrine, and regulated all things concerning the institutions of the New Testament; and this having been accomplished, a cloud and whirlwind enveloped Him, and caught Him up from the sight of men to heaven. His apostles were at that time eleven in number, to whom were added Matthias, in the room of the traitor Judas, and afterwards Paul. Then were they dispersed throughout all the earth to preach the Gospel, as the Lord their Master had commanded them; and during twenty-five years, and until the beginning of the reign of the Emperor Nero, they occupied themselves in laying the foundations of the Church in every province and city. And while Nero reigned, the Apostle Peter came to Rome, and, through the power of God committed to him, wrought certain miracles, and, by turning many to the true religion, built up a faithful and steadfast temple unto the Lord. When Nero heard of those things, and observed that not only in Rome, but in every other place, a great multitude revolted daily from the worship of idols, and, condemning their old ways, went over to the new religion, he, an execrable and pernicious tyrant, sprung forward to raze the heavenly temple and destroy the true faith. It was he who first persecuted the servants of God; he crucified Peter, and killed Paul: nor did he escape with impunity, for God looked on the affliction of His people; and therefore the tyrant, bereaved of authority, and precipitated from the height of empire, suddenly disappeared, and even the burial-place of that noxious wild beast was nowhere to be seen. This has led some persons of extravagant imagination to suppose that, having been conveyed to a distant region, he is still reserved alive; and to him they apply the Sibylline verses concerning "The fugitive, who slew his own mother, being to come from the uttermost boundaries of the earth;" as if he who was the first should also be the last persecutor, and thus prove the forerunner of Antichrist! But we ought not to believe those who, affirming that the two prophets Enoch and Elias have been translated into some remote place that they might attend our Lord when He shall come to judgment, also fancy that Nero is to appear hereafter as the forerunner of the devil, when he shall come to lay waste the earth and overthrow mankind.

Chap. 5. And presently Valerian also, in a mood alike frantic, lifted up his impious hands to assault God, and, although his time was short, shed much righteous blood. But God punished him in a new and extraordinary manner, that it might be a lesson to future ages that the adversaries of Heaven always receive the just recompense of their iniquities. He, having been made prisoner by the Persians, lost not only that power which he had exercised without moderation, but also the liberty of which he had deprived others; and he wasted the remainder of his days in the vilest condition of slavery: for Sapores (Shapur), the king of the Persians, who had made him prisoner, whenever he chose to get into his carriage or to mount on horseback, commanded the Roman to stoop and present his back; then, setting his foot on the shoulders of Valerian, he said, with a smile of reproach, "This is true, and not what the Romans delineate on board or plaster." Valerian lived for a considerable time under the well-merited insults of his conqueror; so that the Roman name remained long the scoff and derision of the barbarians: and this also was added to the severity of his punishment, that although he had an emperor for his son, he found no one to revenge his captivity and most abject and servile state; neither indeed was he ever demanded back. Afterward, when he had finished this shameful life under so great dishonor, he was flayed, and his skin, stripped from the flesh, was dyed with vermilion, and placed in the temple of the gods of the barbarians, that the remembrance of a triumph so signal might be perpetuated, and that this spectacle might always be exhibited to our ambassadors, as an admonition to the Romans, that, beholding the spoils of their captive emperor in a Persian temple, they should not place too great confidence in their own strength. Now since God so punished the sacrilegious, is it not strange that any one should afterward have dared to do, or even to devise, aught against the majesty of the one God, who governs and supports all things?

Chap. 10. Diocletian, as being of a timorous disposition, was a searcher into futurity, and during his abode in the East he began to slay victims, that from their livers he might obtain a prognostic of events; and while he sacrificed, some attendants of his, who were Christians, stood by, and they put the immortal sign on their foreheads. At this the demons were chased away, and the holy rites interrupted. The soothsayers trembled, unable to investigate the wonted marks on the entrails of the victims. They frequently repeated the sacrifices, as if the former had been unpropitious; but the victims, slain from time to time, afforded no tokens for divination. At length Tages, the chief of the soothsayers, either from guess or from his own observation, said, "There are profane persons here, who obstruct the rites." Then Diocletian, in furious passion, ordered not only all who were assisting at the holy ceremonies, but also all who resided within the palace, to sacrifice, and, in case of their refusal, to be scourged. And further, by letters to the commanding officers, he enjoined that all soldiers should be forced to the like impiety, under pain of being dismissed the service. Thus far his rage proceeded; but at that season he did nothing more against the law and religion of God. After an interval of some time he went to winter in Bithynia; and presently Galerius Caesar came thither, inflamed with furious resentment, and purposing to excite the inconsiderate old man to carry on that persecution which he had begun against the Christians. I have learned that the cause of his fury was as follows.

Chap. 11. The mother of Galerius, a woman exceedingly superstitious, was a votary of the gods of the mountains. Being of such a character, she made sacrifices almost every day, and she feasted her servants on the meat offered to idols: but the Christians of her family would not partake of those entertainments; and while she feasted with the Gentiles, they continued in fasting and prayer. On this account she conceived ill-will against the Christians, and by woman-like complaints instigated her son, no less superstitious than herself, to destroy them. So, during the whole winter, Diocletian and Galerius held councils together, at which no one else assisted; and it was the universal opinion that their conferences respected the most momentous affairs of the empire. The old man long opposed the fury of Galerius, and showed how pernicious it would be to raise disturbances throughout the world and to shed so much blood; that the Christians were wont with eagerness to meet death; and that it would be enough for him to exclude persons of that religion from the court and the army. Yet he could not restrain the madness of that obstinate man. He resolved, therefore, to take the opinion of his friends. Now this was a circumstance in the bad disposition of Diocletian, that whenever he determined to do good, he did it without advice, that the praise might be all his own; but whenever he determined to do ill, which he was sensible would be blamed, he called in many advisers, that his own fault might be imputed to other men: and therefore a few civil magistrates, and a few military commanders, were admitted to give their counsel; and the question was put to them according to priority of rank. Some, through personal ill-will towards the Christians, were of opinion that they ought to be cut off, as enemies of the gods and adversaries of the established religious ceremonies. Others thought differently, but, having understood the will of Galerius, they, either from dread of displeasing or from a desire of gratifying him, concurred in the opinion given against the Christians. Yet not even then could the emperor be prevailed upon to yield his assent. He determined above all to consult his gods; and to that end he dispatched a soothsayer to inquire of Apollo at Miletus, whose answer was such as might be expected from an enemy of the divine religion. So Diocletian was drawn over from his purpose. But although he could struggle no longer against his friends, and against Caesar and Apollo, yet still he attempted to observe such moderation as to command the business to be carried through without bloodshed; whereas Galerius would have had all persons burnt alive who refused to sacrifice.

Source: Roberts, Rev. Alexander, and James Donaldson, eds. *The Ante-Nicene Fathers: Translations of the Writings of the Fathers Down to A.D. 325,* vol. 7. Buffalo, NY: Christian Literature Company, 1905, 301–05.

AFTERMATH

The Great Persecution, or the persecution started by Diocletian and Galerius, lasted until 311 CE in the eastern part of the Roman Empire. Galerius, after becoming emperor himself, stopped the persecution. Galerius was in quite a bit of pain from some disease and wanted to make amends towards the end of his life, so he begged the Christians for forgiveness. After his death in 311, the persecution in the East began again, but was soon ended by Emperor Maximinus Daia (ruled 311–313). The Great Persecution, as well as the earlier persecutions, had a long-lasting effect on the lives of Christians. Many who were martyred were remembered later as being heroes for their faith.

ASK YOURSELF

1. As mentioned, there was a fire (called the Great Fire) in Rome in 64 CE, and Emperor Nero blamed the Christians for this. Lactantius, however, does not mention this as the reason for the persecution. Why does Lactantius not mention the Great Fire?
2. Lactantius relates a story about the disappearance of Nero that is not historically accurate. Why would Lactantius tell this story about the emperor? If this story were true, what message would the reader get from reading this?
3. Lactantius goes into detail about the mother of Galerius and her effect she had on her son. Do you think his mother's influence was the sole reason for his reaction against the Christians? If she was not the only reason, what other reasons could there be for his hatred of the Christians?

TOPICS TO CONSIDER

- Consider the importance of sacrifice, the Sibylline Oracles and the worship of Apollo on the Roman people. Consider how these types of religious practice differed from those of the Christians. Can you think of some similarities?
- Diocletian not only forced his own household to sacrifice, but he also forced those in the military to do the same. Consider how this would have affected the readiness and morale of the Roman soldiers.
- Diocletian was the emperor, while Galerius was his Caesar (next in line to become emperor if anything happened to Diocletian). Lactantius, however, implies that Galerius held quite a bit of power, and tried to convince Diocletian to increase the severity of the persecution. Discuss the role of negotiation in the Roman Empire when it came to the emperor making a decision.

DIOCLETIAN AND THE THIRD CENTURY CRISIS

Emperor Diocletian is most famously seen as the promoter of Christian persecution and as the person who rescued the Roman Empire from probable ruin in the late 200s. When Diocletian took the throne, the Empire was in disarray. There had been a string of emperors and this led to multiple civil wars. The empire was also being attacked in the north from the barbarians and in the east by the Persians. This, combined with the civil wars, forced the Roman government to raise taxes in order to pay for the military. This led to rapid inflation. Diocletian took steps that allowed the empire to survive. He instituted a Price Edict, which set the prices of goods all throughout the empire and stopped the debasing of the money supply. Both of these slowed inflation. He also started the Tetrarchy, or the rule of four. He split the empire into two and put an emperor in power in the west, while he ruled the east. Below both emperors were Caesars, and these Caesars were to take power after the death or the retirement (in the case of Diocletian). It was in this way that Diocletian had hoped to stop the cycle of multiple emperors. His new policies allowed the Empire to survive until the late 300s, when again the Empire was attacked from the north by the various barbarian tribes.

Further Information

Barnes, T. D. "Lactantius and Constantine." *Journal of Roman Studies* 63 (1973): 29–46.

Bryant, Joseph M. "The Sect-Church Dynamic and Christian Expansion in the Roman Empire: Persecution, Penitential Discipline, and Schism in Sociological Perspective." *British Journal of Sociology* 44, no. 2 (Jun., 1993): 303–39.

De Ste. Croix, G.E.M. "Aspects of the 'Great' Persecution." *Harvard Theological Review* 47, no. 2 (Apr., 1954): 75–113.

Fisher, Arthur L. "Lactantius' Ideas Relating Christian Truth and Christian Society." *Journal of the History of Ideas* 43, no. 3 (Jul.–Sep., 1982): 355–77.

Keresztes, Paul. "From the Great Persecution to the Peace of Galerius." *Vigiliae Christianae* 37, no. 4 (Dec., 1983): 379–99.

Lactanius. *On the Deaths of the Persecutors.* http://www.ccel.org/ccel/schaff/anf07.iii.v.i.html.

Leadbetter, William L. *Galerius and the Will of Diocletian,* Roman Imperial Biographies. New York: Routledge, 2010.

39. The Edict of Milan

INTRODUCTION

The next selection is the Edict of Milan, issued in 313. Up to this time Christians were still being persecuted through the actions of Roman officials. The persecution was severe, at least according to Eusebius of Caesarea, the church historian. Eusebius states that Christians were tortured, their churches pulled down, and the Bible was burned. In 306 CE, Constantine, the son of Emperor Constantius, became the next emperor. However, Severus was supposed to become the next emperor after the death of Constantius. Ultimately there were three emperors in the west—Constantine, Severus, and Maxentius. Maxentius defeated Severus, and this set the stage for the battle between him and Constantine. The two of them fought for final supremacy at the Milvian Bridge in Rome in October 312 CE. Constantine won his battle and became the sole emperor in the west (with Licinius in the east). It was after his victory that Constantine and Licinius issued the Edict (given in November 313 CE), ending the Great Persecution.

KEEP IN MIND WHILE YOU READ

1. There are two versions of this edict. One is given by Lactantius, a Christian who lived from ca. 240 to 320 CE, in his *On the Deaths of the Persecutors* 48.2–12. This is likely to be the original, written in Latin. The other is given by Eusebius, a Christian historian (ca. 263–339 CE) in his *Ecclesiastical History* 10.5.2–14, written in Greek. The main difference between the two is the opening paragraph, which is found only in the version given by Eusebius of Caesarea. This may have been part of the Edict that was sent out by Emperor Licinius to those living in the eastern part of the Roman Empire. I've given the introduction by Eusebius below, followed by the text found in Lactantius.

2. There is still considerable scholarly debate on whether Constantine became a Christian after his victory over Maxentius or whether he converted later. There are coins representing him as Apollo, which is an image later Christian emperors would not use.

3. Most of the people living in the Roman Empire during the time of Constantine were not Christian. The empire stretched from England in the northwest to Mesopotamia in the west, and Egypt and North Africa in the south.

4. Constantine and Licinius met in Milan, Italy, so that Licinius could marry Constantine's younger half sister, Constantia. This would supposedly firm up their relationship.

The Edict of Milan, Eusebius, Ecclesiastical History *10.5; Lactantius,* On the Deaths of the Persecutors *48*

(Found in Eusebius, *Ecclesiastical History* 10.5): 2. "Perceiving long ago that religious liberty ought not to be denied, but that it ought to be granted to the judgment and desire of each individual to perform his religious duties according to his own choice, we had given orders that every man, Christians as well as others, should preserve the faith of his own sect and religion. 3. But since in that rescript, in which such liberty was granted them, many and various conditions seemed clearly added, some of them, it may be, after a little retired from such observance.

(Found in Lactantius, *On the Deaths of the Persecutors* 48): "When we, Constantine and Licinius, emperors, had an interview at Milan, and conferred together with respect to the good and security of the public, it seemed to us that, among those things that are profitable to mankind in general, the reverence paid to the Divinity merited our first and chief attention, and that it was proper that the Christians and **all others** should have liberty to follow that mode of religion which to each of them appeared best; so that that God, who is seated in heaven, might be benign and propitious to us, and to every one under our government. And therefore we judged it a salutary measure, and one highly consonant to right reason, that no man should be denied leave of attaching himself to the rites of the Christians, or to whatever other religion his mind directed him, that thus the supreme Divinity, to whose worship we freely devote ourselves, might continue to show favor and beneficence to us. And accordingly we give you to know that, without regard to any provisos in our former orders to you concerning the Christians, all who choose that religion are to be permitted, freely and absolutely, to remain in it, and not to be disturbed any ways, or molested. And we thought fit to be thus special in the things committed to your charge, that you might understand that the indulgence which we have granted in matters of religion to the Christians is ample and unconditional; and perceive at the same time that the open and free exercise of their respective religions is granted to all others, as well as to the Christians. For it befits the well-ordered state and the tranquility of our times that each individual be allowed, according to his own choice, to worship the Divinity; and we mean not to derogate aught from the honor due to any religion or its votaries. Moreover, with respect to the Christians, we formerly gave certain

> **all others** Those who follow the Roman religions (sometimes referred to as the pagans). Many gods and goddesses were worshipped in the Roman Empire during the early 300s, and this edict allowed all people to practice their own religion.

orders **concerning the places appropriated for their religious assemblies**; but now we will that all persons who have purchased such places, either from our treasury or from anyone else, do restore them to the Christians, without money demanded or price claimed, and that this be performed peremptorily and unambiguously; and we will also, that they who have obtained any right to such places by form of gift do forthwith restore them to the Christians: reserving always to such persons, who have either purchased for a price, or gratuitously acquired them, to make application to the judge of the district, if they look on themselves as entitled to any equivalent from our beneficence. All those places are, by your intervention, to be immediately restored to the Christians. And because it appears that, besides the places appropriated to religious worship, the Christians did possess other places, which belonged not to individuals, but to their society in general, that is, to their churches, we comprehend all such within the regulation aforesaid, and we will that you cause them all to be restored to the society or churches, and that without hesitation or controversy, provided always, that the persons making restitution without a price paid shall be at liberty to seek indemnification from our bounty. In furthering all which things on behalf of the Christians, you are to use your utmost diligence, to the end that our orders be speedily obeyed, and our gracious purpose in securing the public tranquility promoted. So shall that divine favor which, in affairs of the mightiest importance, we have already experienced, continue to give success to us, and in our successes make the commonweal happy. And that the tenor of this our gracious ordinance may be made known unto all, we will that you cause it by your authority to be published everywhere."

> **concerning the places appropriated for their religious assemblies**
> It was technically illegal for Christians to worship in the empire, but they still managed to build churches in some locations. Eusebius, the church historian, states that during the persecution of Diocletian churches were torn down. Where persecution may have been more severe, Christians would have met in private houses.

Source: Roberts, Rev. Alexander, and James Donaldson, eds. *The Ante-Nicene Fathers: Translations of the Writings of the Fathers Down to* A.D. *325,* vol. 7. Buffalo, NY: Christian Literature Company, 1905, 318–20.

AFTERMATH

The Edict of Milan brought official peace to Christianity, especially those Christians living in the eastern half of the Roman Empire (those who were under the rule of Licinius). It also left the Roman religion and its practices untouched as well, primarily because Constantine was not in a political position to outlaw pagan practices. Many of the Roman senators were still followers of the Roman religion. In 314 CE, civil war broke out between Constantine and Licinius. They met on the battlefield, and Licinius was defeated. However, they kept the empire divided but in 324 went to war again. The result was the same as in 314—Constantine was victorious. Constantine waited a year and then had Licinius killed, leaving Constantine as the sole emperor. All of this had no effect on the outcome of the Edict of Milan, except that Constantine, a Christian, was the sole emperor.

ASK YOURSELF

1. How do you think the marriage of Constantine's half sister, Constantia, affected the role that Licinius played? What might have happened if the marriage had not taken place (or had never been offered) by Constantine?

2. Why would there be two versions of this text (the link to the version found in Eusebius is given below)? Does the opening paragraph, given only by Eusebius of Caesarea, add anything important?

3. How would non-Christians feel about the issuing of the Edict? Would it have affected their day-to-day lives?

TOPICS TO CONSIDER

- Some scholars do not believe that this was an actual edict issued by the two emperors. Examine both views on this topic. If it was not an edict, consider why many believe that it was.

- Freedom of religion is an important concept in many modern-day countries. Consider what the United States would be like if it had adopted one version of Christianity over another.

- Consider the effect this edict had on Christians living in the Roman Empire. How would it have changed their day-to-day lives? How would it change their interactions with the Roman government?

- Consider why the Roman emperors would issue an edict such as this. What benefit did they expect to receive?

Further Information

Armstrong, Gregory T. "Church and State Relations: The Changes Wrought by Constantine." *Journal of Bible and Religion* 32, no. 1 (Jan., 1964): 1–7.

Armstrong, Gregory T. "Imperial Church Building and Church-State Relations, A.D. 313–363." *Church History* 36, no. 1 (Mar., 1967): 3–17.

Betten, Francis S. "The Milan Decree of A.D. 313: Translation and Comment." *Catholic Historical Review* 8, no. 2 (Jul., 1922): 191–97.

Carotenuto, Erica. "Six Constantinian Documents (Eus. 'H.E.' 10, 5–7)." *Vigiliae Christianae* 56, no. 1 (Feb., 2002): 56–74.

Curran, John. "Constantine and the Ancient Cults of Rome: The Legal Evidence." *Greece & Rome,* 2nd ser., 43, no. 1 (Apr., 1996): 68–80.

Eusebius. http://www.ccel.org/ccel/schaff/npnf201.html.

Keresztes, Paul. "From the Great Persecution to the Peace of Galerius." *Vigiliae Christianae* 37, no. 4 (Dec., 1983): 379–99.

Lactantius. *On the Deaths of the Persecutors.* http://www.ccel.org/ccel/schaff/anf07. iii.v.i.html.

CHURCH AND POLITICS

40. Church and State

INTRODUCTION

Justin Martyr received a Greek education, became a philosopher, and then converted to Christianity. The language used in the *First Apology* reflects his philosophical background. Justin appeals to reason and the "love of truth" to convince Emperor Antonius Pius to reconsider his treatment of the Christians. The *First and Second Apologies* are written in the defense of Christianity, especially against the Roman state, which was persecuting them. While the tone of the *Apologies* is sometimes conciliatory, Justin also wrote *The Discourse to the Greeks*. He begins this work by attacking two of the most famous Greek poets, Homer and Hesiod, and continues with attacks on the Greek gods. Justin moved to Rome and began his own school teaching Christians. It was probably the combination of attacking the gods and teaching Christians that ultimately led to his martyrdom in 165 CE.

KEEP IN MIND WHILE YOU READ

1. Christians were being persecuted or harassed by government officials for their beliefs, and Justin tried to appeal to reason to stop this. In the end he was not successful.
2. Justin grew up in Palestine and was highly educated. We know that he went from teacher to teacher looking for the Truth. He claimed to have found this after discussing Christianity with an older man, and soon after he converted.
3. Justin wrote a *Second Apology,* which was addressed to the Roman Senate. Like the *First Apology,* the second attempted to teach Romans the true nature of Christianity.
4. Justin had great respect for the Christian martyrs, even before he converted to Christianity. In his *Second Apology* (2:12), he states that he "heard the Christians slandered, and saw them fearless of death . . ."

Justin Martyr, First Apology, *excerpts*

1. To the Emperor Titus Ælius Adrianus Antoninus Pius Augustus Cæsar, and to his son Verissimus the Philosopher, and to Lucius the Philosopher, the natural son of Cæsar, and the adopted son of Pius, a lover of learning, and to the sacred Senate, with the whole People of the Romans, I, Justin, the son of Priscus and grandson of Bacchius, natives of Flavia Neapolis in Palestine, present this address and petition in behalf of those of all nations who are unjustly hated and wantonly abused, myself being one of them.

2. Reason directs those who are truly pious and philosophical to honor and love only what is true, declining to follow traditional opinions, if these are worthless. For not only does sound reason direct us to refuse the guidance of those who did or taught anything wrong, but it is incumbent on the lover of truth, by all means, and if death be threatened, even before his own life, to choose to do and say what is right. Do you, then, since you are called pious and philosophers, guardians of justice and lovers of learning, give good heed, and listen to my address; and if you are indeed such, it will be clear. For we have come, not to flatter you by this writing, nor please you by our address, but to beg that you pass judgment, after an accurate and searching investigation, not flattered by prejudice or by a desire of pleasing superstitious men, nor induced by irrational impulse or evil rumors which have long been prevalent, to give a decision which will prove to be against yourselves. For as for us, we reckon that no evil can be done us, unless we be convicted as evil-doers or be proved to be wicked men; and you, you can kill, but not hurt us.

3. But unless anyone think that this is an unreasonable and reckless utterance, we demand that the charges against the Christians be investigated, and that, if these be substantiated, they be punished as they deserve; [or rather, indeed, we ourselves will punish them.] But if no one can convict us of anything, true reason forbids you, for the sake of a wicked rumor, to wrong blameless men, and indeed rather yourselves, who think fit to direct affairs, not by judgment, but by passion. And every sober-minded person will declare this to be the only fair and equitable adjustment, namely, that the subjects render an unexceptional account of their own life and doctrine; and that, on the other hand, the rulers should give their decision in obedience, not to violence and tyranny, but to piety and philosophy. For thus would both rulers and ruled reap benefit. For even one of the ancients somewhere said, "Unless both rulers and ruled philosophize, it is impossible to make states blessed." It is our task, therefore, to afford to all an opportunity of inspecting our life and teachings, lest, on account of those who are accustomed to be ignorant of our affairs, we should incur the penalty due to them for mental blindness; and it is your business, when you hear us, to be found, as reason demands, good judges. For if, when you have learned the truth, you do not what is just, you will be before God without excuse . . .

5. Why, then, should this be? In our case, we who pledge ourselves to do no wickedness, nor to hold these atheistic opinions, you do not examine the charges made against us; but, yielding to unreasoning passion, and to the instigation of evil demons, you punish us without consideration or judgment. For the truth shall be spoken; since of old these evil demons, effecting apparitions of themselves, both defiled women and corrupted boys, and showed such fearful sights to men, that those who did not use their reason in judging of the actions that were done, were struck with terror; and being carried away by fear,

and not knowing that these were demons, they called them gods, and gave to each the name which each of the demons chose for himself. And when Socrates endeavored, by true reason and examination, to bring these things to light, and deliver men from the demons, then the demons themselves, by means of men who rejoiced in iniquity, compassed his death, as an atheist and a profane person, on the charge that "he was introducing new divinities;" and in our case they display a similar activity. For not only among the Greeks did reason (Logos) prevail to condemn these things through Socrates, but also among the Barbarians were they condemned by Reason (or the Word, the Logos) Himself, who took shape, and became man, and was called Jesus Christ; and in obedience to Him, we not only deny that they who did such things as these are gods, but assert that they are wicked and impious demons, whose actions will not bear comparison with those even of men desirous of virtue.

6. Hence are we called atheists. And we confess that we are atheists, so far as gods of this sort are concerned, but not with respect to the most true God, the Father of righteousness and temperance and the other virtues, who is free from all impurity. But both Him, and the Son (who came forth from Him and taught us these things, and the host of the other good angels who follow and are made like to Him), and the prophetic Spirit, we worship and adore, knowing them in reason and truth, and declaring without grudging to everyone who wishes to learn, as we have been taught . . .

32. Moses then, who was the first of the prophets, spoke in these very words: "The scepter shall not depart from Judah, nor a lawgiver from between his feet, until He come for whom it is reserved; and He shall be the desire of the nations, binding His foal to the vine, washing His robe in the blood of the grape." It is yours to make accurate inquiry, and ascertain up to whose time the Jews had a lawgiver and king of their own. Up to the time of Jesus Christ, who taught us, and interpreted the prophecies which were not yet understood, [they had a lawgiver] as was foretold by the holy and divine Spirit of prophecy through Moses, "that a ruler would not fail the Jews until He should come for whom the kingdom was reserved" (for Judah was the forefather of the Jews, from whom also they have their name of Jews); and after He (i.e., Christ) appeared, you began to rule the Jews, and gained possession of all their territory. And the prophecy, "He shall be the expectation of the nations," signified that there would be some of all nations who should look for Him to come again. And this indeed you can see for yourselves, and be convinced of by fact. For of all races of men there are some who look for Him who was crucified in Judea, and after whose crucifixion the land was straightway surrendered to you as spoil of war. And the prophecy, "binding His foal to the vine, and washing His robe in the blood of the grape," was a significant symbol of the things that were to happen to Christ, and of what He was to do.

For the foal of an ass stood bound to a vine at the entrance of a village, and He ordered His acquaintances to bring it to Him then; and when it was brought, He mounted and sat upon it, and entered Jerusalem, where was **the vast temple of the Jews** which was afterwards destroyed by you. And after this He was crucified, that the rest of the prophecy might be fulfilled. For this "washing His robe in the blood of the grape" was predictive of the passion He was to endure, cleansing by His blood those who believe on Him. For what is called by the Divine Spirit through the prophet "His robe," are those men who believe in Him in whom abides the seed of God, the Word. And what is spoken of as "the blood of the grape," signifies that He who should appear would have blood, though not of the seed of man, but of the power of

> **the vast temple of the Jews** The Second Temple, which was destroyed by the Romans in 70 CE.

God. And the first power after God the Father and Lord of all is the Word, who is also the Son; and of Him we will, in what follows, relate how He took flesh and became man. For as man did not make the blood of the vine, but God, so it was hereby intimated that the blood should not be of human seed, but of divine power, as we have said above. And Isaiah, another prophet, foretelling the same things in other words, spoke thus: "A star shall rise out of Jacob, and a flower shall spring from the root of Jesse; and His arm shall the nations trust. And a star of light has arisen, and a flower has sprung from the root of Jesse—this Christ. For by the power of God He was conceived by a virgin of the seed of Jacob, who was the father of Judah, who, as we have shown, was the father of the Jews; and Jesse was His forefather according to the oracle, and He was the son of Jacob and Judah according to lineal descent . . .

Source: Roberts, Rev. Alexander, and James Donaldson, eds. *The Ante-Nicene Fathers: Translations of the Writings of the Fathers Down to A.D. 325,* vol. 1. Buffalo, NY: Christian Literature Company, 1885, 163–74.

AFTERMATH

Justin wrote this *First Apology* sometime between 138 and 165, the year of his death. It is not known if the emperor ever read it, and if he did, his response is not known. Justin's appeal to reason did not stop the persecution of the Christians. It was not until the time of Constantine in the early 300s that the Christians were truly safe from governmental persecution. Nor did Justin's passionate plea save his own life, since he was martyred as well. One positive outcome of his *First Apology* is that many Christians afterward used it to defend themselves and other Christians.

ASK YOURSELF

1. Why did Justin's appeal to reason not convince Roman authorities to stop persecuting the Christians? Do you think he could have phrased his arguments differently?
2. Why would Justin direct his letter not only to the emperor but also to his philosopher sons?
3. Justin attacks the traditional Roman gods in this *Apology*. How would the emperor and his sons react to this? Do you think it helped or hurt Justin's argument that the Christians should not be persecuted? Why do you think Justin brought this up?
4. Why would the Christians be considered to be atheists, when they clearly stated they believed in God?

TOPICS TO CONSIDER

- Consider, from Justin's *Apology,* the various reasons why the Roman government attacked the Christians. Consider why this group was singled out by the authorities, as opposed to those who were Jewish.
- Take apart the argument that Justin puts forth in his defense of Christianity. List his reasons why they should not be attacked. Consider whether the emperor (if he had read this *Apology*) would have found the arguments legitimate or not.
- At the end of this section of the *First Apology,* Justin lists a number of prophecies about the coming of Christ, taken from the Old Testament. Consider how this

section would have affected the typical Roman official. Consider how this would have affected other Christians.

> ~ Read Justin Martyr's *Second Apology* and compare the arguments that Justin made to the senate with those he made to the emperor and his sons. If there are differences, why would he argue differently?

Further Information

Droge, Arthur J. "Justin Martyr and the Restoration of Philosophy." *Church History* 56, no. 3 (Sep., 1987): 303–19.

Keresztes, Paul. "The Literary Genre of Justin's First Apology." *Vigiliae Christianae* 19, no. 2 (Jun., 1965): 99–110.

Martyr, Justin. *First and Second Apology.* http://www.ccel.org/ccel/schaff/anf01.html.

Minns, Denis, and Paul Parvis, eds. *Justin, Philosopher and Martyr: Apologies.* Oxford: Oxford University Press, 2009.

Parvis, Sara, and Paul Foster. *Justin Martyr and His Worlds.* Minneapolis, MN: Fortress Press, 2007.

Piper, Otto A. "The Nature of the Gospel According to Justin Martyr." *Journal of Religion* 41, no. 3 (Jul., 1961): 155–68.

Story, Cullen I. K. "Justin's Apology I. 62–64: Its Importance for the Author's Treatment of Christian Baptism." *Vigiliae Christianae* 16, no. 3/4 (Sep., 1962): 172–78.

41. Conversion of Constantine

INTRODUCTION

Lactantius (ca. 240–320 CE) is an important source for the life of Emperor Constantine, the first Roman Christian emperor. He was an advisor to the emperor and became the tutor of Constantine's son, Crispus. His work *On the Deaths of the Persecutors* is Lactantius's eyewitness account of the persecution of Christians that had begun under the reign of Emperor Diocletian. Included in his account is the story of Constantine's conversion to Christianity. Constantine was his hero since he elevated Christianity from a persecuted religion to the preferred religion in the Roman Empire. We are fortunate to have another, slightly different account of Constantine's conversion from Eusebius of Caesarea (260–339 CE), another advisor to Constantine. Eusebius is more famous for his *History of the Church* and the part he played at the Council of Nicea. Eusebius had written the *Life of Constantine* within a few years of the death of the emperor in 337 CE.

KEEP IN MIND WHILE YOU READ

1. The Greek letters chi and rho were used frequently on early Christian art.
2. Lactantius first was appointed the rhetor of Nicomedia by Emperor Diocletian. As a rhetor, Lactantius would have spent his days teaching and writing speeches. He converted to Christianity and resigned his post. Constantine, when he became emperor, then hired Lactantius.
3. Eusebius, bishop of the port city of Caesarea, became involved in the Arian controversy that was raging during the beginning of the 300s. Just before the Council of Nicea in 325, Eusebius was condemned for his views. He redeemed himself, however, at the important council, where his draft statement of faith ultimately became the Nicene Creed.
4. Constantine had come to power by the declaration of his soldiers after the death of his father Emperor Constantius (made emperor in the west in 305 CE) when he was campaigning in Roman Britain in 306 CE. This was a problem because Severus was meant to become the next emperor if anything happened to Constantius. Maxentius, too, wanted to become emperor. The battle described below was Constantine's final victory in his attempts to become the sole emperor in the west.

Lactantius, On the Deaths of the Persecutors *44*

And now a civil war broke out between Constantine and Maxentius. Although Maxentius kept himself within Rome, because the soothsayers had foretold that if he went out of it he should perish, yet he conducted the military operations by able generals. In forces he exceeded his adversary; for he had not only his father's army, which deserted from Severus, but also his own, which he had lately drawn together out of Mauritania and Italy. They fought, and the troops of Maxentius prevailed. At length Constantine, with steady courage and a mind prepared for every event, led his whole forces to the neighborhood of Rome, and camped them opposite to the Milvian Bridge. The anniversary of the reign of Maxentius approached, that is, the sixth of the kalends of November, and the fifth year of his reign was drawing to an end. Constantine was directed in a dream to cause the heavenly sign to be delineated on the shields of his soldiers, and so to proceed to battle. He did as he had been commanded, and he marked on their shields the letter Ch, with a perpendicular line drawn through it and turned round thus at the top, being the cipher of Christ. Having this sign, his troops stood to arms. The enemies advanced, but without their emperor, and they crossed the bridge. The armies met, and fought with the utmost exertions of valor, and firmly maintained their ground. In the meantime a sedition arose at Rome, and Maxentius was reviled as one who had abandoned all concern for the safety of the commonweal; and suddenly, while he exhibited the Circensian games on the anniversary of his reign, the people cried with one voice, "Constantine cannot be overcome!" Dismayed at this, Maxentius burst from the assembly, and having called some senators together, ordered the Sibylline Oracles to be searched. In them it was found that:—"On the same day the enemy of the Romans should perish." Led by this response to the hopes of victory, he went to the field. The bridge in his rear was broken down. At sight of that the battle grew hotter. The hand of the Lord prevailed, and the forces of Maxentius were routed. He fled towards the broken bridge; but the multitude pressing on him, he was driven headlong into the Tiber. This destructive war being ended, Constantine was acknowledged as emperor, with great rejoicings, by the senate and people of Rome. And now he came to know the perfidy of Daia; for he found the letters written to Maxentius, and saw the statues and portraits of the two associates which had been set up together. The senate, in reward of the valor of Constantine, decreed to him the title of Maximus (the Greatest), a title which Daia had always arrogated to himself. Daia, when he heard that Constantine was victorious and Rome freed, expressed as much sorrow as if he himself had been vanquished; but afterwards, when he heard of the decree of the senate, he grew outrageous, avowed enmity towards Constantine, and made his title of the Greatest a theme of abuse and raillery.

Source: Roberts, Rev. Alexander, and James Donaldson, eds. *The Ante-Nicene Fathers: Translations of the Writings of the Fathers Down to* A.D. *325*, vol. 7. Buffalo, NY: Christian Literature Company, 1905, 318.

Eusebius, Life of Constantine *1:28–31*

Chapter 28: Accordingly he called on him with earnest prayer and supplications that he would reveal to him who he was, and stretch forth his right hand to help him in his present difficulties. And while he was thus praying with fervent entreaty, a most marvelous sign appeared to him from heaven, the account of which it might have been hard to believe had it been related by any other person. But since the victorious emperor himself long afterwards declared it to the writer of this history, when he was honored with his acquaintance and society, and confirmed his statement by an oath, who could hesitate to accredit the relation, especially since the testimony of after-time has established its truth? He said that about noon, when the day was already beginning to decline, he saw with his own eyes the trophy of a cross of light in the heavens, above the sun, and bearing the inscription, Conquer by this. At this sight he himself was struck with amazement, and his whole army also, which followed him on this expedition, and witnessed the miracle.

Chapter 29: He said, moreover, that he doubted within himself what the import of this apparition could be. And while he continued to ponder and reason on its meaning, night suddenly came on; then in his sleep the Christ of God appeared to him with the same sign which he had seen in the heavens, and commanded him to make a likeness of that sign which he had seen in the heavens, and to use it as a safeguard in all engagements with his enemies.

Chapter 30: At dawn of day he arose, and communicated the marvel to his friends: and then, calling together the workers in gold and precious stones, he sat in the midst of them, and described to them the figure of the sign he had seen, bidding them represent it in gold and precious stones. And this representation I myself have had an opportunity of seeing.

Chapter 31: Now it was made in the following manner. A long spear, overlaid with gold, formed the figure of the cross by means of a transverse bar laid over it. On the top of the whole was fixed a wreath of gold and precious stones; and within this, the symbol of the Savior's name, two letters indicating the name of Christ by means of its initial characters, the letter P (the Greek Rho) being intersected by X in its center: and these letters the emperor was in the habit of wearing on his helmet at a later period. From the cross-bar of the spear was suspended a cloth, a royal piece, covered with a profuse embroidery of most brilliant precious stones; and which, being also richly interlaced with gold, presented an indescribable degree of beauty to the beholder. This banner was of a square form, and the upright staff, whose lower section was of great length, bore a golden half-length portrait of the pious emperor and his children on its upper part, beneath the trophy of the cross, and immediately above the embroidered banner. The emperor constantly made use of this sign of salvation as a safeguard against every adverse and hostile power, and commanded that others similar to it should be carried at the head of all his armies.

Source: Wace, Henry, and Philip Schaff, eds. *A Select Library of Nicene and Post-Nicene Fathers of the Christian Church,* vol. 1. Oxford: Parker, 1890, 490–91.

AFTERMATH

After winning the battle against Maxentius, Constantine became the sole emperor on the western side of the Roman Empire, while Licinius was the emperor on the eastern side. Soon after his victory, Constantine and Licinius met in Milan, Italy, to finally declare the Great Persecution, started by Emperor Diocletian, to be officially over. For the first time, Christians were allowed to practice their religion without fear of persecution. Although there are debates on when he officially became a Christian, he created a number of laws that protected Christians as soon as he became emperor. As previously mentioned, Lactantius became friends with the new emperor and was appointed to be the tutor of Constantine's son, Crispus. Eusebius was made bishop of Caesarea sometime around 313 CE and in 325 was present at the Council of Nicea. He played a great part in the formulation of the Nicene Creed.

We do not know when Constantine became a Christian. He was baptized at the end of his life (by the Arian bishop Eusebius of Nicomedia), which was common during this period. There are questions about his commitment to Christianity, at least early on in his emperorship, because coins were minted showing Constantine as Apollo. There can be no doubt, however, that he became committed to Christianity, since he spent quite a bit of effort supporting Christians, building churches, and portraying himself as the leader of the church.

ASK YOURSELF

1. Currently there is a debate whether Constantine was Christian before he became emperor. Eusebius indicates that Constantine was in fact a Christian, while in the account of Lactantius it isn't clear. Do you think that Constantine was a Christian, just based on these accounts?
2. Why does Eusebius spend so much time describing the cross that Constantine created? Do you think it added anything to his account?
3. How accurate do you think Lactantius is when he describes the Roman people shouting down Maxentius during the Circensian games?
4. The versions of what happened are obviously different. How can you explain these differences? Do you trust one version over the other? If so, why?

TOPICS TO CONSIDER

- ❧ Eusebius goes into great detail on the creation of the cross that Constantine carried into battle. Consider how the cross was used in later battles.
- ❧ The Sibylline Oracles had a long history in Rome. Consider how these oracles were used by the Roman people and, in particular, by the Roman emperors. Can you think of modern equivalents to these oracles?
- ❧ Consider how Roman emperors were chosen. As mentioned, Constantine was elected by his troops, without the approval of the emperor of the east. Do you think this is an early form of democracy by the Romans? Be sure to include in your discussion the Tetrarchy, or the Rule of Four, which was designed by Emperor Diocletian.

Further Information

Barnes, Timothy D. *Constantine and Eusebius.* Cambridge, MA: Harvard University Press, 1981.

Digeser, Elizabeth DePalma. *The Making of a Christian Empire: Lactantius and Rome.* Ithaca, NY: Cornell University Press, 2000.

Eusebius writings. http://www.ccel.org/ccel/schaff/npnf201.toc.html.

Kousoulas, D.G. *The Life and Times of Constantine the Great.* 2nd ed. Bethesda, MD: Rutledge Books, 2003.

Lactantius writings. http://www.ccel.org/ccel/schaff/anf07.iii.v.html.

Nicholson, Oliver. "Constantine's Vision of the Cross." *Vigiliae Christianae* 54, no. 3 (2000): 309–23.

Stephenson, Paul. *Constantine: Roman Emperor, Christian Victor.* New York: Penguin, 2010.

42. Arch of Constantine

INTRODUCTION

As discussed in the texts written by Lactantius and Eusebius, Constantine had battled against Maxentius in order to become the sole emperor of the west. After his victory in 312 CE, the Roman Senate declared that a triumphal arch should be built to commemorate this victory. The work on the arch began in 312 and continued until 315 (Marlowe 223). By this time Rome had a number of triumphal arches; the most famous today are the Arch of Titus and the Arch of Septimius Severus, both built in the Roman Forum, not too far from where the Arch of Constantine stands. The Arch of Titus was built to commemorate Emperor Titus's various victories in the first century CE, while the other arch was built to commemorate the victories of Emperor Septimius Severus and his sons over the Parthians in the late 190s CE. These triumphal arches all contained dedicatory inscriptions. On the next page are some pictures of the arch along with the dedication and translation.

KEEP IN MIND WHILE YOU READ

1. The images that are surrounded by a circle are called *tondi* (see the next page).
2. The date of completion, 315 CE, was the 10-year anniversary since Constantine became emperor of the west (his *deccenalia*).
3. Many of the images and statues on the arch were not created for this particular arch. The picture with the inscription *liberatorivrbis, liberator of the city*, meaning Rome, is not original. It is believed that they date to the time of Emperor Trajan (ruled 98–117 CE). The tondi were created sometime during the time of Emperor Hadrian (ruled 117–138 CE).
4. Constantine never lived in Rome. His primary residence was at Trier. It is known that Constantine was in Rome in late July 315, and he left in September of the same year (Barnes 72). This is probably when the celebration occurred. The next time he was in Rome was in July 326, probably for his 20th-anniversary celebration. From 330 to 337 (the year of his death), Constantine lived in Constantinople, the city he had built.

Dedication on the Arch of Constantine

Arch of Constantine (Rome). (Library of Congress)

Dedication on the Arch of Constantine. English translation: To the Emperor Caesar Flavius Constantine Maximus, Pius Felix Augustus, the Senate and the Roman People, Since through divine inspiration and great wisdom, he has delivered the state from the tyrant and his party by his army and noble arms, Dedicate this arch, decorated with triumphal insignia (Stedman Sheard, 172). (iStockPhoto.com)

AFTERMATH

The Arch of Constantine was the last triumphal arch built in Rome. After it was completed, Constantine ruled for another 22 years; during that period, he returned to Rome to celebrate his 20th year of rule as well. The arch still stands today, and the fact that it was not pillaged over the centuries shows that the Roman people remembered the importance of Constantine and his impact on Christian history.

ASK YOURSELF

1. As stated above, Emperor Constantine was rarely in Rome (less than four months in the entire time he was emperor). What effect did this have on the Roman people? Ask yourself how this would have affected the city of Rome in particular. Do you think it mattered that the emperor lived elsewhere?
2. Many of the decorations on the arch were recycled from other monuments. What does this say about the state of architecture during the period of Emperor Constantine's rule?
3. As you look through the decorations and statues on the arch, why aren't there specifically Christian inscriptions or artwork? What does that suggest to you regarding the state of Christianity at this time period?
4. If the president of the United States decided to live somewhere else other than Washington, DC, would that have an impact on the function of the government?

TOPICS TO CONSIDER

- Examine the interaction between the emperor and the Roman Senate, both before and during the time of Constantine. Consider their respective roles in Roman society and discuss how they dealt with each other.
- Consider the other triumphal arches in Rome and the impact they would have had on the Roman people. Consider, too, how the arch would have affected the emperor personally.

THE TRIUMPHAL ARCHES

Triumphal arches were built to showcase the power of the emperor or as a "thank you" from the Roman Senate and the people for some act they considered to be especially brave. The arch itself probably did not have a big impact on Constantine because he never lived in Rome. The arch has an interesting history in that many of its parts were pillaged from other Roman structures. This material is called *spolia*. The statues along the very top of the structure are probably from the time of Emperor Trajan, as well as the friezes, or carvings within the arches, which were made during the time of Emperor Trajan (toward the end of the first century). The medallions (the carvings that are placed in a circle) along the middle of the structure were resculpted. The medallions that show Constantine taking part in a boar hunt were originally from the time of Emperor Hadrian (ruled 117–138). There were certainly new elements created during the time of Constantine, such as the frieze showing him rescuing the city. Some scholars have ventured a guess that the original arch was not built during the time of Constantine but had been standing there before; instead of building a brand new one, it was decided to refigure an old one.

Further Information

Barnes, Timothy. *The New Empire of Diocletian and Constantine*. Cambridge, MA: Harvard University Press, 1982.

Jones, Mark Wilson. "Genesis and Mimesis: The Design of the Arch of Constantine in Rome." *Journal of the Society of Architectural Historians* 59, no. 1 (Mar., 2000): 50–77.

Odahl, Charles. "God and Constantine: Divine Sanction for Imperial Rule in the First Christian Emperor's Early Letters and Art." *Catholic Historical Review* 81, no. 3 (Jul., 1995): 327–52.

Stedman Sheard, Wendy. "Tullio Lombardo in Rome? The Arch of Constantine, the Vendramin Tomb, and the Reinvention of Monumental Classicizing Relief." *Artibus et Historiae* 18, no. 35 (1997): 161–79.

Walton, Alice. "The Date of the Arch of Constantine." *Memoirs of the American Academy in Rome* 4 (1924): 169–80.

APPENDIX 1: BIOGRAPHY

Alexander of Alexandria: Alexander was bishop of Alexandria, Egypt, from 312–328 CE. Arius (below) was one of his priests. Alexander firmly believed that God and the Son were coeternal, meaning that both had existed since the beginning. Alexander made his views known to his flock and it was expected that the priests have the same theological beliefs. Arius, however, disagreed. By 319 CE, Alexander had had enough of Arius and had him condemned for his beliefs. Alexander was also present at the Council of Nicea.

Arius: Arius was born around 260 in either Lybia or Alexandria, Egypt, and died in 336 CE. Arius became a priest in 312 in Alexandria, and he openly started to question some beliefs put forth by his bishop, Alexander of Alexandria. Alexander stated that God and Jesus were both coeternal, but Arius believed that God was first, while Jesus came after. Arius was kicked out of Alexandria and his beliefs became known as Arianism. The fighting between the groups ultimately led to the Council of Nicea in 325. Arius was excommunicated and was sent into exile. He died in 336, almost immediately after Constantine told Athanasius to receive Arius back into communion.

Athanasius: Athanasius was born sometime in the late 200s and died in 373 CE. He was first a priest in Alexandria under Alexander of Alexandria and became bishop of Alexandria in 328 after the death of Alexander. He was at the Council of Nicea in 325 and fully supported his bishop. Athanasius was the main person who fought against Arius and Arianism during the whole time he was bishop. Athanasius occasionally had the support of the emperors but was ultimately exiled four times over disagreements over Arianism.

Barnabas: There isn't much known about Barnabas the Apostle. He is mentioned a few times in the New Testament. He met Paul after he had converted to Christianity and the two of them lived in Antioch, converting both the Jewish and Gentile populations. According to Paul's letter to the Galatians, Paul and Barnabas also argued, in particular over the issue of eating practices: should Christians eat joint meals with the new Christians who converted from paganism? Paul said yes, while Barnabas had second thoughts. Paul and Barnabas also argued over traveling companions, and at some point the two parted ways (Acts 15:36–40). Most scholars agree that this Barnabas did not write the *Epistle of Barnabas*.

Celsus: Almost everything we know about Celsus comes from his book called *True Doctrine*, which was preserved only in parts in Origen's *Against Celsus*. He lived sometime in the second century and wrote True Doctrine probably in the late 100s. It isn't known when he died, but it was sometime before 230 CE. Celsus was a pagan and questioned many of the Christian doctrines he had been told about. His *True Doctrine* did not have too much impact on Christianity during this period, but sometime after 230 Origen decided to write *Against Celsus*. It was after this that Celsus's writing was seen as a danger to Christians.

Clement of Alexandria: Clement was born around 150 and died around 215 CE. He converted to Christianity as a young man and proceeded to travel around Asia Minor in search of teachers. He settled in Alexandria, Egypt, although he left when there was persecution in Egypt in the early 200s. While in Alexandria Clement taught and it is possible that Origen was a student of his. Clement wrote many Christian works.

Constantine: Constantine was born around 285 and died in 337 CE. His father, Constantius, was at first Caesar of Britain, Spain, and Gaul in 293, and in May 305 Constantius became Emperor of the west. Constantine traveled to Britain in 305 and fought alongside his father. In 306 Constantius was killed in battle, and the troops raised up Constantine as emperor. Ultimately, Constantine became the emperor of the west in 312, with Licinius being the emperor in the east. Sometime right before this, Constantine became a Christian and made it legal for Christians to openly practice their religion. Constantine became sole emperor in 324 when he defeated and killed Licinius. He was intimately involved in a number of theological controversies, including Arianism. It was under Constantine that the Council of Nicea was called. Shortly before his death he was baptized by Eusebius of Nicomedia, an Arian.

Cyprian: Cyprian was born sometime in the early 200s and died in 258. It appears he converted to Christianity later in life and was baptized, either in 245 or 246 in Carthage, North Africa. Two years later he became bishop of Carthage. Some Christians were against this quick ordination. In 250 CE, persecution of the Christians by Emperor Decius had begun and Cyprian had to go into hiding. A controversy broke out when Cyprian wanted to grant partial forgiveness to those who had denied Christ. In 257 Emperor Valerian began another persecution against the Christians, and in 258 Cyprian confessed to being a Christian and was beheaded.

Eusebius of Caesarea: Eusebius of Caesarea was born in the middle of the 200s and died around 339 CE. Eusebius grew up in Caesarea (Palestine) and ultimately became bishop of Caesarea in 313. Eusebius was a prolific writer, including his *The Martyrs of Palestine and his famous Ecclesiastical History*. Eusebius lived through the Great Persecution, started under Emperor Diocletian. Eusebius sided with Arius and his views, at least early on in the controversy. He was officially condemned at the Council of Antioch in 324, but he redeemed himself at the Council of Nicea where he produced an early version of the Nicene Creed. Minor corrections were made by the majority of bishops, and the Creed was accepted. Eusebius also became friends with Emperor Constantine and wrote *The Life of Constantine*. Later, Eusebius played a part in sending Athanasius into his first of many exiles.

Eusebius of Nicomedia: Eusebius of Nicomedia was born sometime in the late 200s and died in 342 CE. Eusebius gained fame during the Arian controversy when he took the side of Arius. It was also during this period that some bishops complained that Eusebius could not rightly be the bishop of Nicomedia (then the capital city of the eastern Roman empire during the reign of Licinius) because he left his native Berytus (modern day

Beirut) to become bishop in Nicomedia. Eusebius of Nicomedia played an extremely important role in the spreading of the ideas of Arius, but his support was not given during the Council of Nicea when he signed the Nicene Creed, which held that God and the Son were coeternal. However, Eusebius refused to sign a statement that supported the excommunication of Arius. Soon after he was sent into exile, but was allowed back and during this period he continued to support Arius. In 342 he was made bishop of Constantinople but died shortly after taking office.

Hippolytus: Hippolytus was born around 170 and died around 236 CE. Hippolytus, a Christian, was living in Rome and was involved in arguments with the bishop of Rome. This resulted in Hippolytus become a rival bishop in this very same city. He is most remembered for his book *Refutation against All Heresies*. He died in 236 after he was exiled to the island of Sardinia during a persecution under Emperor Maximinus Thrax, who ruled 235–238 CE.

Ignatius of Antioch: Ignatius was bishop of Antioch sometime during the reign of Emperor Trajan (98–117 CE). During this period there was a persecution of Christians and Ignatius was arrested and was taken to Rome. On his way Ignatius wrote many letters to the churches in Asia Minor. His main topic was on the bishop and how the person who held the office should be in control of the church. Related to this was his belief that the church as a whole should be as one in belief and action. Ignatius was looking forward to his upcoming martyrdom in Rome, and he begged the church in that city to not interfere.

Irenaeus of Lyon: Irenaeus was born in the early decades of the second century and died sometime in the early 200s. He moved to Rome and then to Lyons (now in modern-day France). His most famous writing is *Against Heresies*. In particular, he was writing against Christians who believed they received secret knowledge (the Gnostics). His *Against Heresies* was very influential in terms of attacking these Gnostics since it contains his thoughts on what Christianity ought to be, as opposed to what these groups were teaching.

Josephus: Josephus was born around 35 and died around 100 CE. He was Jewish and was involved in a Jewish revolt against Rome in 66–70 CE during the reigns of Nero and then Galba. When the war went badly, he surrendered to the Romans and ultimately served as a translator under Emperor Titus (79–81 CE). He went to Rome and proceeded to write a history titled the *Jewish War and then the Antiquities of the Jews.*

Justin Martyr: Justin died around 165, and it is not clear when he was born. He probably was brought up in a pagan family since he did not convert to Christianity until he was an adult. Justin's writings had a large impact on Christianity because he was very familiar with Greek writings and used them in his defense of Christianity. His more famous writing was *The First and Second Apology*, which are addressed to the emperor and to the Roman Senate. In them he tried to convince the Romans that Christian faith was not a danger to the Roman world. Although he was unsuccessful on this front, many late Christians used his writings. Justin refused to worship the Roman gods and during the reign of Emperor Marcus Aurelius (who ruled 161–180 CE), he was beheaded for his faith.

Lactantius: Lactantius was born sometime around 250 and died around 325 CE. Lactantius began his career as a rhetor under the reign of Emperor Diocletian. During the Great Persecution, Lactantius lost his position because he had converted to Christianity. Later, around 317, he became the tutor to Crispus, the son of Emperor Constantine. Just before this period he had written *On the Deaths of the Persecutors*, which detailed the various punishments that befell the Roman emperors who had persecuted Christians.

Licinius: Licinius was a Roman co-emperor from 308 to 324 CE. He ruled the eastern part of the Roman Empire, and from 312 he co-ruled with Emperor Constantine in the west. It was in this year that Constantine married his sister Constantia to Licinius. In 314, Constantine and Licinius fought to a stalemate. They fought again between 321–324, and this time Licinius was forced to abdicate. He was held under house arrest and was promised that his life would be spared, but Constantine had him put to death.

Mani: Mani was born in 216, somewhere in Mesopotamia, and was executed in 276. As a child, his family was part of the Jewish Christian sect of the Elchasaites. Mani began to have religious visions when he was 12 and again when he was 24. After this he left the Elchasaites and began his own Christian religion, now called Manichaeism. Mani was friends with the great Persian king Shapur, who allowed Mani to travel throughout Persia teaching his new religion. However, during the reign of Bahram I (274–277), Mani and his followers were heavily persecuted, and Mani died in prison. His religion spread both west into the Roman Empire and east as far as China.

Marcion: Marcion was born sometime in the late first century and died in the middle of the second. He was from Sinope on the Black Sea. He was a Christian who believed that Christians did not need to read the Old Testament, that Christians should only read parts of what is now the New Testament, and that there were two gods—one of the New Testament and one in the Old. Marcion traveled to Rome and tried to convince the church leaders that he had the correct interpretation of Christianity. His view was rejected and he was expelled from the church. Marcion then created his own church, which must have been fairly large and popular since many Christians mention its existence. He died around 154 CE, but his churches continued on for centuries after his death.

Montanus: Montanus lived in Asia Minor (now modern-day Turkey) around the middle/end of the second century. He believed that some people were filled with the Holy Spirit or God and spoke in ecstatic speech. His version of Christianity (called Montanism) also allowed women and, in particular, two women, named Priscilla and Maximilla, to be prophets. His movement attracted much attention and spread as far as Rome. It is possible that Tertullian of Carthage became a Montanist in the early third century. The movement died out sometime in the 500s CE.

Muratori: Ludovico Antonio Muratori was born in 1672 and died in 1750. Muratori discovered a manuscript in the Ambrosian Library in Milan. It is called the Muratorian Canon and contains a list of writings that later made up a large part of the New Testament. While there is still debate on the date of the manuscript, it is possible that it is one of the earliest New Testament lists we have and could date to the end of the second century. The Muratorian Canon was published in 1740.

Origen: Origen was born sometime in the 180s and died around 251 CE. He was born in Alexandria and was famous during his life, and certainly after his death, for his prolific writings. It has been thought that he wrote over 2,000 works that covered many different topics. He was forced out of Alexandria, primarily because of his controversial way of reading the Bible. He spent nearly the last 20 years of his life living in Caesarea. Origen's father was martyred for being a Christian during the reign of Septimius Severus, and there is a story that states that Origen wanted to be martyred as well but his mother hid his clothes. Origen almost got his wish 40 years later when he was persecuted under

Emperor Decius (249–251 CE). Origen did not die during the actual persecution but died soon from the wounds he received.

Ossius (or Hosius): Ossius was born sometime around 257 and died around 357 CE. He was a Spanish bishop of Cordova and was very influential, especially during the time of Emperor Constantine. Ossius fought primarily against the Arian Christians. He became the advisor to Emperor Constantine and played a large role in the Council of Nicea in 325 CE. He became a supporter of Athanasius of Alexandria in his own fight against Arianism.

Paul the Apostle: It isn't known exactly when he was born or when he died, but according to tradition, Paul was executed sometime during the reign of Emperor Nero (around 65 CE). Paul (known as Saul before his conversion to Christianity) was raised in Tarsus (modern-day Turkey) in a Jewish family. Paul was persecuting Christians, and on his way to Damascus, Syria, he had a conversion to Christianity. Soon after he became very active in converting both the Jewish and Gentile population to Christianity, especially in Asia Minor, starting in the early 50s CE. Paul was taken into custody by Roman officials in the early 60s and was ultimately taken to Rome. As mentioned, according to tradition he was executed in Rome.

Perpetua and Felicitas: Not much is known about these women except what we know from their martyrdom, which probably contains some of Perpetua's own account. They were both martyred in Carthage, North Africa, in 203 CE, during a general persecution against Christians.

Polycarp: Polycarp was born sometime in the middle/late first century and died around 156 CE. According to Irenaeus, Polycarp knew John the Apostle and in fact had been appointed as bishop of his native city Smyrna by the original apostles.

Suetonius: Suetonius was born between 69 and 75 and died after 130 CE. Suetonius came from a wealthy family and eventually became friends with Pliny the Younger, a Roman senator and then governor of a part of Asia Minor. Primarily because of his close friendship with Pliny, Suetonius became the secretary to Emperor Hadrian, and because of this position he had access to state records. His most famous work is the Twelve Caesars, written in 121 CE.

Tacitus: Tacitus was born in 56 and died in 117 CE. He became a Roman senator, the highest social class below the emperor. He was famous for his oratory skills. After his retirement from politics he wrote his two most famous works, the *Histories and the Annals.*

Tertullian: Tertullian was born around 160, died in the early part of the third century, and lived in Carthage, North Africa. Tertullian began his career as a lawyer and converted to Christianity when he was an adult. His writings were very influential since he combined his classical education with Christian ideas. One of his most popular books was his *Apology,* in which he tried to convince pagans to join Christianity. He might have converted to Montanism, although scholars are still debating this point.

APPENDIX 2: GLOSSARY

Apocryphon: A writing that includes secret knowledge.

Apology: A defense of Christianity.

Asceticism: In early Christianity, asceticism was the self-denial of certain things such as sex or other worldly pleasures.

Canon: A church law, usually created during a conference of church officials. It can also be a list of approved texts that Christians could read.

Codex: A collection of sheets of paper that were then bound together, exactly like a modern-day book. Originally, texts were written on scrolls.

Confessors: These were people who openly confessed to being Christian during times of persecution, which meant that they were usually tortured. They had positions of power in some early communities, both when they were in prison and when they were released when the persecution stopped.

Coptic: An Egyptian language that started sometime in the first century CE. The written language adopted many letters from the Greek alphabet, plus a few native Egyptian letters.

Critical Apparatus: Information found at the bottom of the Greek or Latin Bibles that illustrate the differences between the various manuscripts of these writings.

Donatists: When the Great Persecution finished, many Christians who had cursed Christ, or burned the biblical books, wanted to come back into the church. The Donatists did not want these people back into the church. Donatism was a problem mainly in North Africa during the fourth and early fifth centuries.

Ecumenical: This refers to the Council at Nicea. It is referred to as the first Ecumenical Council because all bishops were invited (although in reality all did not attend).

Edict: A proclamation put out by the emperors that had the force of law.

Enigmatic: Mysterious or obscure.

Eunuch: A castrated male.

Fossores: Those who dug the catacombs. The word comes from the Latin meaning "bone."

Gentiles: Those who were not Jewish or Christian.

Heretic: Someone who believed something different from the accepted norm.

Idol: An object or an image that was considered to be unacceptable to Christians. An idol was usually seen as representing the devil or some other form of evil.

Intended Audience: To whom a letter or book is addressed, as opposed to the modern readers.

Jewish Christians: Christians who followed some of the regulations of Judaism.

Lapsed: These were people who decided to curse Christ and/or worship the emperor during times of persecution, but who wanted back in the church when the persecution ceased.

Lex Julia, or the Julian Law: These were laws passed by the Julian family, which included the first emperor, Augustus. Many of these Julian Laws discussed morals, especially marriage, adultery, and divorce.

Martyrdoms: The stories of the martyrs.

Monasticism: The act of removing oneself from worldly society to worship God.

Proselytize: Actively trying to convert someone to a particular belief.

Recension: A revised text.

Relic: An object that is somehow tied to someone important in the past. This can be a body part, a piece of clothing, or something that the person had touched.

Rhetor: The Roman official who gave speeches. A rhetor almost always was a teacher of rhetoric, or the art of giving speeches.

Sacrament: A religious rite that is considered to be sacred.

Tondi: Pieces of artwork that are created within a circular form.

BIBLIOGRAPHY

Abakuks, Adris. "A Statistical Study of the Triple-Link Model in the Synoptic Problem." *Journal of the Royal Statistical Society,* Series A (Statistics in Society), 169, no. 1 (2006): 49–60.

Aland, Kurt, ed. *Synopsis of the Four Gospels: Greek-English Edition of the Synopsis Quattuor Evangeliorum,* 10th ed. Stuttgart: Biblia-Druck, 1993.

Allberry, C.R.C., ed., with a contribution by H. Ibscher. *A Manichaean Psalm-Book: Part II,* Manichaean Manuscripts in the Chester Beatty Collection, 2. Stuttgart, Germany: W. Kohlhammer, 1938.

Armstrong, Gregory T. "Church and State Relations: The Changes Wrought by Constantine." *Journal of Bible and Religion* 32, no. 1 (Jan., 1964): 1–7.

Armstrong, Gregory T. "Imperial Church Building and Church-State Relations, A.D. 313–363." *Church History* 36, no. 1 (Mar., 1967): 3–17.

Armstrong, Jonathan J. "Victorinus of Pettau as the Author of the Canon Muratori." *Vigiliae Christianae* 62, no. 1 (2008): 1–34.

Baker-Brian, Nicholas J. *Manichaeism: An Ancient Faith Rediscovered.* New York: T & T Clark, 2011.

Bakker, H., P. Van Geest, and H. Van Loon, eds. *Cyprian of Carthage: Studies in His Life, Language and Thought.* Louvain, Belgium: Peeters, 2010..

Balch, David L., and Carolyn Osiek. *Early Christian Families in Context: An Interdisciplinary Dialogue.* Grand Rapids, MI: Eerdmans, 2003.

Barnard, L. W. "The Antecedents of Arius." *Vigiliae Christianae* 24, no. 3 (Sep., 1970): 172–88.

Barnard, L. W. "Athanasius and the Meletian Schism in Egypt." *Journal of Egyptian Archaeology* 59 (Aug., 1973): 181–89.

Barnard, L. W. "The Background of St. Ignatius of Antioch." *Vigiliae Christianae* 17, no. 4 (Dec., 1963): 193–206.

Barnard, L. W. "The Date of the *Epistle of Barnabas:* A Document of Early Egyptian Christianity." *Journal of Egyptian Archaeology* (Dec., 1958): 101–7.

Barnard, L. W. "The *Epistle of Barnabas:* A Paschal Homily?" *Vigiliae Christianae* 15, no. 1 (Mar., 1961): 8–22.

Barnard, L. W. *Justin Martyr.* Cambridge: Cambridge University Press, 1967.

Barnard, L. W. "Justin Martyr's Eschatology." *Vigiliae Christianae* 19, no. 2 (Jun., 1965): 86–98.

Barnes, T. D. *Athanasius and Constantius: Theology and Politics in the Constantinian Empire.* Cambridge, MA: Harvard University Press, 1993.

Barnes, T. D. *Constantine and Eusebius.* Cambridge, MA: Harvard University Press, 1981.

Barnes, T. D. "Lactantius and Constantine." *Journal of Roman Studies* 63 (1973): 29–46.

Barnes, T. D. *The New Empire of Diocletian and Constantine.* Cambridge, MA: Harvard University Press, 1982.

Bassler, Jouette M. "The Widows' Tale: A Fresh Look at 1 Tim 5:3–16." *Journal of Biblical Literature* 103, no. 1 (Mar., 1984): 23–41.

Bazell, Dianne M. "Strife among the Table-Fellows: Conflicting Attitudes of Early and Medieval Christians toward the Eating of Meat." *Journal of the American Academy of Religion* 65, no. 1 (Spring, 1997): 73–99.

Beasley-Murray, G. R. *Baptism in the New Testament.* London: MacMillan, 1962.

Beatrice, Pier Franco. "The Word 'Homoousios' from Hellenism to Christianity." *Church History* 71, no. 2 (Jun., 2002): 243–72.

Beattie, Gillian. *Women and Marriage in Paul and His Early Interpreters.* London: Continuum, 2005.

Becker, Jurgen. *Paul: Apostle to the Gentiles.* Louisville, KY: John Knox Press, 1993.

Beduhn, Jason, and Paul Mirecki, eds. *Frontiers of Faith: The Christian-Manichaean Encounter in the Acts of Archelaus.* Leiden, the Netherlands: Brill: 2007.

Berding, Kenneth. *Polycarp and Paul: An Analysis of Their Literary and Theological Relationship in Light of Polycarp's Use of Biblical and Extra-biblical Literature.* Leiden, the Netherlands: Brill Academic Publishers, 2002.

Betten, Francis S. "The Milan Decree of A.D. 313: Translation and Comment." *Catholic Historical Review* 8, no. 2 (Jul., 1922): 191–97.

Billy, Dennis. *Beauty of the Eucharist: Voices from the Church Fathers.* New York: New City Press, 2010.

Blackmann, E. C. *Marcion and His Influence.* Reprint. Eugene, OR: Wipf and Stock, 2004.

Bokser, Ben Zion. "Justin Martyr and the Jews." *Jewish Quarterly Review,* n.s., 64, no. 2 (Oct., 1973): 97–122.

Bokser, Ben Zion. "Justin Martyr and the Jews: II." *Jewish Quarterly Review,* n.s., 64, no. 3 (Jan., 1974), 204–11.

Bouman, C. A. "Variants in the Introduction to the Eucharistic Prayer." *Vigiliae Christianae* 4, no. 2 (Apr., 1950): 94–115.

Boyarin, Daniel. "Justin Martyr Invents Judaism." *Church History* 70, no. 3 (Sep., 2001): 427–61.

Brakke, David. *Athanasius and Asceticism.* Baltimore: Johns Hopkins University Press, 1995.

Brakke, David. "Canon Formation and Social Conflict in Fourth-Century Egypt: Athanasius of Alexandria's Thirty-Ninth 'Festal Letter.'" *Harvard Theological Review* 87, no. 4 (Oct., 1994): 395–419.

Bratten, Carl E., and Robert W. Jenson. *The Last Things: Biblical and Theological Perspectives on Eschatology.* Grand Rapids, MI: Eerdmanns, 2002.

Brent, Allen. *Cyprian and Roman Carthage.* Cambridge: Cambridge University Press, 2010.

Brent, Allen. *Ignatius of Antioch: A Martyr Bishop and the Origin of the Episcopacy.* New York: T&T Clark International, 2009.

Brooks, Oscar S. "The Johannine Eucharist: Another Interpretation." *Journal of Biblical Literature* 82, no. 3 (Sep., 1963): 293–300.

Brown, Charles Thomas. *The Gospel and Ignatius of Antioch.* Studies in Biblical Literature, vol. 12. New York: Peter Lang, 2000.

Brown, Peter. *Augustine of Hippo: A Biography.* New ed. Berkeley: University of California Press, 2000.

Brown, Peter. *The Body and Society: Men, Women, and Sexual Renunciation in Early Christianity.* New York: Columbia University Press, 1988.

Bryant, Joseph M. "The Sect-Church Dynamic and Christian Expansion in the Roman Empire: Persecution, Penitential Discipline, and Schism in Sociological Perspective." *British Journal of Sociology* 44, no. 2 (Jun., 1993): 303–39.

Bulmer, Ralph. "The Uncleanness of the Birds of Leviticus and Deuteronomy." *Man,* n.s., 24, no. 2 (Jun., 1989): 304–32.

Bultmann, Rudolf. "The New Approach to the Synoptic Problem." *Journal of Religion* 6, no. 4 (Jul., 1926): 337–62.

Butler, Rex D. *The New Prophecy & "New Visions": Evidence of Montanism in the Passion of Perpetua and Felicitas.* Washington, DC: Catholic University of America Press, 2006.

Calder, W. M. "Early-Christian Epitaphs from Phrygia." *Anatolian Studies* 5 (1955): 25–38.

Caner, Daniel F. "The Practice and Prohibition of Self-Castration in Early Christianity." *Vigiliae Christianae* 51, no. 4 (Nov., 1997): 396–415.

Carotenuto, Erica. "Six Constantinian Documents (Eus. 'H.E.' 10, 5–7)." *Vigiliae Christianae* 56, no. 1 (Feb., 2002): 56–74.

Carter, Warren. *The Roman Empire and the New Testament: An Essential Guide.* Nashville, TN: Abingdon Press, 2006.

Castelli, Elizabeth. *Martyrdom and Memory: Early Christian Culture Making.* New York: Columbia University Press, 2004.

Chadwick, Henry. "Origen, Celcus, and the Resurrection of the Body." *Harvard Theological Review* 41, no. 2 (Apr., 1948): 83–102.

Chadwick, Henry. "Faith and Order at the Council of Nicaea: A Note on the Background of the Sixth Canon." *Harvard Theological Review* 53, no. 3 (Jul., 1960): 171–95.

Cheung, Alex T. *Idol Food in Corinth: Jewish Background and Pauline Legacy.* Sheffield, England: Sheffield Academic Press, 1999.

Church, F. Forrester. "Sex and Salvation in Tertullian." *Harvard Theological Review* 68, no. 2 (Apr., 1975): 83–101.

Clark, Elizabeth A. "Antifamilial Tendencies in Ancient Christianity." *Journal of the History of Sexuality* 5, no. 3 (Jan., 1995): 356–80.

Clark, Elizabeth, ed., and Sally Rieger Shore, trans. *John Chrysostom: "On Virginity," "Against Marriage."* Lewiston, NY: Edwin Mellon Press, 1989.

Cochrane, Eric. "Muratori: The Vocation of a Historian." *Catholic Historical Review* 51, no. 2 (Jul., 1965): 153–72.

Cohen, Shaye J. D. "Judaism without Circumcision and 'Judaism' without 'Circumcision' in Ignatius." *Harvard Theological Review* 95, no. 4 (Oct., 2002): 395–415.

Colwell, Ernest Cadman. "The Fourth Gospel and Early Christian Art." *Journal of Religion* 15, no. 2 (Apr., 1935): 191–206.

Curran, John. "Constantine and the Ancient Cults of Rome: The Legal Evidence." *Greece & Rome,* 2nd ser., 43, no. 1 (Apr., 1996): 68–80.

Davies, Stevan L. "The Predicament of Ignatius of Antioch." *Vigiliae Christianae* 30, no. 3 (Sep., 1976): 175–80.

Davis, Leo Donald. *The First Seven Ecumenical Councils (325–787): Their History and Theology.* Collegeville, MN: Liturgical Press, 1983.

De Lubac, Henri. *History and Spirit: The Understanding of Scripture According to Origen.* San Francisco: Ignatius Press, 2007.

Deming, Will. *Paul on Marriage and Celibacy: The Hellenistic Background of 1 Corinthians 7.* 2nd ed. Grand Rapids, MI: Eerdmans, 2004.

Denzey, Nicola. "What Did the Montanists Read?" *Harvard Theological Review* 94, no. 4 (Oct., 2001): 427–48.

De Ste. Croix, G.E.M. "Aspects of the 'Great' Persecution." *Harvard Theological Review* 47, no. 2 (Apr., 1954): 75–113.

DeWitt Burton, Ernest. "The Office of Apostle in the Early Church." *American Journal of Theology* 16, no. 4 (Oct., 1912): 561–88.

Digeser, Elizabeth DePalma. *The Making of a Christian Empire: Lactantius and Rome.* Ithaca, NY: Cornell University Press, 2000.

Donahue, Paul J. "Jewish Christianity in the Letters of Ignatius of Antioch." *Vigiliae Christianae* 32, no. 2 (Jun., 1978): 81–93.

Drake, H. A. "Constantine and Consensus." *Church History* 64, no. 1 (Mar., 1995): 1–15.

Droge, Arthur J. "Justin Martyr and the Restoration of Philosophy." *Church History* 56, no. 3 (Sep., 1987): 303–19.

Dunn, Geoffrey R. *Tertullian.* The Early Church Fathers series. New York: Routledge, 2004.

Eberts, Harry W., Jr. "Plurality and Ethnicity in Early Christian Mission." *Sociology of Religion* 58, no. 4 (Winter, 1997): 305–21.

Ehrman, Bart D. *Forged: Writing in the Name of God—Why the Bible's Authors Are Not Who We Think They Are.* New York: HarperCollins, 2011.

Ehrman, Bart D. "The New Testament Canon of Didymus the Blind." *Vigiliae Christianae* 37, no. 1 (Mar., 1983): 1–21.

Eisen, Ute E. *Women Officeholders in Early Christianity: Epigraphical and Literary Studies.* Collegeville, MN: Liturgical Press, 2000.

Ernest, James D. "Athanasius of Alexandria: The Scope of Scripture in Polemical and Pastoral Context." *Vigiliae Christianae* 47, no. 4 (Dec., 1993): 341–62.

Esler, Philip Francis, and Ronald A. Piper. *Lazarus, Mary and Martha: Social-Scientific Approaches to the Gospel of John.* Minneapolis, MN: Augsberg Fortress, 2006.

Evans, E., ed. *Tertullian's Homily on Baptism.* London: SPCK, 1964.

Evans, G. R. *Augustine on Evil.* Cambridge: Cambridge University Press, 1993.

Farmer, William R. *The Synoptic Problem: A Critical Analysis.* New York: Macmillan, 1964.

Feeley-Harnik, Gillian. *The Lord's Table: Eucharist and Passover in Early Christianity.* Philadelphia: University of Pennsylvania Press, 1981.

Feldman, Louis H. "Origen's 'Contra Celsum' and Josephus' 'Contra Apionem': The Issue of Jewish Origins." *Vigiliae Christianae* 44, no. 2 (Jun., 1990): 105–35.

Ferguson, Everett. *Baptism in the Early Church: History, Theology, and Liturgy in the First Five Centuries.* Grand Rapids, MI: Eerdman, 2009.

Fisher, Arthur L. "Lactantius' Ideas Relating Christian Truth and Christian Society." *Journal of the History of Ideas* 43, no. 3 (Jul.–Sep., 1982): 355–77.

Fonrobert, Charlotte. *Menstrual Purity: Rabbinic and Christian Reconstructions of Biblical Gender.* Stanford, CA: Stanford University Press, 2000.

Francis, Fred O. "Eschatology and History in Luke-Acts." *Journal of the American Academy of Religion* 37, no. 1 (Mar., 1969): 49–63.

Frazee, Charles A. "The Origins of Clerical Celibacy in the Western Church." *Church History* 41, no. 2 (Jun., 1972): 149–67.

Fredriksen, Paula. "Apocalypse and Redemption in Early Christianity from John of Patmos to Augustine of Hippo." *Vigiliae Christianae* 45, no. 2 (Jun., 1991): 151–83.

Gardner, Iain, and Sam N. C. Lieu, eds. *Manichaean Tests from the Roman Empire.* Cambridge: Cambridge University Press, 2004.

Gardner, Iain, and Klass A. Worp. "Leaves from a Manichaean Codex (Pl.s VIII–X)." *Zeitschrift für Papyrologie und Epigraphik* 117 (1997): 139–55.

Geller, M. J. "Early Christianity and the Dead Sea Scrolls." *Bulletin of the School of Oriental and African Studies, University of London,* 57, no. 1 (1994): 82–86.

Goodenough, Erwin R. "Catacomb Art." *Journal of Biblical Literature* 81, no. 2 (Jun., 1962): 113–42.

Grabar, Andre. *Christian Iconography: A Study of Its Origins.* Princeton, NJ: Princeton University Press, 1968.

Grant, Robert M. "Dietary Laws among Pythagoreans, Jews, and Christians." *Harvard Theological Review* 73, no. 1/2 (Jan.–Apr., 1980): 299–310.

Grant, Robert M. "Irenaeus and Hellenistic Culture." *Harvard Theological Review* 42, no. 1 (Jan., 1949): 41–51.

Grant, Robert M. "Religion and Politics at the Council at Nicaea." *Journal of Religion* 55, no. 1 (Jan., 1975): 1–12.

Grubbs, Judith Evans. *Women and the Law in the Roman Empire: A Sourcebook on Marriage, Divorce and Widowhood.* New York: Routledge, 2002.

Haas, Christopher. "The Arians of Alexandria." *Vigiliae Christianae* 47, no. 3 (Sep., 1993): 234–45.

Hahneman, Geoffrey Mark. *The Muratorian Fragment and the Development of the Canon.* Oxford: Clarendon Press, 1992.

Halporn, J. W. "Literary History and Generic Expectations in the Passio and Acta Perpetuae." *Vigiliae Christianae* 45, no. 3 (Sep., 1991): 223–41.

Hamman, André, ed., and Thomas Halton, trans. *Baptism: Ancient Liturgies and Patristic Texts.* New York: Alba House, 1967.

Hannah, Jack W. "The Setting of the Ignatian Long Recension." *Journal of Biblical Literature* 79, no. 3 (Sep., 1960): 221–38.

Hanson, R. P. C. "A Note on Origen's Self-Mutilation." *Vigiliae Christianae* 20, no. 2 (Jun., 1966): 81–82.

Hanson, R. P. C. *The Search for the Christian Doctrine of God: The Arian Controversy, 318–381.* Grand Rapids, MI: Baker Academic, 1988.

Hareog, Paul. *Polycarp and the New Testament: The Occasion, Rhetoric, Theme, and Unity of the Epistle to the Philippians and Its Allusions to New Testament Literature.* Tübingen, Germany: Mohr Siebeck, 2001.

Haugaard, William P. "Arius: Twice a Heretic? Arius and the Human Soul of Jesus Christ." *Church History* 29, no. 3 (Sep., 1960): 251–63.

Heid, Stefan. *Celibacy in the Early Church: The Beginnings of Obligatory Continence for Clerics in East and West.* San Francisco: Ignatius Press, 2001.

Herbert, Judith A., Anne-Marie Korte, and Judith Ann Johnson. *Wholly Woman, Holy Blood: A Feminist Critique of Purity and Impurity.* Harrisburg, PA: Trinity Press, International, 2003.

Higgins, A. J. B. "Jewish Messianic Belief in Justin Martyr's 'Dialogue with Trypho.'" *Novum Testamentum* 9, Fasc. 4 (Oct., 1967): 298–305.

Hirshman, M. "Polemic Literary Units in the Classical Midrashim and Justin Martyr's 'Dialogue with Trypho.'" *Jewish Quarterly Review,* n.s., 83, no. 3/4 (Jan.–Apr., 1993): 369–84.

Hoffmann, R. Joseph. *Marcion, on the Restitution of Christianity: An Essay on the Development of Radical Paulist Theology in the Second Century,* American Academy of Religion Academy Series. Atlanta: Scholars Press, 1984.

Holleman, Joost. *Resurrection and Parousia: A Traditio-Historical Study of Paul's Eschatology in 1 Corinthians 15*. Louvain, Belgium: Brill, 1996.

Honoré, A. M. "A Statistical Study of the Synoptic Problem." *Novum Testamentum* 10, Fasc. 2/3 (Apr.–Jul., 1968): 95–147.

Hopkins, M. K. "The Age of Roman Girls at Marriage." *Population Studies* 18, no. 3 (Mar., 1965): 309–27.

Horrell, David. "Leadership Patterns and the Development of Ideology in Early Christianity." *Sociology of Religion* 58, no. 4 (Winter, 1997): 323–41.

Hülsen, Ch. "The Burning of Rome under Nero." *American Journal of Archaeology* 13, no. 1 (Jan.–Mar., 1909): 45–48.

Jacobs, Andrew S. "A Jew's Jew: Paul and the Early Christian Problem of Jewish Origins." *Journal of Religion* 86, no. 2 (April 2006): 258–86.

Jensen, Robin Margaret. *Understanding Early Christian Art*. London: Routledge, 2000.

Johnson, Luke Timothy. *Religious Experience in Earliest Christianity: A Missing Dimension in New Testament Study*. Minneapolis, MN: Fortress Press, 1998.

Jones, Mark Wilson. "Genesis and Mimesis: The Design of the Arch of Constantine in Rome." *Journal of the Society of Architectural Historians* 59, no. 1 (Mar., 2000): 50–77.

Kaatz, Kevin W. *Early Controversies and the Growth of Christianity*. Santa Barbara, CA: Praeger, 2012.

Kee, Howard C. "The Development of Eschatology in the New Testament." *Journal of Bible and Religion* 20, no. 3 (Jul., 1952): 187–93.

Keresztes, Paul. "From the Great Persecution to the Peace of Galerius." *Vigiliae Christianae* 37, no. 4 (Dec., 1983): 379–99.

Keresztes, Paul. "The Literary Genre of Justin's First Apology." *Vigiliae Christianae* 19, no. 2 (Jun., 1965): 99–110.

Kirschbaum, Engelbert, and John Murray, trans. *The Tombs of St Peter & St Paul*. 1st ed. New York: St. Martin's Press, 1959.

Klawiter, Frederick C. "The Role of Martyrdom and Persecution in Developing the Priestly Authority of Women in Early Christianity: A Case Study of Montanism." *Church History* 49, no. 3 (Sep., 1980): 251–61.

Knipfing, John R. "The Libelli of the Decian Persecution." *Harvard Theological Review* 16, no. 4 (Oct., 1923): 345–90.

Kousoulas, D. G. *The Life and Times of Constantine the Great*. 2nd ed. Bethesda, MD: Rutledge Books, 2003.

Kraemer, Ross S. "The Conversion of Women to Ascetic Forms of Christianity." *Signs* 6, no. 2, Studies in Change (Winter, 1980): 298–307.

Kuefler, Mathew. *The Manly Eunuch: Masculinity, Gender Ambiguity, and Christian Ideology in Late Antiquity*. Chicago: University of Chicago Press, 2001.

Kümmel, Werner Georg. "Futuristic and Realized Eschatology in the Earliest Stages of Christianity." *Journal of Religion* 43, no. 4 (Oct., 1963): 303–14.

Lamberton, Clark D. "The Development of Christian Symbolism as Illustrated in Roman Catacomb Painting." *American Journal of Archaeology* 15, no. 4 (Oct.–Dec., 1911): 507–22.

Launderville, Dale. *Celibacy in the Ancient World: Its Ideal and Practice in Pre-Hellenistic Israel, Mesopotamia, and Greece*. Collegeville, MN: Liturgical Press, 2010.

Laupot, Eric. "Tacitus' Fragment 2: The Anti-Roman Movement of the 'hristiani' and the Nazoreans." *Vigiliae Christianae* 54, no. 3 (2000): 233–47.

LaVerdiere, Eugene A. *The Eucharist in the New Testament and the Early Church*. Collegeville, MN: Liturgical Press, 1996.

Leadbetter, William L. *Galerius and the Will of Diocletian,* Roman Imperial Biographies. New York: Routledge, 2010.

Lefkowitz, Mary R. "The Motivations for St. Perpetua's Martyrdom." *Journal of the American Academy of Religion* 44, no. 3 (Sep., 1976): 417–21.

Lieu, S.N.C. *Manichaeism in the Later Roman Empire and Medieval China*: *A Historical Survey*. Rev. 2nd ed. Tübingen, Germany: Mohr Siebeck, 1992.

Mancinelli, Fabrizio. *The Catacombs of Rome and the Origins of Christianity*. Florence: Scala, 1981.

Martin, Troy W. "The Covenant of Circumcision (Genesis 17:9–14) and the Situational Antitheses in Galatians 3:28." *Journal of Biblical Literature* 122, no. 1 (Spring, 2003): 111–25.

McDonnell, Kilian. *Christian Initiation and Baptism in the Holy Spirit: Evidence from the First Eight Centuries*. 2nd rev. ed. Collegeville, MN: Liturgical Press, 1994.

McNamara, Jo Ann. "Sexual Equality and the Cult of Virginity in Early Christian Thought." *Feminist Studies* 3, no. 3/4 (Spring–Summer, 1976): 145–58.

Methuen, Charlotte. "The 'Virgin Widow': A Problematic Social Role for the Early Church?" *Harvard Theological Review* 90, no. 3 (Jul., 1997): 285–98.

Methuen, Charlotte. "Widows, Bishops and the Struggle for Authority in the Didascalia Apostolorum." *Journal of Ecclesiastical History* 46 (1995): 197–213.

Metzger, Bruce M. *The Canon of the New Testament: Its Origin, Development, and Significance*. Oxford: Clarendon Press, 1987.

Minns, Denis. *Irenaeus: An Introduction*. London: T & T Clark, 2010.

Minns, Denis, and Paul Parvis, eds. *Justin, Philosopher and Martyr: Apologies*. Oxford: Oxford University Press, 2009.

Murphy-O'Connor, Jerome. "The Corinth That Saint Paul Saw." *The Biblical Archaeologist* 47, no. 3 (Sep., 1984): 147–59.

Murphy-O'Connor, Jerome. *St. Paul's Corinth: Texts and Archaeology*. Collegeville, MN: Liturgical Press, 1983.

Musurillo, Herbert Anthony, ed. *The Acts of the Christian Martyrs*: *Texts, Translations, and Introduction*. Oxford: Oxford University Press, 1972.

Nathan, Geoffrey S. *The Family in Late Antiquity: The Rise of Christianity and the Endurance of Tradition*. New York: Routledge, 2000.

Neusner, Jacob. "The Idea of Purity in Ancient Judaism." *Journal of the American Academy of Religion* 43, no. 1 (Mar., 1975): 15–26.

Nicholson, Oliver. "Constantine's Vision of the Cross." *Vigiliae Christianae* 54, no. 3 (2000): 309–23.

Odahl, Charles. "God and Constantine: Divine Sanction for Imperial Rule in the First Christian Emperor's Early Letters and Art." *Catholic Historical Review* 81, no. 3 (Jul., 1995), 327–52.

Osborn, Eric. *Irenaeus of Lyons*. Cambridge: Cambridge University Press, 2005.

Osborn, Eric. *Tertullian, First Theologian of the West*. Cambridge: Cambridge University Press, 2003.

Pagels, Elaine. "Irenaeus, the 'Canon of Truth,' and the 'Gospel of John': 'Making a Difference' through Hermeneutics and Ritual." *Vigiliae Christianae* 56, no. 4 (Nov., 2002): 339–71.

Paget, J.N.B. Carleton. "Barnabas 9:4: A Peculiar Verse on Circumcision." *Vigiliae Christianae* 45, no. 3 (Sep., 1991): 242–54.

Paget, James Carleton. *The* Epistle of Barnabas: *Outlook and Background.* Tübingen: J.C.B. Mohr, December 1994.

Paget, James Carleton. "Paul and the *Epistle of Barnabas.*" *Novum Testamentum* 38, Fasc. 4 (Oct., 1996): 359–81.

Parish, Helen. *Clerical Celibacy in the West, c. 1100–1700.* Burlington, VT: Ashgate, 2010.

Parvis, Sara, and Paul Foster. *Justin Martyr and His Worlds.* Minneapolis, MN: Fortress Press, 2007.

Patout Burns, J., Jr. *Cyprian the Bishop.* New York: Routledge, 2002.

Patzia, Arthur G. *The Making of the New Testament: Origin, Collection, Text & Canon.* Downers Grove, IL: InterVarsity Press, 1995.

Pervo, Richard I. *The Making of Paul: Constructions of the Apostle in Early Christianity.* Minneapolis, MN: Fortress Press, 2010.

Pettersen, Alvyn. *Athanasius.* Harrisburg, PA: Morehouse, 1995.

Pettersen, Alvyn. "Perpetua: Prisoner of Conscience." *Vigiliae Christianae* 41, no. 2 (Jun., 1987): 139–53.

Petzer, J. H. "Luke 22:19b–20 and the Structure of the Passage." *Novum Testamentum* 26, Fasc. 3 (Jul., 1984): 249–52.

Phipps, William E. "The Menstrual Taboo in the Judeo-Christian Tradition." *Journal of Religion and Health* 19, no. 4 (Winter, 1980): 298–303.

Piper, Otto A. "The Nature of the Gospel According to Justin Martyr." *Journal of Religion* 41, no. 3 (Jul., 1961): 155–68.

Pohlsander, Hans A. *The Emperor Constantine.* New York: Routledge, 1996.

Portella, Ivana Della. *Subterranean Rome.* Cologne, Germany: Könemann, 2000.

Porúbčan, Štefan. "Form Criticism and the Synoptic Problem." *Novum Testamentum* 7, Fasc. 2 (Mar., 1964): 81–118.

Quasten, Johannes. *Patrology,* vol. 1. Allen, TX: RCL, 1986.

Quispel, Gilles. "Marcion and the Text of the New Testament." *Vigiliae Christianae* 52, no. 4 (Nov., 1998): 349–60.

Quispel, Gilles. "The Original Doctrine of Valentinus the Gnostic." *Vigiliae Christianae* 50, no. 4 (1996): 327–52.

Quispel, Gilles. "Valentinus and the Gnostikoi." *Vigiliae Christianae* 50, no. 1 (1996): 1–4.

Rawson, Beryl, ed. *Marriage, Divorce, and Children in Ancient Rome.* Oxford: Clarendon Press, 1991.

Reynolds, Phillip L. *Marriage in the Western Church: The Christianization of Marriage during the Patristic and Early Medieval Periods.* Leiden, the Netherlands: Brill, 2001.

Richardson, Cyril C. "The Condemnation of Origen." *Church History* 6, no. 1 (Mar., 1937): 50–64.

Rives, J. B. "The Decree of Decius and the Religion of Empire." *Journal of Roman Studies* 89 (1999): 135–54.

Robinson, Thomas A. *Ignatius of Antioch and the Parting of the Ways: Early Jewish-Christian Relations.* Peabody, MA: Hendrickson, 2009.

Rokeah, David. *Justin Martyr and the Jews,* Jewish and Christian Perspectives Series. Leiden, the Netherlands: Brill Academic Publishers, 2001.

Rossi, Mary Ann, and Giorgio Otranto. "Priesthood, Precedent, and Prejudice: On Recovering the Women Priests of Early Christianity." *Journal of Feminist Studies in Religion* 7, no. 1 (Spring, 1991): 73–94.

Rubenstein, Richard E. *When Jesus Became God: The Struggle to Define Christianity during the Last Days of Rome*. Orlando, FL: Harcourt, 1999.

Salter, Kenneth W. "Canon Law Divorce and Annulment of the Roman Catholic Church at the Parish." *Journal of Marriage and Family* 31, no. 1 (Feb., 1969): 51–60.

Sanders, E. P., and Margaret Davies. *Studying the Synoptic Gospels*. London: SCM Press, 1989.

Schatkin, Margaret A., "Divorce." In *Encyclopedia of Early Christianity*, 2nd ed., edited by Everett Ferguson, 340–341. New York: Garland, 1998.

Selvidge, Marla J. "Mark 5:25–34 and Leviticus 15:19–20: A Reaction to Restrictive Purity Regulations." *Journal of Biblical Literature* 103, no. 4 (Dec., 1984): 619–23.

Shaw, Brent D. "The Passion of Perpetua." *Past & Present*, no. 139 (May, 1993): 3–45.

Skarsaune, Oskar. "A Neglected Detail in the Creed of Nicaea (325)." *Vigiliae Christianae* 41, no. 1 (Mar., 1987): 34–54.

Slingerland, Dixon. "Suetonius 'Claudius' 25.4 and the Account in Cassius Dio." *Jewish Quarterly Review*, n.s., 79, no. 4 (Apr., 1989): 305–22.

Stedman Sheard, Wendy. "Tullio Lombardo in Rome? The Arch of Constantine, the Vendramin Tomb, and the Reinvention of Monumental Classicizing Relief." *Artibus et Historiae* 18, no. 35 (1997): 161–79.

Stephenson, Paul. *Constantine: Roman Emperor, Christian Victor*. New York: Penguin, 2010.

Stevenson, James. *The Catacombs: Rediscovered Monuments of Early Christianity*. London: Thames and Hudson, 1978.

Stevenson, Walter. "The Rise of Eunuchs in Greco-Roman Antiquity." *Journal of the History of Sexuality* 5, no. 4 (Apr., 1995): 495–511.

Stickler, Alphonso M., and Brian Ferme, trans. *The Case for Clerical Celibacy: Its Historical Development and Theological Foundations*. San Francisco: Ignatius Press, 1993.

Story, Cullen I. K. "Justin's Apology I. 62–64: Its Importance for the Author's Treatment of Christian Baptism." *Vigiliae Christianae* 16, no. 3/4 (Sep., 1962): 172–78.

Street, Gail. *Redeemed Bodies: Women Martyrs in Early Christianity*. Louisville, KY: John Knox Press, 2009.

Sundberg, Albert C. Jr. "Canon Muratori: A Fourth Century List." *Harvard Theological Review* 66 (1973): 1–41.

Tabbernee, William. *Fake Prophecy and Polluted Sacraments*. Leiden, the Netherlands: Brill, 2007.

Talbott, Rick. "Imagining the Matthean Eunuch Community: Kyriarchy on the Chopping Block." *Journal of Feminist Studies in Religion* 22, no. 1 (Spring, 2006): 21–43.

Taylor, Gary. *Castration: An Abbreviated History of Western Manhood*. New York: Routledge, 2002.

Thiessen, Matthew. *Contesting Conversion: Genealogy, Circumcision, and Identity in Ancient Judaism and Christianity*. New York: Oxford University Press, 2011.

Thomassen, Einar. "Orthodoxy and Heresy in Second-Century Rome." *Harvard Theological Review* 97, no. 3 (Jul., 2004): 241–56.

Thompson, Leonard L. "The Martyrdom of Polycarp: Death in the Roman Games." *Journal of Religion* 82, no. 1 (Jan., 2002): 27–52.

Thurston, Bonnie Bowman. *The Widows: A Women's Ministry in the Early Church*. Minneapolis, MN: Fortress, 1989.

Torjesen, Karen J. *When Women Were Priests: Women's Leadership in the Early Church and the Scandal of Their Subordination in the Rise of Christianity*. San Francisco: HarperSanFrancisco, 1993.

Trakatellis, Demetrios. "Justin Martyr's Trypho." *Harvard Theological Review* 79, no. 1/3, Christians among Jews and Gentiles: Essays in Honor of Krister Stendahl on His Sixty-Fifth Birthday (Jan.–Jul., 1986): 287–97.

Trevett, Christine. *Montanism: Gender, Authority and the New Prophecy.* Cambridge: Cambridge University Press, 1996.

Trigg, Joseph W. *Origen.* New York: Routledge, 1998.

Tronzo, William. *The Via Latina Catacomb: Imitation and Discontinuity in Fourth-Century Roman Painting.* University Park, PA: Pennsylvania State University Press, 1986.

Tyson, Joseph B. *Marcion and Luke-Acts: A Defining Struggle.* Columbia: University of South Carolina Press, 2006.

Ulrich, Jörg. "Nicaea and the West." *Vigiliae Christianae* 51, no. 1 (Mar., 1997): 10–24.

Van de Sandt, Huub. " 'Do Not Give What Is Holy to the Dogs' (Did 9:5D and Matt 7:6A): The Eucharistic Food of the Didache in Its Jewish Purity Setting." *Vigiliae Christianae* 56, no. 3 (Aug., 2002): 223–46.

Van Winden, J.C.M. "Notes on Origen, Contra Celsum." *Vigiliae Christianae* 20, no. 4 (Dec., 1966): 201–13.

Verheyden, Joseph, Korinna Zamfir, and Tobias Nicklas, eds. *Prophets and Prophecy in Jewish and Early Christian Literature.* Tübingen, Germany: Mohr Siebeck, 2010.

Von Campenhausen, Hans. *The Formation of the Christian Bible.* Philadelphia: Fortress, 1972.

Wallace, Daniel B., ed. *Revisiting the Corruption of the New Testament: Manuscript, Patristic, and Apocryphal Evidence.* Grand Rapids, MI: Kregel, 2011.

Walton, Alice. "The Date of the Arch of Constantine." *Memoirs of the American Academy in Rome* 4 (1924): 169–80.

Webb, Matilda. *The Churches and Catacombs of Early Christian Rome: A Comprehensive Guide.* Brighton, England: Sussex Academic Press, 2001.

Wermelinger, Otto, Gregor Wurst, and Johannes Van Oort, eds. *Augustine and Manichaeism in the Latin West: Proceedings of the Fribourg-Utrecht Symposium of the International Association of Manichaean Studies.* Leiden, the Netherlands: Brill, 2001.

Williams, Rowan. *Arius: Heresy and Tradition.* Rev. ed. Grand Rapids, MI: Eerdmans, 2002.

Witherington, Ben III. *Women and the Genesis of Christianity.* Cambridge: Cambridge University Press, 1990.

Wypustek, Andrzej. "Magic, Montanism, Perpetua, and the Severan Persecution." *Vigiliae Christianae* 51, no. 3 (Aug., 1997): 276–97.

Yarbrough, Anne. "Christianization in the Fourth Century: The Example of Roman Women." *Church History* 45, no. 2 (Jun., 1976): 149–65.

Zeitlin, Solomon. "The Christ Passage in Josephus." *Jewish Quarterly Review,* n.s., 18, no. 3 (Jan., 1928): 231–55.

BIBLIOGRAPHY OF WEBSITES

The Acts of Paul and Thecla. http://www.fordham.edu/halsall/basis/thecla.asp

"Alexander of Alexandria." *Catholic Encyclopedia.* http://www.newadvent.org/cathen/01296a.htm

Ambrose. *The Treatise Concerning Widows.* http://www.ccel.org/ccel/schaff/npnf210.iv.viii.ii.html

Apostolic Constitutions, chapter 8. http://www.newadvent.org/fathers/07158.htm

Athanasius. *The Discourses* (including the fourth, which is generally thought not to have been written by Athanasius). http://www.ccel.org/ccel/schaff/npnf204.xxi.ii.i.i.html

Athanasius. *Festal Letter 39.* http://www.ccel.org/ccel/schaff/npnf204.xxv.iii.iii.xxv.html

"Celsus the Platonist." *The Catholic Encyclopedia* website. http://www.newadvent.org/cathen/03490a.htm

Chrysostom, John. *Homily 31 on Matthew.* http://www.newadvent.org/fathers/200131.htm

Chrysostom, John. *Letter to a Young Widow.* http://www.ccel.org/ccel/schaff/npnf109.vi.iii.html

Clement of Alexandria. http://www.earlychristianwritings.com/clement.html

Clement of Alexandria, *Instructor.* http://www.ccel.org/ccel/schaff/anf02.vi.iii.i.i.html

Cyprian. *On the Dress of Virgins.* http://www.ccel.org/ccel/schaff/anf05.toc.html

Cyprian. *On the Lapsed.* http://www.ccel.org/ccel/schaff/anf05.iv.v.iii.html

Cyprian's works. http://www.ccel.org/ccel/schaff/anf05.iv.ii.html

Didascalia Apostolorum. http://www.bombaxo.com/didascalia.html

Dionysius, *Letters.* http://www.ccel.org/ccel/schaff/anf06.html

Early Church website. http://www.earlychurch.org.uk/polycarp.php

Epistle of Barnabas. http://www.ccel.org/ccel/schaff/anf01.vi.ii.i.html

Eusebius. http://www.ccel.org/ccel/schaff/npnf201.html

Eusebius writings. http://www.ccel.org/ccel/schaff/npnf201.toc.html

The Fourth Century Christianity website. http://www.fourthcentury.com/

Gospel of Peter. http://www.earlychristianwritings.com/text/gospelpeter.html

Gospel of Thomas. http://www.gnosis.org/naghamm/gthlamb.html

Ignatius, *Letters* (audio). http://www.youtube.com/view_play_list?p=CEA5BBE5A9094A43Ignatius, *Letters* (text). http://www.ccel.org/ccel/schaff/anf01.v.html

The Imperial Index: The Rulers of the Roman Empire. http://www.roman-emperors.org/impindex.htm

International Association of Manichaean Studies. http://www.manichaeism.de/

International Catacomb Society. http://www.catacombsociety.org/index.html International Catacomb Society. "Visiting the Catacombs." http://www.catacombsociety.org/visiting_Christian.html

Irenaeus's texts. http://www.ccel.org/ccel/schaff/anf01.ix.html

Lactantius. *On the Deaths of the Persecutors.* http://www.ccel.org/ccel/schaff/anf07.iii.v.i.html

Lactantius writings. http://www.ccel.org/ccel/schaff/anf07.iii.v.html

Martyr, Justin. *Dialogue with Trypho.* http://www.ccel.org/ccel/schaff/anf01.viii.iv.i.html

Martyr, Justin. *First and Second Apology.* http://www.ccel.org/ccel/schaff/anf01.html

The Martyrdom of Polycarp. http://www.ccel.org/ccel/schaff/anf01.txt

Origen. *Against Celsus.* http://www.ccel.org/ccel/schaff/anf04.vi.ix.i.i.html

The Passion of the Holy Martyrs Perpetua and Felicitas. http://www.ccel.org/ccel/schaff/anf03.toc.html

Pliny the Elder. *The Natural History* 28.23. http://www.perseus.tufts.edu/hopper/text?doc=Perseus:text:1999.02.0137Pontius. *Life and Passion of Cyprian, Bishop and Martyr.* http://www.ccel.org/ccel/schaff/anf05.iv.iii.html

Pope Paul VI. "Declaration on the Question of Admission of Women to the Ministerial Priesthood." http://www.papalencyclicals.net/Paul06/p6interi.htm

Synoptic Gospels: Our Primary Sources for the Study of Jesus, by James F. McGrath. http://blue.butler.edu/~jfmcgrat/jesus/synoptics.htm

Synoptic Gospels: Structural Outlines and Unique Materials, by Felix Just, SJ. http://catholic-resources.org/Bible/Synoptic_Outlines.htm

Tertullian. *Against Marcion.* http://www.ccel.org/ccel/schaff/anf03.v.iv.i.html

Tertullian. *Against Marcion.* http://www.ccel.org/ccel/schaff/anf03.pdf

Tertullian. *On the Dress of Women.* http://www.ccel.org/ccel/schaff/anf04.html

The Tertullian Project. http://www.tertullian.org/index.htm

INDEX

ABOUT THE EDITOR

Kevin W. Kaatz, PhD, is a lecturer in the Department of History at California State University, East Bay Campus, Hayward, California. Kaatz authored *Early Controversies and the Growth of Christianity*, coauthored "Hegemonius, Acta Archelai" ("The Acts of Archelaus"), *Manichaean Studies*, vol. 4, and a number of articles on early church history and in the field of neurology.